WALT WHITMAN AND THE CULTURE
OF AMERICAN CELEBRITY

DAVID HAVEN BLAKE

Walt Whitman
and the Culture of
American Celebrity

YALE UNIVERSITY PRESS NEW HAVEN & LONDON

Published with assistance from the foundation established in memory of Philip Hamilton McMillan of the Class of 1894, Yale College.

Set in Scala by Keystone Typesetting, Inc.
Printed in the United States of America.

Library of Congress Cataloging-in-Publication Data
Blake, David Haven.
Walt Whitman and the culture of American celebrity / David Haven Blake.
p. cm.
Includes bibliographical references (p.) and index.
ISBN-13: 978-0-300-11017-3 (alk. paper)
ISBN-10: 0-300-11017-0 (alk. paper)
1. Whitman, Walt, 1819–1892. 2. Poets, American—19th century—Biography. 3. Publicity. 4. Fame—Economic aspects. 5. Popular culture—United States—History—19th century. I. Title.
PS3231.B58 2006
811'.3—dc22

2006009075

A catalogue record for this book is available from the British Library.

The paper in this book meets the guidelines for permanence and durability of the Committee on Production Guidelines for Book Longevity of the Council on Library Resources.

10 9 8 7 6 5 4 3 2 1

GREAT JONES STREET by Don DeLillo
Copyright © 1973 by Don DeLillo
Reprinted by permission of the Wallace Literary Agency, Inc.

For Eben, Eva, and Julie

Fame requires every kind of excess. I mean true fame, a devouring neon, not the somber renown of waning statesmen or chinless kings. I mean long journeys across gray space. I mean danger, the edge of every void, the circumstance of one man imparting an erotic terror to the dreams of the republic.

—Don DeLillo, *Great Jones Street*

CONTENTS

Long before Walt Whitman wrote *Leaves of Grass*, poets had addressed themselves to fame. Horace, Petrarch, Shakespeare, Milton, and Keats all hoped that poetic greatness would grant them a kind of earthly immortality. Whitman held a similar faith that for centuries the world would value his poems. But to this ancient desire to live forever on the page, he added a new sense of fame. Readers would not simply attend to the poet's work, they would be attracted to the magnificence of his personality. They would see in his poems a vibrant cultural performance, an individual springing from the book with tremendous charisma and appeal. Out of the political rallies and electoral parades that marked Jacksonian America, Whitman defined poetic fame in relation to the crowd. Others might court the muses on Mt. Parnassus or imagine themselves in the laureates' sacred grove. Whitman's poet sought the approval of his contemporaries. In the turbulence of American democracy, fame would be contingent on celebrity, on the degree to which the people exulted in the poet and his work.

This book tells the story of how an obscure Brooklyn poet, better known for his political journalism than verse, immersed himself in the culture of celebrity that was then emerging in the United States. Hoping to redress the mounting divisions in his country, he declared that the poet would become the center of American civic life, that he would command more power and sway than the political representatives he expected to supersede. As Whitman imagined it, the story of celebrity would be the story of democracy. He hoped that the nation's narrow political institutions would undergo an extraordinary transformation once they encountered the populist power embodied in the poet's fame.

Whitman would have to wait a long time for his celebrity to appear, and even then, it came not in the overflow of spontaneous affection he had envisioned as a younger man but in the respect and admiration expressed by his fellow dignitaries. Uncomfortable with the magnetic, sexual rebel depicted in the first editions of *Leaves of Grass*, the culture finally accepted Whitman as a majestic, grandfatherly poet, a patriotic wound dresser with his long white beard. But this book is not a study of Whitman's reputation, of how he was eventually accepted into the canon and became the complex national icon that he is today.[1] I am interested in how Whitman's ideas of celebrity helped shape *Leaves of Grass,* how the meanings he granted to fame influenced the relationship he established with his readers. Sketched out in his notebooks, advertisements, conversations, and poetry, Whitman's celebrity was as much a form of advance publicity as it was a biographical achievement.

The fact that Whitman's fame was largely imagined makes his case more distinctive and revealing than those of the many entertainers and athletes who have achieved stardom since the poet's death in 1892. Neal Gabler has suggested that, as an art form wrought in the medium of life, celebrity is primarily narrative in orientation.[2] One of my goals in this book is to reflect on the lyric components of fame, the fleeting, sometimes fantastical moments and gestures that bear the imprint of celebrity culture even when divorced from celebrity stature itself. I use the word *lyric* regretfully, cringing at the too-clever allusion it implies to *Leaves of Grass,* but the word can help us recognize these components outside the dramas of narrative and biography. Contemporary life is filled with such lyric expressions of celebrity: the six-year-old who dons a pair of sunglasses and poses like a movie star, the middle-aged accountant who struts like a rock 'n' roll icon during karaoke night at the local pub. Although he would frown at the high incidence of mimicry, I suspect that were he alive today, Whitman would recognize in such gestures the desire for personality that permeates *Leaves of Grass.*

I began this book after observing how frequently Whitman teaches us what we should value in his poems. *Leaves of Grass* struck me as being particularly interesting in this regard, for so much of the poetry seemed dedicated to proclaiming its cultural relevance. I wondered whether Whitman had coaxed us into believing that the things he said about himself were true. "I give the sign of democracy," he announced in "Song of Myself," and in the classes I had attended and the books I had read, democracy was precisely the yardstick by which he was measured, the rubric through which he was understood (*LG* 1855, 48). (This book is no exception.) Whitman, to my mind, was the Muhammad Ali of American literature, the man whose bombast and epithets were so overwhelming that they had gloriously taken root. Whitman's capacity to fuse poetry with advertisement first led me to investigate his engagement with celebrity.

In researching this topic, I became increasingly aware of the strong presence of Whitman's contemporaries. What I had been observing in Whitman was not simply a personal predilection; it was a window into the growth of celebrity culture in the United States. My original intention was to compare Whitman's treatment of fame to that of such writers as Ezra Pound, Gertrude Stein, Anne Sexton, and Allen Ginsberg, but the more I read about antebellum New York, the more these voices receded into the background, where they await another book. The Whitman this work explores is the poet who was immersed in the life of his times, immersed in the actors, lecturers, publishers, showmen, novelists, and poets who helped define celebrity culture in the United States. To borrow a phrase from "Song of Myself," Whitman was both in and out of the game, at once alert to the pressing crowd and alert to posterity. The result was a book of poems that viewed the celebrity of poets as integral to a visionary democracy.

I would like to express my grateful acknowledgement to the following libraries and agencies for permission to reproduce images in this book: the Thomas B. Harned and Charles E. Feinberg Collections of the Library of Congress; the Henry W. and Albert A. Berg Collection of English and American Literature at the New York Public Library; the Picture Collection, the Branch Libraries, New York Public Library; the Special Collections Department of the University of Virginia Library; and the Smithsonian Institution's National Portrait Gallery.

For permission to quote from Don DeLillo's novel *Great Jones Street*, I thank the author and the Wallace Literary Agency, Inc.

One of the great pleasures in working on this project has been working with many excellent librarians. I am grateful for the friendly help of the librarians and staff at Duke University's Rare Book, Manuscript, and Special Collections Library, the Historical Society of Pennsylvania, the Library of Congress, the Library Company of Philadelphia, the New York Public Library, and Princeton University's Firestone Library.

The library staff at my home institution, The College of New Jersey (TCNJ), has provided unstinting support. Writing this book would have been nearly impossible without the help of Marc Meola and Dina Carmy and without the resourcefulness, ingenuity, and commitment of Judy Cobb, Dolores Davis, and Elizabeth Maziarz in the interlibrary loan office.

Key support for this book was provided by Susan Albertine, dean of the School of Culture and Society, and by the committee on faculty research, SOSA, which generously awarded me the time to research and write from 2001 to 2005.

It has been a real pleasure working with the people at Yale University Press. I have learned a great deal from John Kulka, Lindsay Toland, Jessie Hunnicutt, Robin DuBlanc, and the two anonymous readers who reviewed my manuscript. Thank you for your patience, confidence, and high standards.

In the background of this book are three wonderful teachers, each of whom has influenced both my sense of the profession and my love of the word: Peter Balakian, Robert Milder, and Steven Zwicker.

My students at The College of New Jersey, particularly those in my seminars on Whitman and the Nineteenth Century and Literary Theory and the Long Poem, have had an immeasurably positive impact on this work.

I have been blessed with many interested friends and colleagues at TCNJ and elsewhere, all of whom have helped this become a better book: Donald Anderson, James Bailey, Juda Bennett, Peter Blake, Scott Dierks, Betsy Erkkila, Ed Folsom, Ted Genoways, Ameen Ghannam, Janet Gray, JoAnne Gross, Harvey J. Kaye, Andrew Loesberg, Angela Miller, Jean Noosinow, William Pannapacker, Catie Rosemurgy, Ralph

Savarese, David Venturo, Gary Woodward, and the TCNJ English department chair Jo Carney.

I am especially grateful to Ezra Greenspan and Ken Price, who read early drafts of this manuscript and provided invaluable advice and encouragement.

My colleague and fellow Whitmaniac Michael Robertson has been extraordinarily generous with his time, materials, and commentary. His dedication and enthusiasm have been wonderful living reminders of the premium Whitman placed on friendship and community.

Ed Schwarzschild has been a friend to this project for many years; his good sense, confidence, and gusto have been steady and remarkable.

This book reflects the exceptional support of my mother, Susie Blake, my father, David Blake, and my grandmother Haven Blake Groening, each of whom has helped bring this project to fruition.

Finally, at the very center of this work are my children, Eben and Eva—who speak of Walt as if he were another member of the family—and my wife, Julie—who has shared in this book from its beginning, responding to its various stages with clarity, humor, and warmth. With love, awe, and gratitude, this book is dedicated to Eben, Eva, and Julie.

DN   Walt Whitman, *Daybooks and Notebooks*, 3 vols., ed. William
White (New York: New York University Press, 1977).

EPF   Walt Whitman, *Early Poems and Fiction*, ed. Thomas L.
Brasher (New York: New York University Press, 1963).

LG 1855   Walt Whitman, *Leaves of Grass: The 1855 Edition*, ed. Malcolm
Cowley (New York: Penguin, 1959).

LG 1860   Walt Whitman, *Leaves of Grass: A Facsimile Edition of the 1860
Text*, ed. Roy Harvey Pearce (Ithaca: Cornell University Press,
1961).

LGNC   Walt Whitman, *Leaves of Grass and Other Writings: A Norton
Critical Edition*, ed. Michael Moon (New York: Norton, 2003).

LGV   Walt Whitman, *Leaves of Grass: A Textual Variorum of the
Printed Poems*, 3 vols., ed. Sculley Bradley, Harold W.
Blodgett, Arthur Golden, and William White (New York: New
York University Press, 1980).

PW   Walt Whitman, *Prose Works 1892*, 2 vols., ed. Floyd Stovall
(New York: New York University Press, 1963, 1964).

WPP   Walt Whitman, *Complete Poetry and Collected Prose*, ed. Justin
Kaplan (New York: Library of America, 1982).

WWC   Horace Traubel, *With Walt Whitman in Camden*, 9 vols.
(Various publishers, 1906–96).

Frontispiece

SPEAKING WITH THE photographer Mathew Brady, Walt Whitman once speculated that history could best be absorbed through a series of photographs. Compared to the contradictory accounts that eyewitnesses and historians had provided of men such as Caesar, Socrates, and Epictetus, it would be much more beneficial, Whitman surmised, to "have three or four or half a dozen portraits—very accurate—of the men: that would be history—the best history—a history from which there could be no appeal" (*WWC*, 3:553). Of the more than 120 photographs we have of Whitman, I am particularly drawn to a photograph that appeared, among other places, in the special "birthday" edition of *Leaves of Grass* (1889).[1] Featured as the volume's frontispiece, the portrait presents Whitman in profile as he admires a butterfly resting on his extended forefinger. Seated in a rustic chair, wearing a cardigan sweater, he appears keenly delighted by this visit from an unexpected friend. The image suggests a moment of remarkable balance and serendipity as the "Good Gray Poet" ventures into nature and is fondly greeted by one of its most blatantly poetic creations. Although the photograph was widely admired, suspicions about its authenticity had vexed Whitman's supporters since the 1880s. These suspicions were confirmed in 1936 when a scholar working at the Library of Congress discovered that the butterfly was made of cardboard and that, with the help of some twine, the poet had worn it around his finger like a

Whitman and his butterfly, 1877. Courtesy of the Library of Congress, Prints and Photographs Division, LC-USZ62-124410.

ring. The staging of the portrait makes it particularly valuable as a historical document. Notoriously artificial, the photograph has much to disclose about Whitman's relation to the culture of American celebrity.

The origins of the butterfly photograph were long a mystery. The picture does not seem to have been a part of a larger series, which made it difficult for scholars to determine who the photographer was and where his studio was located. Theories about the date of composition ranged widely from 1873 to the early 1880s, until it was recently disclosed that W. Curtis Taylor took the photograph in the spring of 1877.[2] The image attracted a good deal of commentary among Whitman's contemporaries. In January 1883, a reviewer in the *Critic* called attention to the image, describing the poet as "lounging in smoking-jacket and broad felt hat, gazing at his hand, on which a delicate butterfly, with expanded wings, forms a contrast to the thick fingers and heavy ploughman's wrist."[3] Whitman described the photograph simply as "2/3 length with hat outdoor rustic," but he plainly admired it himself.[4] Thomas Donaldson, a loyal friend and financial supporter throughout the 1880s, recalled that the photograph was the poet's favorite, a recollection that Whitman's nurse Elizabeth Keller agreed to as well.[5] As a young man, the biographer William Roscoe Thayer frequently visited Whitman's house on Mickle Street where one afternoon the poet gave him several photographs, one of which was the "unusually beautiful" butterfly portrait. Years later, Thayer still found the photograph delightful, but he remained disturbed by the possibility that somehow it had been staged: "How it happened that the butterfly should have been waiting in that studio on the chance that it might drop in to be photographed, or why Walt should be clad in a thick cardigan jacket on any day when butterflies would have been disporting themselves in the fields, I have never been able to explain. Was this one of the petty artifices by which Walt carried out his pose?" To Thayer's mind, the photograph was important evidence that despite Whitman's poetic genius, he remained "a poseur of truly colossal proportions, one to whom playing a part had long before become so habitual that he had ceased to be conscious that he was doing it."[6] Thayer died before the cardboard butterfly turned up in the Library of Congress's holdings and revealed the true extent of that posturing.

The butterfly descends to us today as a testament to Whitman's remarkable merger of poetry and publicity. This "poseur of truly colossal proportions" shrewdly understood that photography was one of several cultural developments that would change the way in which literature was promoted and produced. At times in his old age, Whitman grew weary of the number of photographers who commercially sold his image while not paying him royalties. "They have photographed me all ages, sizes, shapes," he complained in 1889. "They have used me for a show-horse again and again and again" (*WWC*, 2:446). But at each stage of his career, Whitman had courted the camera, displaying himself like a show horse repeatedly. The metaphors of exhibition that surface in descriptions of the portrait point to the poet's position as both the subject and producer of publicity. The *Critic* connected the photograph to Whitman's literary style in describing the poet as the large-hearted "manager of a literary interstate exhibition or American institute fair."[7] Thayer took the image a step further. Grappling with his skepticism, he compared Whitman to the most famous American showman of the nineteenth century: "We must remember that he was a contemporary of P. T. Barnum and agreed with that master-showman's views of publicity; so he chose a style both in prose and verse which at once arrested attention; he did not blush to write for the newspapers puffs of himself and his works; he craved notoriety even of the flimsiest sort. 'The public,' he said to me, 'is a thick-skinned beast, and you have to keep whacking away at its hide to let it know you're there.' "[8] The butterfly portrait is one of Whitman's many attempts to whack at the public's thick-skinned hide, to let it know that he was there. Whether a petty artifice or ingenious advertisement, the portrait was one of a series of attempts to raise the public's awareness of *Leaves of Grass* and its author.

The poet's efforts to promote himself, to pronounce and realize his fame, have provided many humorous anecdotes to students of American literature, but they have yet to receive the kind of sustained, analytical attention that they warrant. Whitman's fantasies of popular acceptance form an important part of his biography. Not only did he stage photographs of himself, he made outlandish claims about his popularity and published anonymous reviews of his work. The same promotional energy also surfaces in the speech acts and lyric persona of *Leaves of Grass*, where it makes a vital contribution to his poetics. Thayer compared Whitman to Barnum as a way of contextualizing and therefore excusing what he considered to be the poet's embarrassing excess and vanity. That connection, however, also provides an opportunity to understand the import of Whitman's desire for popular acclaim. The poet's interest in being celebrated by the crowd raises questions that rarely appear in studies of American literature. How can poetry operate as a vehicle for reflecting on fame? What happens to a literary text when its author invokes his or her popularity? Is celebrity a form of exalted individualism, or does it signify a broader communal identity? What is the distinction between the value of a literary text and the promotion that surrounds it? Is there a meaningful relationship between poetry and advertising, between the rhetoric of the lyric and the rhetoric of hype?

For Whitman the lived experience of celebrity was less significant than how the idea of celebrity impacted his thinking and his poetry. By the end of his life, he had achieved considerable fame. People throughout the world sent the poet letters telling him how much they admired *Leaves of Grass*. Photographers, painters, and sculptors made pilgrimages to Mickle Street in order to capture his image. The later editions of *Leaves of Grass* became collectors' items soon after they were released; the special birthday edition, with its butterfly portrait, doubled in value within four years of its publication.[9] Newspapers paid considerable attention to the poet's travels, health problems, reputation, visitors, and anniversaries. After Oscar Wilde spent an afternoon with Whitman at his brother's Camden home, both men were interviewed by reporters curious about the meeting.[10] On the day that Queen Victoria's comments on the poet appeared in the press, he received his copy of *Celebrities of the Century* (1887), a two-volume dictionary of famous Americans and Europeans in which he prominently appeared (*WWC*, 6:463).

A study that focused exclusively on Whitman's experience as a celebrity, however, would make for a very slim book. Harriet Beecher Stowe, Henry Wadsworth Longfellow, Henry James, and of course Mark Twain are just some of the nineteenth-century writers who led more prominent public lives than did Whitman, and scholars have done a superb job examining the impact that fame had on their careers. Scattered across these lives, readers can find the tales of wealth, glamour, social access, and prestige that form such an important part of celebrity narratives today. Whitman, in contrast, remained poor for much of his life, and while he counted writers such as Twain and Wilde among his supporters, he did not seek the company of famous people and, with a few important exceptions, he did not court their favor. The poet's experience of celebrity was ultimately subordinate to his interest in developing a poetry that would position him in relation to the crowd, a crowd of supporters whose affection would give him unparalleled cultural legitimacy. In these respects, Whitman's vision of celebrity markedly differs from the celebrity culture we know in the twenty-first century.

Whitman's attention to the legitimizing power of the crowd has led me throughout this study to use the words *fame* and *celebrity* interchangeably. Among the growing number of studies focused on the subject, some writers have chosen to distinguish between the two terms, using *fame* to signify real and lasting accomplishment and *celebrity* to describe the meretricious notoriety they see as being prevalent today. Whitman, by nearly universal account, would be a poet who had achieved fame, the kind of immortal status Western cultures have traditionally granted to geniuses, statesmen, heroes, and others of exceptional virtue, courage, or skill. It would be convenient to differentiate the poet's fame from the mere celebrity of such nineteenth-century writers as Martin Tupper and N. P. Willis. In using the words interchangeably, I don't deny these differences as much as acknowledge the importance Whitman placed on being embraced by the crowd. At the heart of Whitman's poetics was the conviction that the people could grant and ratify a poet's identity; as he wrote in 1855, "The proof of a poet is that his country absorbs him as affectionately as he has absorbed it" (*LG* 1855, 24). To be a celebrity meant that one had been celebrated by one's fellow citizens, that one had been affectionately absorbed. Celebrity for Whitman was ultimately a political identity, the cultural manifestation of the principles of popular sovereignty.

Leaves of Grass almost seamlessly meshes the language of poetry and publicity, making self-promotion not simply an extratextual activity but something integral to the themes and symbols of his work. The portrait of Whitman holding his cardboard butterfly explains this point well, for it was clearly a deliberate and largely successful effort to court iconographic stature. As Esther Shepherd pointed out in 1936, the photograph acts out an image that first appeared in the 1860 *Leaves of Grass:* a simple line drawing of a butterfly perched upon a hand.[11] Whitman used two other drawings in the 1860 volume (a sun over a landscape and a view of the planet from the cosmos), but he gave the butterfly drawing particular prominence by placing it at the beginning and end of the volume. On the most simple level, the drawing conveys the poet's union with nature, a union that in the photograph becomes his embrace of the rustic. The butterfly introduces a more symbolic dimension to this association, for it represents the kind of personal metamorphoses that Whitman regularly promises his readers. *Leaves of Grass* presents the poet as an agent of conversion; the poems can inspire a miraculous rebirth, a transformation that will bring readers into a fuller sense of their own individuality. "Your true Soul and body appear before me," Whitman writes in "To You, Whoever You Are," inviting readers to see a more glorious version of themselves than the one to which they are accustomed (*LG* 1860, 391). The poet can turn these caterpillar readers into timeless butterflies.

Printed in the 1860 *Leaves of Grass* and then enacted in the photograph, the butterfly adds a graphic component to what I describe throughout this book as Whitman's civic evangelism. Poets in the early Republic had hoped to use literature to make their readers fit for self-government. Wary of literature's traditional ties to leisure and the courts of European monarchies, the nation's earliest poets sought a civic role for their verse, often combining the didactic and panegyric modes.[12] Despite their different political agendas, Timothy Dwight in *Greenfield Hill* and Joel Barlow in *The Columbiad* both structured their poems around celebratory visions of American nationalism and instructions to the reader on the need for virtue. Barlow prefaced *The Columbiad* by explaining that his objective in the poem was "of a moral and political nature": "to encourage and strengthen in the rising generation, a sense of the importance of republican institutions; as being the great foundation of public and private happiness."[13] Whitman both drew upon and radicalized this tradition in stating his desire to remake the Republic by enlightening and transforming its citizens. *Leaves of Grass,* he would later explain, had a specifically public ambition: "to help the forming of a great aggregate Nation . . . altogether through the forming of myriads of fully develop'd and enclosing individuals" (*WPP,* 668). In this fusion of republicanism and romanticism, the poet served the state by functioning as an agent of conversion, an evangelist seeking to bring his readers into a wider, more reflective consciousness.

The evangelical mode of Whitman's address led him to make astonishing claims for what his poems might offer. The public would not only enjoy *Leaves of Grass* and be edified by its wisdom. Reading Whitman would produce a radical transformation. In 1855, he cast himself in the role of a biblical prophet as he beautifully aligned his text with the reader's metamorphosis and redemption:

> This is what you shall do: Love the earth and sun and the ani-
> mals, despise riches, give alms to every one that asks, stand up
> for the stupid and crazy, devote your income and labor to others,
> hate tyrants, argue not concerning God, have patience and in-
> dulgence toward the people, take off your hat to nothing known
> or unknown or to any man or number of men, go freely with
> powerful uneducated persons and with the young and with the
> mothers of families, read these leaves in the open air every sea-
> son of every year of your life, re-examine all you have been told
> at school or church or in any book, dismiss whatever insults
> your own soul, and your very flesh shall be a great poem and
> have the richest fluency not only in its words but in the silent
> lines of its lips and face and between the lashes of your eyes and
> in every motion and joint of your body. (*LG* 1855, 10)

The passage directs readers to bring about their own personal and aesthetic awakening by attending to the wonders in *Leaves of Grass*. Reading the poems in open air is consonant with the kind of radically egalitarian spirit the passage celebrates. The caterpillar becomes a butterfly, the reader a poem. Whitman effects the transformation.

Housed at the Library of Congress (and displayed on its website), the actual cardboard butterfly embodies this spirit of civic evangelism. Though Whitman does not use it for a Christian purpose, his butterfly had apparently been one of many produced for an Easter celebration. On one side, the butterfly is decorated with a rainbow's assortment of colors, on the other the lyrics to an Easter hymn. The word *Easter* itself appears on the abdomen and thorax. The portrait does not capture this level of detail, but Whitman certainly knew the spiritual purpose of the butterfly when he attached it to his finger. As both a symbol and an object, the butterfly associates multiple images of resurrection with the poet's relation to his

---

Two views of Whitman's butterfly. The lyrics to John Mason Neale's Easter hymn read: "The first begotten of the dead / For us He rose, our Glorious Head, / Immortal life to bring. / What though the saints like Him shall die, / They share their Leader's victory, / And triumph with their King." Courtesy of the Library of Congress, Manuscript Division, LCMS-45443-5, LCMS-45443-6.

readers. It manages to register Whitman's spiritual, political, and aesthetic themes at the same time, elegantly conveying the sense of personal possibility that animates *Leaves of Grass.*

The portrait's symbolism deftly coincides with its larger promotional purpose. Offering readers the potential for rebirth, Whitman stages the rather extravagant expectations he has for his work. The secularized Christian narrative implied by the butterfly shrewdly promotes the real and imagined advantages of reading the book. As a form of publicity, however, the portrait is designed to augment the poet's public profile and readership. It acknowledges that he needs his readers as much as they need him. Whitman's friend Dr. R. M. Bucke saw in the portrait an image of Whitman's perfectly aligned personality: "The butterfly . . . represents, of course, Psyche, his soul, his fixed contemplation of which accords with his declaration: 'I need no assurances; I am a man who is preoccupied of his own soul.' "[14] Bucke's notion of needing no assurances, of being perfectly engrossed with the soul, overlooks Whitman's use of the butterfly to structure his reception as a recognizably public man.

The butterfly functions quite literally as a prop, one of the many items Whitman used to advertise and support different versions of himself. As Michael Davidson remarks, the poet seems to have pioneered the promotional use of the literary photograph: "It is hard to think of another writer of his era who so thoroughly exploited the possibility of the camera for staging versions of self, from Broadway dandy to rough-hewn outdoorsman, from kindly preceptor to visionary sage. In all these representations, clothing, props, and body language are important adjuncts to the effect desired. . . . What is remarkable about all such performances is that Whitman saw them as serving an essential authenticity."[15] Although he does not discuss it specifically, Davidson illuminates the complex function of Whitman's butterfly. Symbolizing the poet's union with nature and the outdoors, offering readers an emblem of their potential metamorphoses, the butterfly signifies the authentic world of *Leaves of Grass.* At the same time, the photograph creates an illusion aimed at preparing the poet for public consumption. The butterfly is an advertiser's cardboard prop. In projecting Whitman's ambitions for his readers, it ultimately suggests his ambitions for *Leaves of Grass.*

Before Wilde adopted his velvet breeches and Twain his white suit, Whitman had begun to experiment with establishing a signature symbol for himself. The butterfly produces a new promotional discourse about Whitman's work, one that extends rather than illustrates the world created by *Leaves of Grass*. The portrait, for example, has a very different effect than that of a roughly contemporaneous photograph of Whitman seated next to a boy. On one print, someone drew blades of grass in the child's hand and underneath wrote these lines from "Song of Myself": "A child said to me, '*What is the grass?*' fetching it to me with full hands.—How could I answer the child?"[16] The experiment produced rather comic results, and Whitman did not duplicate the image in any of his promotional materials.

The butterfly portrait, in contrast, was widely distributed. Whitman frequently autographed the portrait for admirers and included copies in several books. In *Specimen Days and Collect* (1882), the photograph serves to illustrate a description of the butterflies Whitman had seen during his retreat at Timber Creek in rural New Jersey: "Over all flutter myriads of light-yellow butterflies, mostly skimming along the surface, dipping and oscillating, giving a curious animation to the scene. The beautiful, spiritual insects! Straw-color'd Psyches!" (*WPP*, 828). But while the child's photograph was altered decades after the first publication of "Song of Myself," the butterfly image actually predated its textual counterpart. When Whitman wrote in *Specimen Days*, "I have one big and handsome moth down here, knows and comes to me, likes me to hold him up on my extended finger," he was seeking to anchor his promotional image in an autobiographical anecdote (*WPP*, 829).[17] Preceding *Specimen Days* and standing apart from the poems, the butterfly photograph creates a set of external associations meant to inform the public's perception of the poet and his books. Whitman the author becomes Whitman the image, a personality performed on the public stage.

The promotional value of those associations continues to thrive today, though their meaning now centers on the inspirational impact of the poet's fame. In the nineteenth century, Whitman used the butterfly to cultivate his celebrity; at the end of the twentieth century, his adopted city of Camden hoped to trade on this fame in an effort to revive its own beleaguered circumstances and stature. Notorious for its crime and poverty, the city purchased street signs that displayed the image of a hand with a butterfly perched on it. Just a few blocks from Mickle Street on the revitalized waterfront, the city erected a statue of Whitman and his butterfly at the center of the Camden Children's Garden. The possibility for

Whitman and child with drawn leaves of grass. Courtesy of the Walt Whitman Collection (#3829-H), Clifton Waller Barrett Library of American Literature, Special Collections, University of Virginia Library.

renewal enacted in the photograph has become for the city the possibility for a meaningful urban renaissance. Whether or not the image proves to be effective for Camden remains to be seen, but the logic of its campaign seems perfectly consistent with that of its most prominent literary citizen. Out of the artifice of publicity comes a symbol of civic rebirth.

Reflecting on Whitman's butterfly can help reclaim his persona as an impresario and master of hype. Criticism has paid scant attention to the poet's self-promotions, despite their forming such a large part of his lore. In the past two decades, students of *Leaves of Grass* have grown used to thinking about Whitman alongside an array of sociopolitical topics: abolition, capitalism, class solidarity, constitutionality, democracy, gay sexuality, gender, masculinity, representation, and the role of women, to name just a few. With the rise of New Historicism, Whitman has proven to be an ideal candidate for these historical assessments of his poems. He suggested this path in 1888 when he commented that *Leaves of Grass* could never have emerged "from any other era than the latter half of the Nineteenth Century, nor any other land than democratic America" (*WPP*, 661). The poet who first presented himself as a working-class redeemer instigated a tradition of criticism in which many commentators continue to measure him in largely heroic terms. Across a striking range of issues, some scholars have celebrated the poet for his sociopolitical vision, while others have faulted him for failing the same visionary goals.[18] Whether praising Whitman's politics or pointing to their shortcomings, such conclusions ultimately reinforce the original heroic mode.

Whitman's penchant for self-advertisement has historically posed a challenge for readers accustomed to viewing him in these terms. With increasing dismay, the poet's admirers grappled with this problem in the years before and after his death. Thayer was not alone in condemning the poet for the "petty artifices" by which he promoted himself. Writing to Horace Traubel, Bucke once commented that Whitman's "self-advertising was a shock to many people. I myself would have had him above that sort of thing, tho' I see how it came about. When he retired into himself and wrote his poems he was a god; when in his idle moments he faced the indifference of the public he was often a child."[19] The statement presumes a binary that continues to exist today: the god who writes the poems and the child who descends to advertise their worth. Scholars may not feel the same repulsion as men such as Bucke and Thayer did, but they have only recently turned to the subject in depth. Since the groundbreaking work of David Reynolds's *Walt Whitman's America*, there have been several illuminating discussions of Whitman's relation to advertising, promotion, and the culture of celebrity, though as of this writing, no sustained, book-length analysis of the topic exists.[20]

The butterfly portrait is a revealing index of the growing scholarly interest in Whitman's self-promotions. Until it appeared on the back cover of Michael Moon's critical edition of *Leaves of Grass,* the image was rarely reproduced, and its position in Whitman's career received only brief mention in biographies.[21] The historic lack of attention is strangely mirrored in the cardboard butterfly's fate. Placed in a carton with other Whitman materials, the butterfly disappeared from the Library of Congress's holdings when it was transferred to a more secure location during World War II. Apparently stolen, it seemed forever lost when scholarly interest in the poet began to rise in the 1950s and 1960s. However, just in time for a more receptive cultural climate, the butterfly surfaced (along with some missing notebooks) at Sotheby's auction house in 1995, and that spring it was safely returned to the Thomas B. Harned Collection at the Library of Congress. The Library has since made digitized pictures of the butterfly permanently available on its website. The outcome seems fitting for a poet who was so interested in promulgating and disseminating himself. Not unlike the speaker in "Song of Myself," the butterfly is now both everywhere and nowhere. Digitally preserved, electronically circulated, the cardboard prop is now "the occupant and expression of a virtual America," its ubiquity challenging a new generation of scholars to grapple with the desire for celebrity that it represents.[22]

Whitman would be pleased at this turn of events, for he seems to have been careful about preserving the object for posterity. Indeed, perhaps the most revealing part of the butterfly's history is that somehow it survived. For a poet who proclaimed the virtues of being "undisguised and naked," Whitman fiercely protected both his image and his privacy (*LG* 1855, 25). Although Traubel filled nine volumes recording his conversations with the poet, researchers continue to know little about his experience in New Orleans, the gestation of *Leaves of Grass* in the early 1850s, and his much-discussed sexuality. The poet's secrecy about his love affairs with men and women is legendary, and despite his promise to reveal a "Big Secret" to Traubel in the last years of his life, that revelation never came to pass. The poet's concern for privacy was so intense that in one of his journals, he developed a code to disguise the male recipient of his passion. When asked about the butterfly photograph, Whitman claimed that it was authentic, but his answers seem more arch than defensively sincere. "Yes—that was an actual moth," he told one inquisitor. "The picture is substantially literal: we were good friends: I had quite the in-and-out of taming, or fraternizing with, some of the insects, animals."[23] Adopting what may have been a rural accent, he told the skeptical Thayer, "I've always had the knack of attracting birds and butterflies and other wild critters. They know that I like 'em and won't hurt 'em and so they come."[24] Surely if Whitman had been embarrassed by his artifice he would not have kept the butterfly as a souvenir. And surely he would have destroyed the evidence before his literary executors took control. The butterfly's survival indicates that rather than feel shame about his embrace of publicity, he seemed to enjoy it. That shamelessness appears throughout the poet's life—from his un-authorized publication of Emerson's 1855 letter congratulating him on the beginnings of a great career to his filing wildly exaggerated newspaper reports of his 1879 tour of the West.

In seeking a suitable critical approach toward the poet and the culture of celebrity, readers would be well served by following the pose that Whit-man struck in the original photograph. Holding the butterfly aloft, he seems unmistakably delighted by his "fraternizing" with this insect. At the same time, the photograph records a more playful, mischievous mo-ment. It records the pleasure that arises from Whitman's embrace of his own superficiality. As he holds his prop up for the camera, Whitman appears pleasantly amused by his participation in this photographic trick. He is Barnum entertained by his own bit of humbuggery, his cultivation of artifice for the purposes of publicity. Neil Harris once coined the term "operational aesthetic" to explain Barnum's ability not only to fool the public but to have it delight in the revelation of the trick.[25] Like Barnum happily revealing the secrets behind an exhibit (and in the process charg-ing his customers twice), Whitman seems to have willed his cardboard butterfly to posterity. Without the poet's consent, future generations would not understand the deception behind what was reportedly his fa-vorite portrait of himself.

Rather than fault Whitman for somehow failing both democracy and Parnassus, readers might share in his satisfaction with this artifice. The sociologist Joshua Gamson has examined the enjoyment that some con-temporary audiences experience in observing the construction of celeb-rity by media and public relations specialists: "The activity that engages audiences in this reading position is the pleasure that comes from recog-nizing manipulation, from deconstructing the encoding process, from dwelling on the visible machinery itself and on the play of images."[26] Reading *Leaves of Grass* is a categorically different activity than observing the star industry at work, but Gamson's description can be quite valuable when considering not just the butterfly portrait but Whitman's poetic manipulation of the crowd. In the years before the Civil War, Whitman relied almost entirely on a synthetic form of celebrity, one in which he fabricated and enacted the illusion of his popularity. As if he were relentlessly courting public opinion, he invented armies of admirers and at times addressed his readers as fervent, nearly fanatical followers. Such fictions permeate Whitman's poems, rhetorically positioning the poet amid a celebratory populace. With its focus on biographical and cultural criticism, my book does not offer a comprehensive reading of *Leaves of Grass*, and I leave many important works aside in recognition that no single critical perspective could hope to encompass its broad aesthetic achievement. At the same time, however, I firmly believe that seeing Whitman's promotional machinery at work can significantly enhance the pleasure we take from some of his most significant poems.

Although his response may have been especially meaningful and unique, Whitman was not alone in feeling the influence of antebellum America's emergent culture of celebrity. As the first chapter explains, the first editions of *Leaves of Grass* appeared after a period of widespread growth in popular culture and entertainment. New York and Philadelphia were the centers of this growth, but innovations ranging from the lyceum to the penny press allowed even rural Americans to have contact with an identifiable group of celebrities. With his proximity to Manhattan, Whitman was in an unusually good position to observe what Leo Braudy has described as "the frenzy of renown," and from an early age, he found himself reflecting on fame, ambition, and the political import of applause.[27] The first chapter explores the history of antebellum celebrity, tracing its roots in the early Republic, its flowering during the Jacksonian age, and its significance to a range of American authors including Nathaniel Hawthorne, Harriet Beecher Stowe, Edgar Allan Poe, and Emily Dickinson. None of these authors shared Whitman's enthusiasm for the crowd, and their concerns that fame would destabilize traditional concepts of value and identity sound remarkably similar to those offered by such twentieth-century critics as Dwight MacDonald and Daniel Boorstin. Whether or not their cultural influence was warranted, celebrities such as

Jenny Lind, Fanny Fern, and Henry Ward Beecher were quickly woven into the cultural fabric. Their sheer popularity made them part of the representational technology by which the nation came to know itself.

I have organized my discussion of Whitman into four chapters, each focused on a theme that is central to the analysis of celebrity: personality, publicity, intimacy, and campaigns. It is tempting to see a chronology in these chapters as Whitman moves from his early faith in popularity to the position, at the end of his life, when he achieved celebrity by exaggerating his critical and popular neglect. To a certain extent that chronology holds true, as Whitman's fame grew throughout his lifetime and transformed him along the way from a neglected working-class hero to a revered cultural icon. Following this narrative too closely can be misleading, however, for the poet who gloried in the freedom to contradict himself often experimented with contradictory ideas before making one a definitive part of his literary and promotional practice several decades later. Organized by theme, the chapters acknowledge the complexity of Whitman's practice, focusing both on the poetics of fame and its biographical attainment.

The work of Braudy, Richard Schickel, and P. David Marshall has been quite helpful to this analysis, for in very different ways, they have pioneered a topic of critical inquiry that will become increasingly relevant over time.[28] I have freely borrowed concepts from these and other writers, even when those concepts were originally derived to explain the function of television and movie stars. Adopting this strategy obviously risks charges of anachronism from literary scholars focused on the nineteenth century. I acknowledge this anachronism at specific points in the text, but let me offer a blanket apologia for my applications of cultural theory to *Leaves of Grass*. Whitman, of course, encourages us to read him in light of our own cultural concerns; as he writes in "Crossing Brooklyn Ferry," "I am with you, you men and women of a generation, or ever so many generations hence" (*LGNC*, 136). The challenge for scholars is how to ground an analysis in the complexities of Whitman's age while also exploring *Leaves of Grass* with the knowledge and interests of our own historical moment. Thinking about Whitman alongside the insights of cultural and media critics can help us reexamine some commonly held assumptions about the poet in *Leaves of Grass*. What is the purpose of Whitman's self-definition? Why does he demand an intimacy with his readers? Why the insistence that the public has constituted itself in him? Why does he

claim to be larger than the medium that distributes him? Whitman scholars have long considered these and other questions. A vocabulary forged
in the analysis of Hollywood and the public relations industry will help
energize and reframe such inquiries.

The advantages of this approach may be particularly apparent in the
book's second chapter, an exploration of Whitman's concept of personality. In both their antebellum and twenty-first century formulations, celebrities may seem to be the logical outgrowth of Emerson's representative men, prime specimens of the doctrine of romantic individualism. As
Jay Grossman and others have shown, scholars have been too quick in
assuming that Emerson and Whitman had similar ideas about what constituted the representative in the United States.[29] A different model for
understanding the poet than the Concord sage is Whitman's predecessor
Tom Paine, who suggested a type of literary celebrity that made a republican virtue out of fame. Paine's example recommends that rather than an
expression of glorified individualism, celebrity is a collaborative form of
identity, one that presumes the public's role in determining personality.
In asserting his own celebrity, Whitman may appear to be denying the
social roots of fame, but a closer look at *Leaves of Grass* reveals his efforts to
authenticate the poet by fabricating his own impact and popularity. As we
will see, despite its populist roots, Whitman's poetics sharply diverges
from the more popular verse of Longfellow and other Fireside poets. His
emphasis on personality, as opposed to character, resulted in a poetics that
radically challenged his nineteenth-century readers.

Celebrities are both advertisements and commodities. The portrait of
Whitman holding his butterfly is a case in point. The poet's image promotes the desirability of his person, and while readers cannot purchase
that person outright, they can purchase the books associated with him.
Chapter 3 turns to the subject of publicity, a concept that had both a
political and promotional meaning in antebellum America. The chapter
examines Whitman alongside the rise of advertising, comparing his long,
unrhymed lines to the jingle of commercial verse. In Park Benjamin, P. T.
Barnum, and other contemporaries, the poet found examples of the ways
in which public attention could be manufactured, manipulated, and even
counterfeited. He adapted the lessons to an array of promotional activities, finding ways to advertise himself as a popular author—first in the
novel *Franklin Evans* and then later in *Leaves of Grass*. Drawing on the

many advertisements for health tonics and vegetable pills that flourished in antebellum America, Whitman created a poetics that promised to improve his readers' lives.

Chapter 4 continues this focus on the reader in exploring the intimacy that Whitman presumes with his audience. From the beginning of his career, the poet championed his sympathy—a quality that his early admirers as well as twenty-first century scholars have singled out in praising his efforts to get inside readers' lives. Chapter 4 draws on Schickel's important book *Intimate Strangers* in analyzing how Whitman's renowned sympathy constructs "the illusion of intimacy" that the public frequently has with celebrities. Intimacy is often presented as an antidote to publicity, but a number of antebellum writers shrewdly invoked their sympathy as a sign of their celebrity. The Calamus poems highlight the promotional and rhetorical advantages that come from the poet's professing an intimate, secret relation with his audience. The chapter examines the degree to which Whitman addresses his readers as fans, establishing the kind of intimate, confidential relationship that forms such an important part of celebrity culture today. While the crowds of admirers that populate the early poems failed to materialize, the strategy of intimacy seems to have had a direct and material impact. Now known as a series of love poems for men, Calamus was particularly effective in the mid-nineteenth century in arousing the affection of several women readers who wrote the poet passionate, sexually charged letters promising their undying affection.

The final chapter addresses the subject of campaigns, the organization of publicity around a particular topic, issue, or theme. Of all the aspects of American politics that influenced Whitman's work—liberty, equality, independence, the individual, the public good—perhaps the most neglected has been the logic of the campaign, the relentless need to win elections by persuading others of one's talents, suitability, and popular acceptance. *Walt Whitman and the Culture of American Celebrity* closes with a discussion of the poet's last decades, when he turned away from the powerful confidence in celebrity that he had expressed in the 1850s. If in 1856 Whitman had exaggerated the number of people who had bought *Leaves of Grass,* by the 1870s he was misleading the public by describing himself as the United States' most neglected and overlooked poet. In clothing himself in what Braudy has called the "sanction of neglect," he was both echoing the thoughts of his poetic ancestors and looking forward to his modernist progeny.[30] Reflecting on the implied narrative structure of the promotional campaign, the chapter positions this extended promotional strategy alongside two other campaigns from Whitman's career: how his rivalry with the presidency during the antebellum era became an appropriation of Lincoln's image in the 1870s and 1880s and how he deployed the jeremiad as a means of holding the nation responsible for his lack of popularity. Whitman's exaggeration of his neglect is a fitting conclusion to the book, as it demonstrates the ironic outcome of his original populist understanding of fame.

In the twenty-first century, people around the world dream of becoming superstars, of garnering the riches and applause that only a few Cinderellas will achieve. Whitman invites us to see celebrity itself as a kind of dream, an identity brimming with visionary possibility for both ourselves and democracy. This vision appeared throughout the twentieth century—sometimes in the homage Hollywood stars made to their audiences, sometimes in the cynically populist inflections of television's talk shows and reality series. Most notably, Whitman's vision survives in Andy Warhol's well-known prediction that in the future every American would have fifteen minutes of fame. Warhol's comment pithily expresses the ways in which democracy *ironically* commingles with celebrity, the ways in which the people become "personalities." Rooted in the populist promise of Jacksonian political and cultural reforms, Whitman's relation to American celebrity is a story about how the poet's thinking responded to the culture he observed developing around him. The interplay between Whitman's imagination and experience illuminates both the possibility and the tenuousness of his democratic dream.

CHAPTER ONE

Celebrity

ANTEBELLUM OVATIONS

CELEBRITY CAME LATE TO WALT WHITMAN. An old man, half paralyzed by strokes, he could hardly appreciate the attention he attracted
during the height of America's Gilded Age. From around the world people wrote the poet asking for his autograph, and on at least one occasion,
he used a pile of such requests to light the kindling in his fireplace (*WWC,*
4:351–52). Admirers frequently traveled to Camden, hoping to meet the
author of *Leaves of Grass.* When Oscar Wilde arrived in 1882, the poet was
living with his brother and sister-in-law in a respectable working-class
neighborhood. The two drank homemade elderberry wine and took tremendous satisfaction in each other's company. In March 1884, Whitman
moved to the two-story shanty where he would reside until his death.
Located at 328 Mickle Street, the house had six small rooms and no
furnace. By arrangement, the previous owners lived with the poet, but
when they moved ten months later, they left him alone and with no
furniture. Eventually Mary Davis, a sea captain's widow, agreed to move
into the home as Whitman's housekeeper, bringing with her a dog, a cat, a
few birds, and the much-needed furniture.[1]

Surrounded by the sounds of factory whistles, train yards, and ped-
dlers hawking in the street, admirers such as Bram Stoker and Thomas
Eakins visited with the famous man. They climbed the narrow staircase to

a plainly decorated room where the poet sat in a rocking chair amid piles of old newspapers, photographs, notebooks, and manuscripts. A lifetime's worth of correspondence was seemingly scattered about the room, though Whitman seemed able to locate any single letter with ease—the congratulations from Emerson, a rejection from a New York magazine, a note from an English sailor expressing admiration for *Leaves of Grass*. Although many were filled with praise, a number of these letters revealed the complications that came with fame. One reader contacted Whitman, offering to bear him a child; he marked on the envelope containing her letter "?insane asylum." A letter from a prominent Englishman inquired whether the Calamus poems hinted at sexual relations between men. The poet responded with anger and astonishment, claiming that he had fathered six illegitimate children. In 1888 he refused to endorse a California woman's plan to produce a Walt Whitman calendar with each month illustrating a passage from his poems. "I not only don't enthuse—I do not even approve," he commented. "*Leaves of Grass* does not lend itself to piecemeal quotation" (*WWC*, 2:115).[2] Earlier that year, however, the poet had greeted the sight of his portrait on a box of cigars with the amused pronouncement "That is fame!" (*WWC*, 7:386).

With their invasions on both his privacy and his work, such incidents suggest an unexpected conclusion to the kind of fame that Whitman had imagined for himself in the decades before the Civil War. In none of these situations would he find the type of deep-seated popularity he observed in the carnival atmosphere of antebellum New York.[3] Though his understanding would change over time, celebrity for Whitman was less a biographical marker than a broad cultural orientation. Its capacity to signify individual achievement was subordinate to its role in expressing the popular will. Never at ease with the increasingly invasive forms of publicity that arose in the late nineteenth century, Whitman fondly remembered the spontaneous enthusiasm with which audiences had greeted their favorite actors in 1830s New York:

> Recalling from that period the occasion of either Forrest or
> Booth, any good night at the old Bowery, pack'd from ceiling to
> pit with its audience mainly of alert, well dress'd, full-blooded
> young and middle-aged men, the best average of American born
> mechanics—the emotional nature of the whole mass arous'd by

the power and magnetism of as mighty mimes as ever trod the
stage—the whole crowded auditorium, and what seeth'd in it,
and flush'd from its faces and eyes, to me as much a part of the
show as any—bursting forth in one of those long-kept-up tempests of hand-clapping peculiar to the Bowery—no dainty kid-
glove business, but electric force and muscle from perhaps
2000 full-sinew'd men—(the inimitable and chromatic tempest
of one of those ovations to Edwin Forrest, welcoming him back
after an absence, comes up to me this moment). (*WPP*, 1189)

Published in 1888, the passage from *November Boughs* touches on
many of the themes that Whitman had employed in earlier depictions of
the crowd: the manly and polite working class, the magnetic pull of the
star, the eruption of muscular applause setting the Bowery theater apart
from its aristocratic counterparts. As Whitman's next paragraph makes
clear, the actors attracted a highly diverse audience, one that included
such "notables" as John Quincy Adams, Andrew Jackson, and James
Fenimore Cooper along with its native-born workers and mechanics. The
crowd's "inimitable and chromatic tempests" attested not only to the
strength of the actors but to its own strength as well. Edwin Forrest and
Junius Brutus Booth (the father of Lincoln's assassin) were both celebrated for their broadly expressive style of acting. In their celebrity, Whitman sees a kind of election, a representative system in which individuals
could be sanctioned with public approval and sanctified in national pride.
Just as they stirred and electrified their admirers, the performers were
transformed by the audience applauding them. They were not simply
actors with individual talents and skills; they were emblems of democratic
nationalism.

In contrast to much of *November Boughs,* the passage returns Whitman to antebellum New York and the emergent celebrity culture that had
played a prominent role in his conception of *Leaves of Grass.* Although the
poet's own fame came during a later age of magazine profiles, testimonial
dinners, and "star lectures," it was the reception of figures such as Forrest
and Booth that excited his imagination and exerted a deep influence on
his poems. Whitman's recollection of the Old Bowery attests to the rich
potential he had seen in the democratization of fame and the rise of
American celebrity. Among the many political, economic, and social

changes that occurred during the Jacksonian era, substantial popular audiences began to appear in urban centers stretching from New York and
Philadelphia to such far-off towns as Pittsburgh and Cincinnati. Building
on the growing significance of celebrity in eighteenth-century London
and Paris, American cities saw the emergence of a highly fluid and often-
times politicized concept of fame. Though it is colored by nostalgia, Whitman's portrait is indicative of a society that in coming years would turn
people as diverse as Tom Thumb and Harriet Beecher Stowe into objects
of public appeal and scrutiny.

In the years between Jackson's election and the start of the Civil War,
urbanization and the opening of commercial markets resulted in the
proliferation of new forms of popular entertainment.[4] Whitman thinks
back to a period of cultural growth that would affect nearly every segment
of urban society. While these changes influenced aristocrats and profes-
sionals alike, their biggest impact was on the middle and working classes
that were forming in towns and cities along the eastern seaboard. Particularly in New York, common laborers could join their bourgeois counterparts in attending an array of operas, plays, lectures, and recitals. At the
same time, the rise of the penny press was making newspapers, books,
and magazines available to readers of all incomes. Among the most influ-
ential—and visible—members of antebellum society were the great "national" publishers James Gordon Bennett, Robert Bonner, and Horace
Greeley.

For some Americans, the growth of popular culture resulted in "the
deep, horizontal comradeship" that Benedict Anderson has associated
with nationalism.[5] As individuals attended common performances, read
common newspapers, and consumed common goods, they developed a
spirit of both power and fraternity. The sense of cultural ownership could
produce the unity that Whitman recalled in *November Boughs,* but it could
also intensify the boisterous, sometimes volatile nature of his society. The
antebellum public sphere was a disorderly place in which performers,
writers, reformers, and discourses competed for the public's attention.
Out of this period came the first campaign slogans, the first campaign
biographies, the first advertising agencies, and the first programmatic
efforts to understand hype. The men behind these innovations aimed to
adapt to the country's newly competitive environment. At the center of this
competition was the public, and audiences quickly felt their newfound

power, often associating their participation in cultural matters with their political identity. The nearly utopian class mixing Whitman appreciated at the Old Bowery was short lived. In the 1840s, he informs us, "cheap prices and vulgar programmes came in," and the audience of assorted mechanics, writers, and statesmen gave way to "the pandemonium of the pit" (*WPP*, 1190). Over the next decades, spectators from the bourgeois and working classes gravitated toward different kinds of entertainment. The sense of national camaraderie became a class-based identification with specific amusements, venues, and celebrities.[6] With a striking fusion of pride, defiance, and urgency, laborers formed a deep connection to the purveyors of popular entertainment, a connection often expressed as a competing form of nationalism.

That sense of competition was evident in the celebrity of Edwin Forrest, Whitman's favorite actor and one of the most notorious stars of his age. As the passage from *November Boughs* illustrates, Forrest's American style of acting had won him broad praise in the 1830s, particularly among the working classes, who admired his patriotism and hypermasculine roles. (Forrest was known internationally for his performance as the oppressed slave Spartacus in *The Gladiator*.) By 1849, however, Forrest's rivalry with the English Shakespearean James Macready would play a central role in the Astor Place riot. Over the years, the two actors had traded insults through the press, most of which focused on the national character expressed by their divergent styles. The rivalry grew dangerously intense when the two men offered competing productions of *Macbeth* at theaters separated by just a few blocks. With the press aggravating the conflict, Forrest's working-class supporters hissed and heckled Macready's performances at the genteel Astor Place Opera House. Despite pleas from leading writers and intellectuals (Herman Melville among them), the disturbances continued. Eventually the militia was called in, and on the night of May 10, 1849, the ten thousand protestors outside the opera house turned violent. The fighting killed twenty-two people.[7] There are many lessons to be drawn from the Astor Place riot—the depth of class antipathy, the blinding force of nationalism, the long-lived tension between high and popular culture. The riot also indicated the extent to which Whitman's working-class New Yorkers identified themselves with their celebrities.

By the 1850s, a much broader cross-section of society would share

In this 1861 Mathew Brady photograph, Edwin Forrest poses as the Roman slave Spartacus. Courtesy of the National Portrait Gallery, Smithsonian Institution; gift of the Edwin Forrest Home for Retired Actors.

that sense of value, choosing among a group of actors, musicians, writers, and promoters a few select individuals whom they would vest with sociopolitical meaning. The phenomenon extended to all segments of society, affecting not just entertainment but the ministry, publishing, business, lecturing, and poetry. Whether people rejected or sought it, thinking about the meaning of fame and publicity became a prominent concern on both sides of the Atlantic. Some, like Forrest, would experience the hazards of fame firsthand and find themselves beset with overeager fans or invasions of their privacy. Others, like Whitman, would observe such behavior from a distance, reflecting on what celebrity meant to the development of democratic society. The roots of this new world lay in the eighteenth century.

ORIGINS

Determining the beginnings of celebrity culture is a difficult if not futile exercise, particularly since most scholars of the subject view it as roughly corresponding to the lives of the specific men and women they are studying. (While one scholar, for example, observes the phenomenon in the mid-eighteenth century, another claims that the concept did not exist until the advent of film and television.) In the seventeenth century, *celebrity* was used to describe a solemn religious observance; it was a quality that might be attributed to a ritual or ceremony that had been performed with due respect for its office. The *OED* cites Edward Brerewood's *Enquiries Touching the Diversity of Languages and Religions* (1612): "Their general synods . . . have frequently been held with great celebrity." By the eighteenth century, the word's meaning had expanded to include "the condition of being extolled or talked about; famousness, notoriety."[8] Mirroring the increased importance of the public sphere (and the subsequent devaluation of church authority), the word now signified the public's possession of a renowned individual through conversation and colloquy. In this respect, it came closer to its original Latin meaning of being famous or *thronged*. Samuel Johnson—whose dictionary lists celebrity as being synonymous with fame and renown—used the word in *Rambler* 165, wryly remarking that he did not find himself "enriched in proportion to [his] celebrity."[9]

The emergence of this new definition of celebrity coincides with the beginnings of what Leo Braudy has described as "an international European fame culture" in the eighteenth century. As the power of both the church and monarchies waned, "an enormous variety of new social, economic, and political groups" used the press to push their way into "the vacuum of cultural authority."[10] That sense of opportunism, of concerted efforts to publicize one's self, shows up in the example of the novelist Laurence Sterne. In 1760, Sterne traveled to London to promote *Tristram Shandy*. Dressed in character as either the digressing Tristram or the amiable Parson Yorick, he circulated through London as a walking advertisement for his book. As Peter Briggs describes it, the stunt played upon the "illusion of presence already established in the novel" and won for Sterne notoriety in both the press and polite society.[11] Nearly a hundred years before Whitman adopted the costume of a working-class rough, the novelist was achieving enviable success in thinking of publicity as a series of public performances.

Sterne exploited a phenomenon that, as Briggs points out, Johnson and Boswell had observed as well: "that audiences were increasingly interested in authors as 'personalities' rather than simply as artistic makers; idiosyncrasies that had gone unreported in an earlier generation were now seized upon as symptoms of personal character, pieces in a mosaic of personality which the reading public wished earnestly to complete."[12] A more dramatic eighteenth-century expression of this trend centered on Jean-Jacques Rousseau. Unwilling to admire the writer from afar, people traveled hundreds of miles to see and engage him in conversation. The posthumous publication of Rousseau's *Confessions* (1781) provided a fitting conclusion to the publicity surrounding a life known for its singularity. With its insight into the private life of an intellectual celebrity, the autobiography turned Rousseau into "an object not of attention but of curiosity," a writer valued less for his dialogue with the ancients than for his willingness to open his private life to public view.[13]

Both the drive for and construction of celebrity continued in the first decades of the new century. With their emphasis on subjectivity and individual voice, the romantic poets lent themselves to the kind of public scrutiny that Rousseau's *Confessions* had initiated. The cult of personality that rose up around Lord Byron and the wave of Byromania that swept through Europe approached a fervor nowadays associated with popular musicians. In 1814, readers purchased ten thousand copies of Byron's poem *The Corsair* on its first day of publication, effectively buying up the entire release. As one of his contemporaries put it, the poet's power lay in his ability to put a spell on his readers: "the spell is pronounced, the witches['] song is sung—the reader listens, trembles, admires, dreads, condemns . . . and prays for liberation, yet he admires."[14] By the time Mary Shelley wrote the introduction to her 1831 edition of *Frankenstein,* it was quite natural to acknowledge the motivating power of fame: "It is not singular that, as the daughter of two persons of distinguished literary celebrity, I should very early in life have thought of writing. . . . My husband . . . was from the very first anxious that I should prove myself worthy of my parentage and enroll myself on the page of fame."[15]

At roughly the same time, references to celebrity were likewise appearing in the United States. Along with the theatrical term *star* (which Mrs. Trollope liberally used in *Domestic Manners of the Americans* [1832]), the word *celebrity* saw regular use by the end of the 1820s.[16] In 1827, the *Vermont Gazette* wrote that Anna Letitia Barbauld's learned prose writings had "gained her great celebrity."[17] Caroline May used the word similarly in a biographical sketch of Anne Bradstreet she wrote in her 1853 anthology, *The American Female Poets:* "Although 'merrie olde Englande' claims her birthplace, the honour of her poetical fame belongs to America; for we find her recorded as the earliest poet of New England, where she gained much celebrity by the spirit and power of her writings."[18] The usage is consistent with antebellum notions of celebrity, for it does not connote the kind of meretriciousness that the word frequently has today. To have celebrity was to have enrolled oneself "on the page of fame," to have achieved both public acceptance and, through that, a kind of cultural legitimacy. When Emerson used the word as a noun in *English Traits* (1856), he contrasted it with the idleness of British nobility. "A feeling of self-respect," he reported, "is driving cultivated men" out of aristocratic society, for the noble's "pride of place" stubbornly denied the era's "democratic tendencies." In Emerson's discussion, the "celebrities of wealth and fashion" represent a leveling influence that threatens the established aristocracy.[19] Celebrity had evolved into more than a quality granted by the public; it was also a distinct category of democratic identity.

Nineteenth-century celebrity culture occurred in a surprisingly trans-Atlantic context. In fact, as Mary Cayton has argued, it was Emerson's reputation in Great Britain that first brought him fame in the United States.[20] Thomas N. Baker's study of Nathaniel Parker Willis has done a particularly good job demonstrating how international the performance of celebrity could be. After graduating from Yale and publishing several well-received books of poetry, Willis rose to new prominence as a travel correspondent who published private, gossipy information about British luminaries in the American press. The attention and outrage these letters attracted combined a growing interest in the secrets of the famous with the fanning of national rivalries. Collected in book form, Willis's *Pencillings by the Way* (1835) stands at the forefront of a host of other constructions of celebrity which, like the Forrest-Macready feud, drew upon cultural comparisons and rivalry.[21] Mobs of admirers greeted Charles Dickens during his 1842 tour of the United States, leading the novelist to complain that he could not walk down a city street without being "followed by a multitude."[22] In the early 1850s, the singer Jenny Lind embarked on a two-year tour of the States that grossed more than seven hundred thousand dollars. With P. T. Barnum serving as her business partner, tour manager, and all-around impresario, the "Swedish nightingale" was greeted by hordes of adoring Americans, most of whom had never heard of her before Barnum's elaborate promotions. Over twenty thousand people gathered to welcome Lind to the country when her ship arrived in New York.[23] Hoping to attract similar attention, the singer Henrietta Sontag traveled to the city in September 1852, and the crowd that came to greet her quickly devolved into an unruly, rioting mob.

American luminaries traveling abroad met with similar frenzy. Barnum toured England and France with the diminutive Tom Thumb, attracting first royal and then popular attention. When Harriet Beecher Stowe embarked on her 1853 lecture tour of Britain, she encountered increasingly large and hysterical crowds. The country was overtaken by a kind of "national dementia," as one biographer put it, with thousands of spectators gathering at Liverpool's docks to await her arrival. Admirers lined the streets in Liverpool, Glasgow, and London, each hoping to get a look at the author of *Uncle Tom's Cabin*. Two thousand people gathered in Glasgow to sing the American abolitionist a musical greeting. A crowd inside a lecture hall waiting for Stowe grew so excited upon her arrival that they rushed the entrance, trampling and nearly killing a woman in the commotion.[24]

While early-nineteenth-century celebrity developed in a trans-Atlantic context, Americans such as Whitman also drew upon the republican conception of fame they had inherited from the nation's founders. The revolutionary generation had politicized the classical regard for fame, associating virtue with what Ovid described as the mental "spur" to accomplish great things. In *Federalist* 72, for example, Alexander Hamilton described "the love of fame" as "the ruling passion of the noblest minds," a passion "which would prompt a man to plan and undertake extensive and arduous enterprises for the public benefit." Writing in support of Thomas Jefferson's candidacy for president, Hamilton pointed to Aaron Burr's indifference to fame as a sign that his ambition might go unchecked and that, in the end, he was not to be trusted.[25] The links between celebrity and virtue were quite clear to James Wilson, one of Pennsylvania's delegates to the Constitutional Convention: "The love of honest and well-earned fame is deeply rooted in honest and susceptible minds. Can there be a stronger incentive to the operations of this passion, than the hope of becoming the object of well founded and distinguishing applause? Can there be a more complete gratification of this passion, than the satisfaction of knowing that this applause is given—that it is given upon the most honourable principles, and acquired by the most honourable pursuits?"[26]

In our post-Barnum age, the correlations between fame, honor, and honesty may seem comically naïve. As the historian Douglass Adair first explained, however, for men such as Washington, Adams, Jefferson, and Madison, "the pursuit of fame . . . was a way of transforming egotism and self-aggrandizing impulses into public service." The founders "had been taught that public service nobly (and selfishly) performed was the surest way to build 'lasting monuments' and earn the perpetual remembrance of posterity." The goal was to attain the kind of cultural respect that would grow over time. "To be famous or renowned" meant "to be widely spoken of by [one's] contemporaries" and yet at the same time to "act in such a way that posterity" would also remember one's "name and actions."[27] With both admiration and envy, Benjamin Rush wrote his friend John Adams that "the French and American Revolutions differed from each other in many things, but they were alike in one particular—the former gave all its *power* to a single man, the latter all its *fame.*"[28] Feeling that they had failed to win over their contemporaries, both Rush and Adams dedicated their later years to addressing posterity, a figure they conceived as being a more just and republican arbiter than the hagiographers they saw surrounding the memory of Washington.

The coherence of the founders' vision had a complicated fate as it encountered the more carnivalesque atmosphere of Jacksonian America. Stripped of its classical roots, fame became an achievement itself rather than a statesman's purest reward. More significantly, the politicized understanding of celebrity that attracted Whitman became increasingly identified with popularity, something clearly incongruous to eighteenth-century thinkers. As Adair points out, Enlightenment intellectuals on both sides of the Atlantic considered fame or celebrity to be a far superior achievement to mere acclaim. More public and inclusive than glory or popularity, fame looked "to the largest possible human audience, horizontally in space and vertically in time." Fame rewarded "the action or behavior of a 'real man,' who stands out, who towers above his fellows in some spectacular way." The ephemeral nature of popularity made it the "copper coinage of the 18th-century." Adair quotes Oliver Goldsmith in what might be regarded as a concise expression of the founders' views: "Of praise a mere glutton he swallowed what came, / and the puff of a dunce, he mistook for fame."[29] As early as 1813, Adams was stewing over his countrymen's lack of respect for the distinction. Noting its growing significance, he complained to Jefferson that America had developed into a country "where Popularity had more omnipotence than the British Parliament had ever assumed."[30] Just over twenty years later, Alexis de Tocqueville would see a "tyranny of the majority" operating in American political and cultural life.

Despite the dramatic differences, aspects of this republican version of fame survived well into the nineteenth century. The notion that posterity would serve as the final arbiter of fame remained a staple of intellectual thought, at times mixed with a faith in Christian humility and, at others, with the consolation of the avant-garde. Meanwhile the culture continued to see prominent individuals—now ranging from generals to entertainers to abolitionists—as possessing a kind of political legitimacy particularly suited to American society.

The proliferation of lyceums across the country in the 1820s and 1830s did much to strengthen the connections between democratic republicanism and fame. As conceived by Josiah Holbrook, its principal theorist and architect, the lyceum was initially developed to instruct working-class men in both the practical sciences and virtue. Individuals with particular expertise would instruct their townsmen on the kinds of skills and knowledge that would help them become more successful members of the community. The series of public lectures quickly became popular, appealing not just to laborers but to working- and middle-class families. By 1835, the United States had more than three thousand lyceums in towns ranging from Eastport, Maine, to Savannah, Georgia, to Little Rock, Arkansas.[31] Organized by groups of interested citizens, villagers met in a variety of venues—church basements, rooms above courthouses, schools, and private homes. Some lyceums would rent a private hall for their series, while particularly wealthy communities could spend about a thousand dollars to build a meeting place of their own. In 1831, the Salem lyceum premiered its unusually impressive building. As Carl Bode reports, the Salem hall could accommodate "700 persons in semicircular tiers of seats around the speaker's platform."[32]

Tickets to the lyceums were relatively inexpensive, and thus they often attracted husbands, wives, and their school-age children. Societies traditionally sold subscriptions to an entire series of lectures, but they also offered individual tickets for as low as twenty-five cents. Impressed by the number of children who attended the events, a visiting member of the British parliament remarked on the thousands of Americans no more than ten years old who knew astonishing amounts about geology, mineralogy, botany, and other topics useful to living in the United States. Drawing on both civic and family structures, the organizations institutionalized the republican pattern of making the instruction of virtue a rite of citizenship and consensus. Indeed, at the 1831 national convention, the Lyceum board affirmed its political purpose. "*The Lyceum is a Republican Institution*," the delegates agreed. "It has for its object the universal diffusion of knowledge, which has ever been considered the strongest, and surest, if not the only foundation of a republican government." As the organizers saw it, the education and improvement of citizens was vital to the nation's success: "While the Lyceum holds itself high above the vulgar abuse and angry contentions of *party politics*, it would gladly teach the privileges of citizens, the rights of freemen, and an enlightened and sound policy of republican governments."[33]

Local lyceums organized themselves to reinforce these republican principles. Founded in September 1843, the West Philadelphia Lyceum was dedicated to "the moral and intellectual improvement of its members and the general diffusion of useful knowledge." By "useful knowledge," the lyceum meant morality, history, and literature in addition to more practical and scientific topics. The list of questions that members wished to address in the first six months is remarkably varied: Is an animal or vegetable diet healthier in a cold climate? What is the color of snow in Greenland? Should capital punishment be abolished? What cause keeps planets in their orbits? Was Coriolanus justified in heading the Volsci against his native country? Of the thirty-one people who signed the lyceum's constitution, two were doctors, two were lawyers, and thirteen were women. Within six months, the lyceum had sixty-three paying members who paid twenty-five cents apiece to hear speakers from the city. Although their topics were varied, a disproportionate number of the speakers were lawyers.[34]

This republican vision persisted as the local character of the early lyceum briefly gave way to a series of lecture circuits, many organized around historical, evangelical, and reformist themes.[35] The Salem Lyceum in 1838–39 featured lectures as diverse as "The Honey Bee," "The Life of Mohammed," "The Legal Rights of Women," and "The Capacity of the Human Mind for Culture and Improvement."[36] By the late 1840s, however, the boundaries between education and entertainment had grown more porous. Out of the lyceum grew a nationally organized public lecture system that brought a series of prominent lecturers to each community. What had begun as a republican rite of citizenship gradually shaded into a collective performance of celebrity.

F.A.M.E.

At the opening of Nathaniel Hawthorne's *The Blithedale Romance* (1852), the poet Miles Coverdale visits his village's lyceum hall. It is the evening before he plans to leave for the experimental farm Blithedale where he will join a "knot of dreamers" in living and working communally. Hawthorne based the novel on his own experience at Brook Farm, an experimental commune where he lived from April to October 1841. He had initially gone to the farm because he thought it would be a good environment for his writing, but he quickly found the labor deadening. By September, he was describing himself as only a "spectral" participant in the commune's dreamy enterprise. Less than three weeks later, he confessed to his fiancée, Sophia Peabody, that he had "grown apart from the spirit and manners of the place." In *Blithedale* Coverdale goes to the lyceum in preparation for his departure, but the event he attends is not, as we might expect, a lecture on the latest agricultural methods, nor is it a disquisition on the socialist Charles Fourier, whose teachings are debated later in the novel. Instead, the young poet attends an exhibition of the "Veiled Lady," a mesmerist whose "now forgotten celebrity" belies the significant wonder she was then exciting in her spectators.[37] Coverdale shares the audience's amazement, and he asks the prophetic Lady if she can augur the success of the Blithedale experiment. Her response, he says, is nonsensical and sibylline, though open to interpretation.

The presence of such a performer in the village lyceum hall says much about the changes in antebellum America as the edifying lecture both competed and converged with the culture of celebrity. (Coverdale pointedly describes "the Lecture" as a "sober and pallid, or rather, drab-colored, mode of winter-evening entertainment."[38]) Hawthorne takes characteristic interest in the mesmerist's veil and its ability to isolate her from earthly concerns so she can commune with the spiritual realm. The veil, however, is also a veil of publicity, for underneath its shiny, ethereal fabric sits the anemic Priscilla, the youngest and seemingly frailest woman in the Blithedale community. The veil allows Priscilla to perform her celebrity, for it hides her personal self beneath her starring role in the spectacle. Priscilla is so far removed from the celebrated lady that she remains impervious to public sensation (she does not flinch, for example, when two farm boys are encouraged to shout and lift her chair to make her recognize their presence), and yet she seems to know her audience intimately. When Blithedale's leader, the reformer Hollingsworth, eventually rescues Priscilla from her servitude, when he publicly pulls off her veil, he releases her from the erotics of publicity—only to reclaim her for his single-mindedly virtuous pursuit: reforming the nation's prisons.

The Veiled Lady offers an allegory for the lecture's evolution from republican ritual to the public exhibition of celebrity.[39] Hawthorne witnessed this evolution directly when he served as secretary of the Salem Lyceum. Drawing on his prominent friends and acquaintances, he brought Horace Mann, Henry David Thoreau, Ralph Waldo Emerson, and Daniel Webster to the platform during the 1848–49 season. The shift in programming dramatically increased the public's interest in the popular lecture. By 1862, the editor of *Harper's* was estimating that lectures attracted a nationwide audience of about five hundred thousand people a week.[40] Rather than recruit local citizens to discuss optics or the steam engine (as the Salem Lyceum had done in 1830), lecture committees drew from a group of established speakers that included well-known professors, doctors, publishers, writers, lawyers, and, most of all, members of the clergy.[41] Average lecturers spoke to a total of about fifty thousand people in the four to six months they traveled each year.[42] The most popular speakers—a group that included Henry Ward Beecher, Ralph Waldo Emerson, Oliver Wendell Holmes, Orson Fowler, Horace Greeley, Sylvester Graham, William Alcott, and the poet Bayard Taylor—addressed even more. During the 1854–55 season, for example, Taylor traveled from Maine to Iowa, giving a total of 128 lectures, work for which he earned over six thousand dollars, "almost three times what was considered a top clerical salary."[43] For others, too, the work paid quite handsomely, and lecturers' fees frequently indicated an individual's desirability. Audiences thought that a speaker who was willing to lecture for free or receive a token honorarium lacked the authenticity of a true professional.[44] The Brooklyn minister Henry Ward Beecher, arguably the most celebrated figure of the antebellum period, charged up to two hundred dollars per speech.[45] It was much more common, however, for committees to pay fifty dollars an evening. As one man explained, he lectured for "F.A.M.E.—$50 and my expenses."[46]

With its new emphasis on attracting prominent speakers, the lecture system became easily associated with celebrity. While the initial lyceums depended on the private reputation of speakers, audiences in the 1850s preferred speakers who had been in the public eye. Offering an incidental jab at Barnum's newly won respect, the editor at *Harper's* looked back on the decade, recalling that "if a man had done any thing, from inventing a mermaid to writing a history, he was instantly bagged by the lecture committees and carried throughout the country. There was a natural curiosity to see the man of whom much had been said."[47] With speakers now recognized and referred to as "stars," the lectures both fed and created a general desire to know more about the famous. An 1857 editorial in *Putnam's* suggested that the lecture "secures to the insatiable Yankee the chance, for an hour long, of seeing any notability about whom he was curious."[48] The *Harper's* editor speculated in 1862 that the major lecturers were "personally more widely known than any other class of public men in this country."[49] The publicity created a cycle of renown in which the construct of celebrity lent legitimacy to both the speaker and the audience.

Cayton has shown that when Emerson traveled to Cincinnati, the newspapers seized the opportunity to burnish the city's image in the glow of his stature: "The press continually reinforced the renown of the speaker before, during, and after his arrival and thus promoted the notion that the audience was cultured and brilliant. The 'justly celebrated Emerson' was praised; journalists were certain that 'the fame of the lecturer will undoubtedly draw a crowded hall'; 'the poet and the philosopher, who is universally recognized as one of the great thinkers of the age' was coming to speak."[50]

The lecture's popularity was just one sign of the growing import of antebellum celebrity. From Beecher to Greeley to Holmes, speakers competed for the public's attention with a variety of traveling plays, concerts, museums, and novelty performances. In *The Blithedale Romance*, Coverdale expresses great enthusiasm for the "rich and varied series" of carnivallike exhibitions that share the lyceum stage: the magician with his doves and plates, the ventriloquist speaking in many tongues, the choir of African melodists, and the itinerant professor demonstrating, in separate classes, male and female physiology with manikins from Paris. As with the Veiled Lady, the stage becomes the site of a highly visible form of celebrity. The description dwells upon a traveling "museum of wax figures, illustrating the wide catholicism of earthly renown." In this virtual gallery of fame, Coverdale sees "heroes and statesmen, the Pope and the Mormon Prophet, kings, queens, murderers, and beautiful ladies." "Every sort of person" appears represented, he tells us, "except authors, of whom I never beheld even the most famous, done in wax."[51]

Coverdale's lament has less to do with historical reality, however, than with Hawthorne's own concerns about the convergence of celebrity and authorship. Behind the figure of the Veiled Lady Richard Brodhead has seen "the new female celebrities who, first in the 1840s, then more decisively around 1850, began to appear before newly huge audiences and to be *known* to publics much greater yet."[52] Some of these women were performers such as Lind, but Brodhead argues that Hawthorne was especially alarmed by the first wave of popular women novelists who were entering the literary marketplace. Just as it reflects widespread changes in the lecture system, *Blithedale* expresses considerable anxiety about the phenomenon of celebrity authorship. Compared to *The Scarlet Letter* (1850), which by the end of the 1850s had sold only 11,800 copies, books such as *Uncle Tom's Cabin* (1851) and Susan Warner's *The Wide, Wide World* (1850) had astonishing sales. Stowe's figures dwarf all others (*Uncle Tom's Cabin* sold over three hundred thousand copies in its first three years of publication), but Warner's novel sold an impressive forty thousand copies in less than a year. These two books indicated a dramatically new trend in publishing, and the successes kept coming. Maria Cummins's *The Lamplighter* (1854) sold seventy-three thousand copies in its first year of publication, while Fanny Fern's *Ruth Hall* (1855) sold more than fifty thousand copies just eight months after its release.[53]

Not only did these books attract an enormous audience, they gave their authors an increasingly public profile. The success of Fern's books, for example, led to Robert Bonner's very public campaign to serialize her next story in the pages of the *New York Ledger*, a campaign that resulted in her being hired as a featured columnist. *Blithedale* may reveal Hawthorne to be ill at ease with the new literary competition, the "mobs of scribbling women" he is so notorious for damning. As Brodhead argues, however, the Veiled Lady's celebrity reflects not just a gendered rivalry but the embodiment of "the new social conditions of literary production" under which Hawthorne found himself working, conditions that now included the demands of exposure and publicity.[54] Hawthorne knew the rhetoric of publicity firsthand, having written in 1851 a campaign biography for his college friend Franklin Pierce. The year after *Blithedale* was published, he helped write Richard Henry Stoddard's famous promotional essay about his work, an essay largely responsible for creating the myth of Hawthorne's aloof otherworldliness.[55] Against the stifling virtue of Hollingsworth and the candid sexuality of Zenobia Hawthorne positions the ambiguous power of antebellum fame.

The prevalence of celebrity was directly related to the growth of publicity from the Jacksonian period to the start of the Civil War. The "republic of letters" that had been so compelling to the founders developed into an industry of dizzying literary production. From 1820 to 1856, the number of books published in the United States rose from 2.5 to 16 million. (The publishing climate led Whitman to write Emerson that the many authors, editors, and publishers working in the country were building the stairs that American giants would one day ascend [*WPP*, 1329].) An equally dramatic expansion occurred in the popular press. According to census reports, in 1840 there were 551 newspapers and periodicals published in the United

States; by 1869, the number had risen to more than four thousand, each contributing to the nearly billion copies of text sold each year.[56] Since the 1830s, New York City had been the center of American publishing, but in the 1850s, its publishers began to play a dominant role over the entire country. New commercial magazines such as *Graham's*, *Putnam's*, and *Harper's* assumed a distinctly national orientation. Along with the Boston-based magazine the *Atlantic*, they provided a far-reaching but centralized counterpart to the popular lecture. With the added attraction of fiction and verse, the magazines featured the same combination of education and entertainment that was the staple of the local lecture series—biographical profiles, historical essays, travel sketches. To read *Putnam's* or *Harper's* was to enter into a nationally based public sphere as constructed by the commercial press.

The new forms of media did much to promote the concept of celebrity to a public eager for individuals possessing that kind of distinction. Ezra Greenspan has observed that in the early 1840s, *Graham's* began to put its contributors' names on the title page, using the names of Cooper, Longfellow, and Poe to advertise the issue.[57] Like virtually any celebrity that arises from the commercial sphere, authors became advertisements for themselves as well as for the media that conveyed them. Fifteen years later, the promotional value of celebrity seemed unmistakably clear. In a front-page story complete with banner headlines, Bonner announced that he had successfully wooed Fern to write for him: "the most popular authoress in this or in any other country—FANNY FERN, is now engaged in writing a Tale for the *Ledger*."[58] Though employing a more restrained tone, newspapers and magazines followed similar principles in covering lecture series. The Cincinnati press was typical of many local newspapers in featuring articles on visiting speakers both before and after their appearances. Such promotional pieces reported on speakers' performances in another city or offered an assessment of their current work. News about prominent lecturers was of continuing interest to people outside the visited community. As Donald Scott has demonstrated, local newspapers regularly published "reports and excerpts from lectures by stars like Henry Ward Beecher, Emerson, and Holmes taken from the metropolitan newspapers." The *New York Tribune* began to publish a special weekly section entitled "Sketches of Lectures" that covered the lectures that had recently been delivered in New York City. By the 1850s, the supplement had a weekly press run of nearly 175,000 copies that included subscriptions from reading rooms and local newspapers around the country.[59]

With the burgeoning interest in celebrity also came the kinds of invasion and harassment familiar to students of the twentieth century. The scandalous divorce trial of the actor Edwin Forrest and his wife, Catherine, received wide, though presumably unwanted, exposure in both the New York and national press. With its stories about brothels, charges of adultery, and violent eruptions, the trial offered an intimate glimpse into the domestic life of an already controversial hero of the stage.[60] Jenny Lind's tour of the United States was marred by overeager fans who wanted to know the smallest details of her private life. Stowe encountered so many groping, desperate admirers in England that her husband left the country early, "tired to death of the life" the couple was there leading. Michael Newbury has analyzed these and other incidents in arguing that antebellum celebrity was "figuratively imagined through the dynamics and particular inflections of slavery."[61] The country's major celebrities described themselves as slaves to the public sphere. No matter how inappropriate such comparisons may have been, they attest to how unprepared many antebellum writers and performers were for this new world of publicity. *Blithedale*'s Priscilla is virtually enslaved to her promoter Professor Westervelt, and Hawthorne's depiction of their relationship corresponds with the many antebellum performers who were bewildered by public life.

NOBODIES AND SOMEBODIES

What distinguishes the Veiled Lady from a Stowe or Lind is that her anonymity conveys a refusal to participate in the public's unreasonable demands. The hushed breathing with which audiences greet the mesmerist's appearance and the rapt attention to Zenobia's voice as she invents a legendary history for her underscore the unanswered question of the Lady's mysterious identity. In this, her plight is unusual. Presented as a cipher, the Veiled Lady proves to be quite successful. As a "visible obscurity," however, she radically undermines what in antebellum America was fast becoming a central expectation of fame: that celebrities be both visible and knowable, that their personalities appear to be discernible to the general public.[62] Hawthorne presents us with half of a celebrity, allowing the spectacle to take place while eliminating the singular personality who remains famous outside of it. The Veiled Lady deconstructs a culture increasingly interested in having its celebrities circulate through the public sphere, their bodies becoming both advertisements and commodities.

The most obvious example of the new fascination with personality comes from the popularity of daguerreotypes, photographs, and lithographs. The invention of the daguerreotype in 1839 culminated the movement toward visible authority that had begun in the late eighteenth century. As Braudy has shown, men such as Washington, Napoleon, and Franklin were well aware of the need to demonstrate their newly conceived power in a broad visual display, and thus they sat for dozens of sculptures and portraits, candidly facing the public they represented. Upon its arrival in the United States in 1844, the daguerreotype spread quickly, and by 1851, New York City boasted over a hundred studios. The ubiquity of the daguerreotype, and later the photograph, democratized the process of image making, affording middle-class families the opportunity to record themselves for posterity.[63] At the same time, however, the daguerreotype and photograph—along with their complement the lithograph—promised new access to the renowned, an access that underscored the significance of personality. In 1850 Mathew Brady, who was rapidly becoming famous in his own right, published the first volume of his *Gallery of Illustrious Americans,* a twelve-portrait collection populated largely by sober-looking soldiers and statesmen. As Alan Trachtenberg has argued, the portraits and their accompanying text combined a solemn plea for union with a patrician endorsement of republican virtue. To these qualities, the volume added a stern advertisement for the new technology and its ability to produce a pantheon of national greats.[64]

With its Roman bustlike portraits of men such as John Calhoun and Daniel Webster, the volume provided a very different perspective on fame than did the experience of visiting Brady's popular Manhattan galleries, and the volume was not a commercial success. The series of Broadway galleries attracted large crowds, mixing traditional portraits of statesmen and generals with those of Barnum, Lind, Greeley, Willis, Forrest, and the actresses Harriet Hosmer and Charlotte Cushman. Brimming with enthusiasm after his own visit in 1846, the young Whitman commended the gallery to his readers at the *Brooklyn Evening Sun.* In its various incarnations, the gallery featured so many images of the renowned that in 1863 *Harper's Weekly* proclaimed, "For the past twenty years there has hardly been a celebrity in this country who has not been photographed here."[65]

In much the same way that motion pictures and television would do in the twentieth century, the camera transformed and intensified the way antebellum Americans looked at celebrity. However, there were plenty of other opportunities for society to feed its hunger for personalities. In the 1840s, magazines began to publish facsimile autographs of their chief contributors, building off the hobby of autograph collecting that had arisen in Europe in the 1780s and would remain in the United States throughout the nineteenth century. (Autograph collecting provided enough annoyance to Henry James that he satirized the practice in his 1894 story "The Death of the Lion.") Like the phrenologist studying the keys to behavior in head bumps, romantic-era collectors took particular delight in the autograph, viewing it as a revealing symbol of the inner life of the renowned. As Tamara Thornton remarks, the autograph represented "a reification of self in script" or, as one beleagured writer put it, an "exhibition of one's private personality."[66] To publish a facsimile of the autograph in a journal or book—as Whitman did in the 1856 *Leaves of Grass*—was to expose this intimate expression to advertisement and public scrutiny. Like the photograph—and later the *carte de visite*—the facsimile autograph created the illusion of cultlike aura in an age of mechanical reproduction.[67]

At the same time, magazines and newspapers began devoting greater amounts of column space to the personal qualities of the people they covered. Publications in Europe and the United States included information about what leading figures "looked like, what they wore, what they ate, and what they said."[68] The inclusion—and, indeed, featuring—of such information suggests a growing tendency to elevate persona over content, to value the performance, background, or inner life of individuals alongside their substantive accomplishments. From different pen and pencil marks, we know that Whitman was quite typical of antebellum readers in his attraction to personality and anecdote. When he read an 1849 essay in the *North British Review,* for example, he regularly marked passages about Chaucer's life and career while noting very little about the verse. He marked a footnote describing the poet's physical characteristics with particular vigor, writing in the margins "Person."[69]

American newspapers started to direct their stories to readers like

Whitman, covering lecturers and authors with a new focus on profiling their private lives rather than engaging with their thought. The novelist Mary Virginia Terhune reported that not only was Cummins's novel *The Lamplighter* in every home but that "gossip of the personality of the author was seized upon greedily by press and readers."[70] When writing about Emerson's visit, the *Cincinnati Gazette* included a variety of anecdotes about his private life, describing his eccentricities, his habits, and how his genius was a source of amazement to his puzzled wife. Cayton's survey of the newspaper coverage reveals a striking fascination with Emerson the personality over Emerson the thinker: "Emerson surprised audiences with his gaunt and homely appearance, his narrow forehead, and his long, hooked nose. In his habitual 'plain suit of ill-fitting black,' he was 'not unlike a New England schoolmaster.' He was by turns bashful, ungraceful, embarrassed, and half-apologetic, but each designation only added to his mystique as an uncalculating soul of pure wisdom and character. 'He rarely looks his hearers full in the face,' the [*Daily Cincinnati*] *Gazette* observed, 'but at emphatic expressions has a habit of turning his eyes backward as if to look in at himself.' "[71] The attention to Emerson's physical form and habits speaks to what Richard Sennett has described as the nineteenth-century's fundamental "faith in immanent appearances."[72] In England, France, and the United States, the cult of personality presumed that meaning was manifest in physical forms. Phrenology and daguerreotyping exemplified great confidence in the readability of the material world. The exaltation of romantic personality into celebrity followed a similar logic, suggesting that the celebrity expressed a kind of public (if not divine) immanence.

From Emerson's exploration of representative men to Brady's gallery of famed Americans, the producers of American culture clearly tried to capitalize on the rhetorical power of fame. Known for his lectures on foreign travel, Bayard Taylor was asked to endorse *Colton's General Atlas* in New England newspaper advertisements. Marietta Alboni's fame was so significant that the New York company Mantillas named a formal gown after the singer, advertising the Alboni for evening wear in 1853.[73] When Beecher was given the chance to build a new church designed specifically for his talents, he directed the architects to create a pulpit that extended far into the congregation: "I want the audience to surround me," he said, "so that they will come up on every side, and behind me, so that I shall be in the center of the crowd and have the people surge all about me." Lecturing at Yale Divinity School on the qualities of good preaching, he instructed his students that "one's message to his hearers should be so delivered as to bring his personality to bear upon them."[74] Beecher maintained a remarkable faith in the power of personality to attract and impress itself on a crowd. Barnum worked from a similar conviction, but unlike the Brooklyn preacher, he believed that with the right promotion, celebrity could be constructed and conferred. Barnum created much of the hoopla that greeted Jenny Lind in New York. A central part of the promotion was to freely distribute a specially prepared biography of the singer, one that detailed her talents and charity work to newspapers around the country.

Looking for higher profits, the publishing industry similarly intensified the attention to celebrity by focusing on the personal experiences of the renowned. The lessons had been clear since Boswell's *Life of Johnson* and Rousseau's *Confessions* had appeared to such great success in the late eighteenth century. Later biographies of Byron and Scott confirmed the public's interest in intimate portraits of literary greats, as did the appearance of volumes collecting their correspondence. By the 1850s, the American market was awash with celebrity memoirs and biographies, each putting forward a famous individual to be the object of public scrutiny. Part of the attraction to Fern's novel *Ruth Hall* lay in its exposing the insensitivity of her famous brother Willis. Readers were not just at ease with promotional forms of identity; they actively consumed them. "Autobiographies are multiplying, as everybody knows," the *Brooklyn Daily Eagle* complained after a spate of memoirs were released in 1855. "What a world! Every one striving to merit an edition, pay or no pay to the printer; every one striving for one line—one immortal line on the *momentum ære perennius*—striving to leave a fadeless autograph on the imperishable pillar of fame."[75] The popularity of autobiographies disgusted one reviewer of Barnum's 1855 autobiography: "There was a time when people must have lived lives before they could sell them," he wrote, but now "dead or alive, great or little, famous or infamous—the author of a code or the man who was hanged under it—everyone has his equal chances of a life."[76] Upholding a traditional correlation between accomplishment and biography, the reviewer saw an erosion in posterity's power to determine an individual's cultural value. What the overemphasis on promotion had produced, he reasoned, was a culture in which popularity determined

THE WORK TABLE.

JENNY LIND CAP.

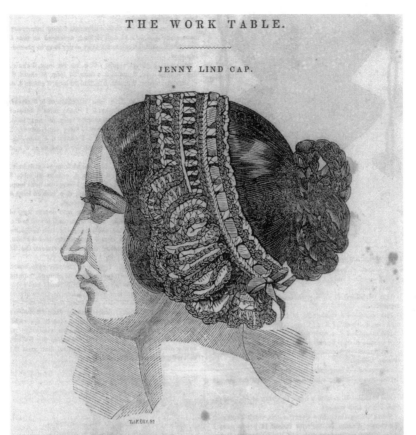

T. H. DLY. S?

Materials—half an ounce of scarlet and half an ounce of white Berlin wool; crochet needle No. 2.

Work a chain fifteen inches long in scarlet double wool.

1st row.—Scarlet. Double crochet.

2d row.— White. Double open crochet, by working a long stitch into every third loop of the foundation, and two chain stitches between each of the long stitches.

3d row.—Scarlet. Double crochet.

4th row.—White. Double open crochet, leaving three inches for the back.

5th row.—Scarlet. Double crochet.

6th row.—Work on each side nine long stitches in double open crochet to form the ears.

7th row.—Scarlet. Double crochet.

Work the border in single wool.

1st row.—White. Double open crochet, worked very loose, two stitches in every loop, except in the front where it should be worked flat.

2d row.—Scarlet. Double open crochet worked in every other loop.

The upper border to be worked the same as the lower, but only at the sides.

For the rosette, make a chain in white single wool three-eighths in length; work a row of double open crochet very loose.

Finish with an edging by working a loose chain of scarlet.

LADY'S PURSE.

Materials—two skeins purse silk, one hank gold beads, and one small gold tassel. D. c. means double crochet.

Make a chain of 5 stitches.

1st round.—D. c.

2d round.—1 d. c., 1 chain into every stitch.

3d round.—D. c., with a bead in every stitch.

4th round.—D. c., increasing after every stitch.

5th round.—Same as 3d.

6th round —1 long stitch into every loop.

7th round.—D. c. Work this round so as to have forty stitches.

291

GY May 1849

The Jenny Lind cap, *Godey's Lady's Book,* May 1849. Even before she performed in the United States, Jenny Lind was associated with elegance and fashion. Courtesy of the Picture Collection, the Branch Libraries, the New York Public Library, Astor, Lenox and Tilden Foundations.

social legitimacy. Publication, as Emily Dickinson put it, had become the auction of one's life.

In the midst of this prevalent commodification of personality Dickinson wrote her well-known indictment of the need to be a "somebody." The 1861 poem has received considerable attention, but in the context of antebellum celebrity, its satire seems particularly trenchant:

> I'm Nobody! Who are you?
> Are you—Nobody—Too?
> Then there's a pair of us!
> Don't tell! They'd advertise—you know!
>
> How dreary—to be—Somebody!
> How public—like a Frog—
> To tell one's name—the livelong June—
> To an admiring Bog![77]

The poem responds to the new discourse of advertising and promotion with a comment about the ubiquity of its values. "No one, in this age of dear flour and high rents can afford to be a nobody," the *Brooklyn Daily Eagle* joked. "Be somebody,—biographically, poetically or historically. A biography of the Mermaid would sell."[78] In a culture in which celebrities were in heavy demand and increasing supply, Dickinson teases that being a nobody was a distinction in itself, a form of identity so unique that it made one vulnerable to exposure and promotion. The poem's intimate address preserves the pair of nobodies as a kind of endangered cultural species. Toying with the distinctions between the somebodies and nobodies, she satirizes the arrogant ease with which the culture associates selfhood with public identity. While the Veiled Lady had found a way to achieve celebrity by renouncing the cult of personality, Dickinson questions the categories themselves, conveying her skepticism in an elaborate offstage whisper.

The poem makes fun of the high regard Americans had not just for the famous but for fame. Adams's fears about the tyrannical power that popularity was exercising over the country proved to be quite prescient, for by the 1850s, many viewed it as being a reliable index of talent or skill. In the lecture system, for example, audiences tended to shy away from unknown or local speakers, thinking instead that lecturers' popularity had much to do with their quality. As a commentator in *Putnam's* put it, "Hundreds of men have lectured, yet there are but a score or two whose names figure upon the lists of every lyceum, and who are first invited everywhere." What "the universal popularity of these men" implied, he continued, was that "they are the intellectual leaders of an intelligent progress in the country."[79] To its proponents, the lecture system seemed to work democratically, with public acclaim granting stature as opposed to wealth or birth. As Scott explains, the lecture came to be closely associated with the workings of democracy: "The popular lecture not only provided people with the comprehensive vision they wanted; it did so in a form that embodied what was widely referred to as the 'democratic spirit' of American society. As a public event, it appeared to make knowledge readily accessible to the common man. More important, it presented a quintessentially democratic form of knowledge, which gained its legitimacy from the people's sanction rather than by imposition."[80] The lecturer's popularity was the center of that legitimacy; the people conferred celebrity by their own will.

Whitman's admiration for the Hutchinson Family Singers exhibits this thinking quite well. Like many Americans, Whitman was attracted to the four New Hampshire siblings for their popular nativist music and commitment to reformist politics. Coming from a family of thirteen children, the Hutchinsons were famous throughout the country; they toured with Frederick Douglass, sang at women's rights conventions, and entertained several presidents, including Abraham Lincoln. Clearly "somebodies" in antebellum America, the singers combined a faith in democratic nationalism with a bold assertion of personality. Whitman particularly liked the group's performance of "The Old Granite State," an immensely popular song that wove the family's history into a spirited affirmation of American democracy. David Reynolds speculates that the song's combination of "egotistical personalism and unabashed patriotism" may have influenced Whitman's own practice of working autobiography into his poems.[81] Whitman's reviews championed the family's construction of community through the frank egotism of celebrity. "Fearless, republican, outspoken, and free" were the national qualities he attached to the Hutchinsons in an 1843 review. He saw the "musical embodiment of the American character" not in the family's performance, however, but "in the enthusiastic reception invariably accorded to these children of the Granite State."[82]

VALUES

While the Hutchinsons' fame may have been easy to integrate into republican political values, they circulated in a world that was at once more boisterous and volatile than their rustic charm would suggest. As Reynolds describes it, in the raucous, freewheeling atmosphere of antebellum America, "rigid cultural hierarchies did not yet exist," and thus artists and performers freely borrowed from one another's work, mixing aesthetic categories and promoting "a fluid exchange between different cultural idioms."[83] In this environment, sensationalism emerged as a dominant cultural mode. In part an expression of the new legitimacy given to popular individuals and works, in part an endorsement of the public spectacle itself, the American taste for sensation spread across multiple idioms and forms, affecting the development of cheap novels, the penny press, and the antebellum stage. The popularity of Barnum's American Museum suggests that in the increasingly competitive world of antebellum culture, people could be sensationalized as well. Situated directly across the street from Brady's studio, the museum exhibited an array of "living curiosities" from the leopard-skin boy to the albino family to Barnum's most famous attraction, the forty-inch Tom Thumb. Relying on elaborate costumes, exotic scenery, and a heavy dose of hype, Barnum made each of these characters exhibit a wild exoticism that visitors found fascinating.[84]

Barnum's ability to create and capitalize on notoriety directly challenged traditional conceptions of reason's supremacy in the public sphere. His triumphs point to a much larger issue confronting antebellum Americans: the problem, as Jackson Lears puts it, of how to "represent value, meaning or personal identity in a society where all values, meanings, and identities seemed subject to change."[85] The country seems to have faced this problem in every decade since its birth, but in the antebellum period, questions of value and identity were unusually fierce. Particularly in the North, society struggled with constitutional, moral, and racial crises while at the same time trying to adapt to capitalism's tremendous variability and growth. The growing interest in fame was a telling symptom of this environment, for like capitalism itself, fame both depended on and promoted a culture of illusory value. As early as 1835, Poe had lampooned the counterfeit kinds of distinction that lay in fame and popularity. His short story "Lionizing" centers on a narrator—a once "great man"—who recounts his reputation throughout Europe for his remarkably conspicuous nose and his highly successful pamphlet, "Nosology." Having been welcomed into the company of Europe's most impressive nobles and thinkers, the man is shocked when he experiences a fast decline into oblivion and disgrace.[86] Thought to be a satire of Willis's celebrity worship, the story turns celebrity into an absurd and short-lived illusion, a phenomenon indicating the naïveté of the renowned and the stupidity of their admirers.

Though it takes place among European nobility, the story eloquently speaks to the growing significance of fame in American cities. Under the influence of promoters like Barnum, celebrity did not simply indicate the problem of shifting values: it flourished in all the ambiguity, incoherence, and potential for misrepresentation that arose in the period. To its many critics, popular culture was making fame an arbitrary sign; buoyed by public interest (if not support), it was a condition bestowed by the people rather than God. Celebrity, with all its surrounding commotion and hype, was democracy's ironic cousin, a system of value that did not measure virtue or talent as much as an individual's cultural profile. As Barnum's reviewer put it, everyone now seemed capable of "having a life." The extent to which the values of celebrity pervaded American culture can be seen in Lincoln's suspending a cabinet meeting during the war to greet the country's most famous newlyweds, General and Mrs. Tom Thumb.

This lack of distinction, this disregard for the differences between popularity and accomplishment clearly vexed an unknown poet living in Amherst, Massachusetts. In the more than a dozen poems she devoted to the subject, Dickinson grappled with the complex, somewhat contradictory meanings that fame had accrued by the Civil War. Like generations of New Englanders before her, she tended to view worldly fame as the nineteenth century's version of Fortune. "Fame is a fickle food / Upon a shifting plate," she comments. Even the crows decline its crumbs and sound "ironic" caws as they move to the farmer's corn (F-1702). For Dickinson, the hunger for fame led people to live in earthly vicissitude, committing themselves to a life of never-ending illusion and change. Whereas Poe ridiculed the arbitrary construction of the social lion, Dickinson pointed to the ironic transience of popular acclaim. In a late poem she compares fame to a bee on the principle that each has a song and a sting. What disturbs the poet most, however, is the recognition that, like the bee, fame also "has a wing" (F-1788).

The only way Dickinson could envision eating from fame's ever-shifting plate was to transfer the entire banquet to a realm outside of time. As she insists in another poem, meaningful recognition would not come until after one's death:

> Fame is the one that does not stay—
> It's occupant must die
> Or out of sight of estimate
> Ascend incessantly— (F-1507)

Dickinson's caution about popularity or acclaim in no way diminishes her faith that one might live forever in posterity. She draws on the well-established vision of the republican founders. Fame, she tells us, is one of the piers above oblivion, one of the heights to which an "effaceless 'Few'" can actually lift themselves (F-1552). As with Hamilton and Adams, fame spurs one to accomplishment, offering a few talented individuals a redeeming grace. Dickinson's interest in this kind of fame was so strong that she struggled for a language that might distinguish the popularity of men such as Barnum from the honor of being among the pantheon of greats. Fame may not stay, but to be one of "Fame's boys and girls" means that one never has to die (F-892). Popularity is full of caprice, but fame lasts eternally.

Divided over her sense of the word, the poet would sometimes use *immortality* as a synonym for the kind of life she envisioned through literary fame. While Rush had appealed to future readers, Dickinson looked to immortality to establish a more stable system of value than what currently ruled the earth. She interestingly conflates posterity's judgment with that of the divine:

> Some—Work for Immortality—
> The Chiefer part, for Time—
> He—Compensates—immediately—
> The former—Checks—on Fame—
>
> Slow Gold—but Everlasting—
> The Bullion of Today—
> Contrasted with the Currency
> Of Immortality—

A Beggar—Here and There—
Is gifted to discern
Beyond the Broker's insight—
One's—Money—One's—the Mine— (F-536)

The poem employs traditional Christian imagery in establishing a virtual economy of fame. Popularity may have a direct and immediate payoff, but Dickinson wants the slow gold, the mine from which all currency descends. Like Hercules, she aims to earn immortality through her earthly endeavors. The poem's references to eternity may obscure its cultural critique, but Dickinson's concerns are quite similar to this 1855 complaint from a writer at the *Southern Quarterly Review:* "biographies used to be written upon a tombstone. They are now issued as a continuous periodical posted up to the last paragraph of the distinguished subject. . . . Men ambitious of fame might at least postpone the narrative of their life till it is over. But they discount their posthumous fame for a present pittance of notoriety."[87] Both writers lament the democratization of fame, the ways in which the culture was fawning over fleeting reputations rather than lasting accomplishments. The authors agree that the "pittance of notoriety" seemed valueless next to the slow gold of posthumous fame.

Dickinson's yearning for immortality led to an extreme distrust of publicity. In an America pervaded by unreliable systems of value, the gravest error would be to participate in one's renown, to immerse one's self in a deliberate courting of the crowd. Keats had described the futility of seeking fame in a sonnet published in the United States in 1838. Drawing on a set of images once linked to Lady Fortune, he compared fame to a "wayward girl" who "will still be coy / To those who woo her with too slavish knees." "Repay her scorn for scorn," Keats advised poets and artists alike. "Make your best bow to her and bid adieu— / then, if she likes it, she will follow you."[88] Whether she knew the poem or not, Dickinson echoed its advice. As the "Nobody" poet who worried that "they'd advertise" her status to the bog, she reserved her strongest critique for people who actively sought their own celebrity. Like her much-loved Keats, she personified fame as a single, potential lover rather than a vast, applauding crowd:

To earn it by disdaining it
Is Fame's consummate Fee—

He loves what spurns him—
Look behind—He is pursuing thee— (F-1445)

The conceit is typical of Dickinson's tendency to distance herself aggressively from the inconstancy of promotion and publicity. In rejecting the pursuit, she turns from puffery and self-delusions and chooses instead the more difficult but ultimately more stable goal of achieving immortality.

Despite her focus on Parnassus, Dickinson remained strikingly aware of the need to court and please an audience. The poet may have limited her self-promotional activities to a series of private letters, but her poems reveal a stunning mastery of the language of publicity. Consider the stylized version of audience address that begins what is commonly thought to be a spiritual poem:

Dare you see a Soul *at the White Heat?*
Then crouch within the door—
Red—is the Fire's common tint—
But when the vivid Ore
Has vanquished Flame's conditions,
It quivers from the Forge
Without a color, but the light
Of unanointed Blaze.
Least Village has its Blacksmith
Whose Anvil's even ring
Stands symbol for the finer Forge
That soundless tugs—within—
Refining these impatient Ores
With Hammer, and with Blaze
Until the Designated Light
Repudiate the Forge— (F-401)

In this emotionally and theologically intense poem, Dickinson assumes the role of a carnival barker, inviting us to observe her soul's dramatic conflicts. With its enticing invitation, subtle emotional registers, and final dramatic act, the poem presents the poet as both promoter and exhibit, the Barnum challenging the public and the "living curiosity" itself. Dickinson's address is remarkably clear and unimpeded, and the dashes surrounding "within" create a touch of suspense. The various Gothic identities Dickinson adopted through the years—the woman with goblin lovers, loaded revolvers, and funerals in her brain—suggest a poet who understands the self as a kind of audience-directed performance.

Dickinson's distrust of fame was not unusual among ambitious young writers. The young Whitman also disparaged renown as a site of deceptive value. In two of his earliest (and most self-conscious) poems, he treated the subject with due censure and piety. At twenty years old, he published "Fame's Vanity" (1839) in the *Long Island Democrat,* and three years later he revised and republished the poem under the hardly more interesting title "Ambition." Both works concern a young man whose dreams of fame and grandeur are dashed away when he realizes that fame is an illusion that can only mask death's total disregard for human station. As Whitman suggests in the poem's first version, fame is a wholly secular obsession that seems to inspire a self-destructive zealotry:

> Fame, O what happiness is lost
> In hot pursuit of thy false glare!
> Thou, whose drunk votaries die to gain
> A puff of viewless air. (*EPF,* 23)

Similar in tone and content, both versions associate the desire for celebrity with the type of mortal pride that ignores the world's duplicity, and they firmly punish the youth for indulging in his egocentric fantasies. "And it pierced him sore," the later poem concludes, "To have his airy castles thus dashed down" (*EPF,* 22).

Unlike Poe and Dickinson, Whitman's condemnations never led to a dismissal of the public sphere. The desire for renown may reveal one's naïveté and vanity, but he boldly sees fame as popular acceptance. For all their sermonizing about the ruinous aspects of ambition, the poems maintain deep respect for the public's interest in the famous. This passage comes from "Fame's Vanity":

> Shall I build up a lofty name,
> And seek to have the nations know
> What conscious might dwells in the brain
> That throbs aneath this brow?
>
> And have thick countless ranks of men
> Fix upon me their reverent gaze,

And listen to the deafening shouts,
> To *me* that thousands raise? (*EPF*, 23)

Whitman would frequently imagine such scenes as he prepared *Leaves of Grass*. What is striking about this early version of the fantasy is that although he expects the cosmos to ridicule a mortal's reputation, the public nonetheless appears as a stable, powerful force that can transform popularity into representation.

Like much reformist literature of the period, the poet's moralizing barely conceals his real attraction to celebrity.[89] As if to distance himself from these immodest but genuine goals, Whitman eventually revised his original poem by turning its first-person narrative into a seemingly objective account of an "obscure youth" eager for literary glory. The revisions reveal a writer who is anxiously being conventional about a subject of intense personal significance. With time, Whitman would see different values operating in the workings of celebrity culture. If fame was an illusion reflecting earthly appetite, then he would learn to seize that illusion as a strategy for promoting the self. Rather than veil his fantasies in moralizing cant, he would incorporate them into his faith in popular sovereignty. Keats and Dickinson disdained the fame they expected most poets to desire; they would earn their reputations by courting eternity rather than the crowd. Perhaps because he was so familiar with the inconstancies of public life, Whitman would develop a poetic that perpetually announced and confirmed his cultural relevance as if that were a value worthy in itself.

CELEBRITY AND REPRESENTATION

Whitman's early interest in the crowd is consistent with his focus on the political possibilities within fame rather than the wealth, access, or luxury that others might prize in it. Even as a newspaper editor in the 1840s and 1850s, he understood his papers' circulation in political, not economic terms. "It *aint* their ninepences we want so much," he wrote in the *Daily Eagle*, as the "daily communion" of the editor and his readers, the "sense of brotherhood and sisterhood between the two parties."[90] Politics in the antebellum period was emerging as a kind of public theater, with war heroes and politicians being made into national celebrities. To those with an entrepreneurial spirit, the identification of democratic politics with fame was open to exploitation. After Henry Clay made plans to attend a tragedy performed by the English actor Macready, one theater manager gave the senator "equal billing" with the star. The manager of a Nashville theater complained that for all of their expense, his stars never drew as large a crowd as did Martin Van Buren on the night he attended a performance. The success of Van Buren's visit was so great, he quipped, that he would like to engage him "on his *own terms,* for the season."[91] The conflation of these two concerns raised the question of how the concept of celebrity would integrate itself into representative politics.

Perhaps more than any of his contemporaries, Nathaniel Willis devoted concerted attention to the political ramifications of celebrity. From Willis's point of view, celebrities would form "a kind of new aristocracy of fashion" in the United States, an aristocracy that would help curtail the vulgarities of democratic culture. Developing his concept of the "Upper Ten Thousand," he envisioned a special class of citizens whose sentiment and refinement would help instruct a population that had little sense of values, manners, or comportment. As Willis first summarized his position in 1844, New York City sorely needed a "class whose judgment is made from elevated standards—a class whose favor is alike valuable to the ambitions of both sexes—a class . . . to quote as unquestionable authority." He included in this distinguished group the city's wealthiest families and celebrities, what he described as an assortment of "artists, authors, journalists, 'stars,' and that sort of people."[92] In much the same way that James Madison had described the representative structure of the Union as "a Republican remedy for the diseases most incident to Republican Government," Willis saw the celebrity as "a most republican solution" to the unbridled power of American public opinion.[93] Willis had warm praise for the "very republican operation" he had observed during Lind's tour, particularly in the way that she had brought Italian music—"the luxury of the exclusives"—to the common people.[94] (That Barnum had paid Willis to write a book about the tour was apparently beside the point—as was the fact that ticket prices for the concerts far outpaced the average worker's pocketbook.)

The celebrity, in Willis's estimation, was basically a form of education and social control. Descending from Jefferson's notion of a natural aristocracy, the "Upper Ten Thousand" would serve as models for cultured behavior. Although he strongly associated this group with wealth and sentimental feeling, Willis insisted that such a group be open to anybody, regardless of his or her station at birth. The penny press ridiculed Willis's pretense, but the notion that celebrities could serve a positive political function received surprising support. Greeley's paper, the *New York Herald Tribune*, commended Willis's thinking, arguing that the cultural power accorded to these celebrities would serve as "the talisman of a self-sustaining, unprivileged Aristocracy, which shall furnish a counter-poise and barrier against the tyranny of Public Opinion."[95] By century's end, the "Upper Ten Thousand" would be whittled down to "The Four Hundred," prominent families expected to wield their natural cultural power.

In sharp contrast were the many commentators who regarded celebrity not as a check against the people's opinion but rather as an expression of it. Willis urged the renowned in his audience to take their relationship to the culture more seriously, to use the vertical nature of their fame to instruct the people beneath them. To many, however, fame represented the embodiment of democracy's strong horizontal bonds, with celebrity attesting to the public's achievement in choosing representatives both for and of themselves. Recall the editor at *Putnam's* who concluded that the "universal popularity" of the nation's most prominent lecturers made them the nation's "intellectual leaders." "The word 'popular,'" as one critic complained, had become in America "a synonyme of 'excellent.'"[96] Although Whitman would write of the need to ventriloquize public opinion, to speak for a population that had a limited ability to speak for itself, he nonetheless saw a more interactive relation between the celebrity and crowd than did Willis. The poet's reminiscence about the Bowery theater is a case in point. The audience applauding Forrest and Booth both creates and is created by the actors it invests with popularity. With notables and workers alike, it becomes a public of spectators freely choosing which performers will bind them. Whitman's faith in this dynamic formed the cornerstone of his poetic.

To say that the celebrity and public simultaneously create each other is to depend on the fiction of representation. As Scott concludes about the lecture system, the stars who spoke to each audience were selected by a committee of villagers who acted in the public's name. Though many lauded it for creating a broad national culture out of the popular will, "the public lecture system was in fact an institution for the consolidation of the collective cultural consciousness by which" northern, Anglo-Saxon, Protestant men asserted the claim that they were "the real American public."[97] The same thing might be said about celebrities, that whether selected from literature, the newspapers, politics, or the stage, they served as instruments of consensus, representations of the public's attention as much as its will. The celebrity was a kind of medium that could convey a range of political meanings determined by promoters and the public. Barnum found Stowe's popularity to be a valuable resource in his efforts to attract visitors to his museum. But when he put on a stage production of *Uncle Tom's Cabin,* he chose a dramatic interpretation that eliminated the novel's abolitionist sentiments, thus deliberately courting audiences put off by the more politically faithful play being staged at the National Theater.[98] Both productions traded on the notoriety of Stowe's text; both were a financial success.

The ease with which a celebrity's image could be co-opted by another suggests that in antebellum America, celebrity functioned as kind of representational technology. In the highly politicized, sometimes volatile, and ever-shifting environment, celebrities emerged as a new and rather effective means for representing the public to itself. Though antebellum Americans were inclined to see in the famous an expression of exalted individualism, the public's construction and use of celebrities gave them a function analogous to the sermons, editorials, and advertisements the culture used to know itself. In their different ways, people such as Stowe, Lind, Willis, and Booth conveyed as much cultural knowledge, as much political identity, as the media through which their significance was conveyed. In fact, as both a human text and a form of media, the celebrity provided a figure of public attention that appeared to come from the people while simultaneously being represented before them.

Poe satirizes the representative potential of celebrity in his story "The Man That Was Used Up." First published in 1839, the story stands at the beginning of the many changes that would make celebrity so significant in the 1850s. The story concerns a narrator who becomes obsessed with a war hero—Brevet Brigadier General John A. B. C. Smith, a famed Indian fighter and recent veteran of the Bugaboo and Kickapoo campaigns. The general's good looks, distinguished air, and reputation as "a perfect desperado" spur the narrator to search out the history of this mysterious and remarkable man. From the beginning, this quest seems doomed to fail. In church, at cards, during a performance of *Othello,* the narrator approaches a variety of gossips imploring them to relate the general's well-known tale. They allude to Smith's horrid treatment by the Bugaboo and Kickapoo Indians, they echo him in marveling at the inventiveness of the age, and then each conversation abruptly breaks off, leaving the narrator angry and frustrated. Burning for information, he rushes to the general's home, where he discovers a heap of body parts in his private bedchamber. A slave appears and begins to assemble the heroic man from the shoulders, eyeballs, bosom, legs, and teeth lying on the floor. Smith's disembodied voice alternates between abusing the weary valet, recounting the tortures inflicted upon his body, and cheerfully advising the narrator about the finest merchants for each prostheses. The story concludes, "Brevet Brigadier General John A. B. C. Smith was the man, was the man that was used up."[99]

The general challenges romantic perspectives of celebrity as a form of exalted individualism. As he did in "Lionizing," Poe satirizes the manner in which communities confer celebrity on select individuals. A synthetic hero, the general has been shot, scalped, tortured, and then remembered for the public sphere.[100] Whatever biological self he once possessed has been wholly replaced by prostheses, and the value of his personality now lies in his exhibition to the community. Arising out of a culture that supports and reveres him, the general is, as Jonathan Elmer has remarked, a figure whose "mystery and singularity" reside "in his very publicity, the abstraction and literalization of the public itself."[101] Passing through the community, he is an instrument of unity and consensus. At the height of Jacksonian individualism, the general's personal story is far less significant than its ideological function. As his generic name suggests, the general's identity is indistinguishable from how he is used by the culture that has constructed his renown. "The Man That Was Used Up" quite literally portrays the representational function of fame in antebellum society. From Fanny Fern to Horace Greeley, celebrities served as a kind of representational technology, their identities pieced together in a collaborative performance between their individual selves and the supporting community. For Whitman the challenge would be to construct his renown rhetorically, to make his essays, advertisements, and poems all intimate a personality that was buoyed by popularity. The task would lead him into the mysteries and contradictions of democratic life.

CHAPTER TWO

Personality

THE PROOF OF A POET

OF THE MANY PROCLAMATIONS Whitman made throughout his career, perhaps the boldest was his conclusion to the Preface for the 1855 *Leaves of Grass:* "The proof of a poet is that his country absorbs him as affectionately as he has absorbed it" (24). Whitman wrote the Preface as he was seeing the manuscript through press, and its final sentence was less the guiding principle of his grand poetic experiment than its culminating act. Revolutionary in its bravado and inventiveness, the statement was predicated on Whitman's belief that the public's embrace was vital to his own poetic identity. Throwing out conventional notions of literary value, he hinges a poet's credibility on the country's affection for his work. Throughout the Preface Whitman had worked to define the poet in nationalistic terms, but here he asserts that the most reliable evidence of his national character would be the degree to which he commanded his fellow citizens' support. Many might profess to be the voice of their nation, but in Whitman's thinking, only the people could determine who actually filled that role. The statement grounds American letters on the electoral principles that underlie republican government. A poet's civic worth, he reasons, would be most registered in his popularity or acclaim, for the people essentially elected their poets into positions of cultural prominence.

Whitman structures this radically new definition of literary value

around the legitimizing aspects of celebrity. Rather than invoke the immortal fame to which Dickinson was attracted, he envisions popularity as
a standard by which nations might measure their poets. In Whitman's
formulation, Americans will know their poet when they see him consort-
ing with crowds of readers who have affectionately absorbed his words.
This dramatically populist version of poetic fame says much about Whitman's conception of the writer's role in the country. Seemingly unin-
terested in Parnassus and the company of Shakespeare, Milton, and other
literary greats, Whitman aims to become a public figure, the embodiment
of democracy's horizontal bonds. Strong, magnetic, self-assured, his personality would forever be realized in his readers' esteem.

What made Whitman's conclusion particularly risky was the implica-
tion that *Leaves of Grass* would meet the critical standard he had just set
forth. The poet had little patience for writers who pandered to the crowd,
appealing to its most basic tastes. In imagining an art that would legit-
imately arouse the audience's affection, he was challenging American
poets and readers with a rigorous set of expectations. For a year Whitman
maintained the fiction that his book had found its audience, and in 1856
he wrote in an open letter to Emerson that he expected the second edition
to sell "several thousand copies" (*WPP*, 1327). Even then, however, he
seemed to recognize that *Leaves of Grass* would not come close to attracting popular acclaim. In a poetic version of the Preface (later titled "By
Blue Ontario's Shore"), he revised the pronouncement to read, "The
proof of a poet shall be sternly deferr'd till his country / absorbs him as
affectionately as he has absorb'd it" (*LGV*, 204). As if to soften this already
tempered boast, he would later enclose the statement in parentheses. In
his later years, Whitman backed further away from the hope that the
public would prove his literary identity. He dropped the closing sentence
from every republication of the Preface after the Civil War.

This is not to say that Whitman was without admirers. Reviewers and
readers commented on the poet's looks, his sympathy, and his treatment
of men and women; they praised his self-reliance, showing a keen regard
for his character's strength and power. And yet, even in old age, when
surrounded by friends and disciples, he was haunted by the sense that his
project had been left incomplete, that his public had never materialized.
"[T]he people, the crowd—I have had no way of reaching them," he complained to Horace Traubel early in 1889. "I needed to reach the people . . .

but it's too late now" (*WWC*, 3:467). The man who had confidently proclaimed that poets were indebted to their audience, that their discursive
identities would be proved by their emergence in the public's mind, admitted in the end that his aspirations had gone unfulfilled. Whitman, of
course, had possessed many ways to reach the people. Having been ap-
prenticed to a printer in his youth, he knew the newspaper and book
publishing trades quite well. Over the years, he had produced advertisements, pamphlets, photographs, collector's editions, and a gamut of other
texts to bring the people in contact with *Leaves of Grass*. But the considerable attention he had attracted seemed only to underscore the feeling that
he had failed to meet the mark of popularity. His poems had spoken to
many kindred spirits, but they had never interested the masses.

Whitman's frustration appears quite graphically in "The Two Vaults,"
an unpublished poem he wrote in the early 1860s. The poem is set in
Pfaff's, a Broadway beer cellar and restaurant that was a favorite meeting
place among bohemian intellectuals. From 1858 until he left New York
during the Civil War, Whitman frequented the saloon, usually keeping to
himself but also enjoying the antic conversation among the writers and
performers who had gathered around Henry Clapp, the editor of the
Saturday Press. Though the patrons at times teased the poet about his bad
reviews, they generally held him in high regard.[1] Clapp not only published a number of Whitman's poems in his magazine (including "A
Child's Reminiscence," later titled "Out of the Cradle Endlessly Rocking"), he also tried to place the poet at the center of critical attention. As
Justin Kaplan reports, from December 1859 to December 1860, the *Saturday Press* published "at least twenty-five items by or about Whitman,
including reviews, commentary, controversy, imitations and parodies."[2]
One regular at Pfaff's, the actress Ada Clare, had publicly praised Whitman for being "centuries ahead of his contemporaries."[3]

Although not its central figure, Whitman clearly enjoyed bohemia's
attention and support. At a time when others were downright hostile to
his work, the writers at Pfaff's considered the poet to be among the age's
most significant writers. For Whitman, though, such backing was not
enough, and in "The Two Vaults," he compared the basement saloon to a
grave that goes wholly ignored by the average person on the street. The
contrast reveals his investment in populist forms of identity:

—The vault at Pfaffs where the drinkers and laughers meet to
  eat and drink and carouse
While on the walk immediately overhead pass the myriad feet of
  Broadway
As the dead in their graves are underfoot hidden
And the living pass over them, recking not of them

The myriad walkers pay no attention to the conversations beneath their feet. While Whitman casts the saloon's proceedings in a convivial light, he also sees the basement drinkers heading for another vault, the grave. Sitting among the dead, the poet pines for the people that idly walk by:

Overhead rolls Broadway—the myriad rushing Broadway
The lamps are lit—the shops blaze—the fabrics vividly are seen
  through the plate glass windows
The strong lights from above pour down upon them and are
  shed outside,
The thick crowds, well-dressed—the continual crowds as if they
  would never end
The curious appearance of the faces—the glimpse just caught of
  the eyes and expressions, as they flit along (*LGNC*, 576)

In these atmospheric lines, Whitman seems condemned to haunt the basement regions of the avant-garde. As the drinkers drink and the talkers talk, his interest strays to the crowds above, the well-dressed men and women whose attention is focused on the various well-lighted commodities on display.[4]

The poem expresses Whitman's frustration that he does not capture the attention of the passersby. Hidden in the vault, he cannot circulate among the crowds. Whether he envies the commodities or sees himself rightfully among them, his isolation is a kind of death, for to be alive in *Leaves of Grass* is frequently to be on display. The storefronts "blaze," the fabrics "vividly" attract the eye. The poet's eye moves from the objects to the people to the people's flitting interest in each other on Broadway. If thriving as a poet meant that one had been consumed by the people, then reaching these crowds would make both Whitman and his book complete. As long as he sat in the basement saloon, his identity as a poet would amount to an unsubstantiated claim. Clapp and his followers could not *prove* that he was a poet; only the public could confer that distinction, a distinction that presupposed a measure of popularity.

In *Celebrity and Power,* P. David Marshall argues that "the celebrity's power is derived from the collective configuration of its meaning," that "the audience is central in sustaining the celebrity sign."[5] There is no such thing, we might say, as a self-reliant celebrity, for celebrities do not exist independently. The word itself presumes a collaborative identity, the self as it is defined in relation to an external group. The personality that emerges from *Leaves of Grass* frequently suggests a collaboration between the individual and the community whose attention he receives. Not unlike the fabrics vividly displayed behind plate glass, the poet's personality strives to hold the readers' gaze, to fix their attention and endow them with both wonder and desire. *Leaves of Grass* seems attuned to what Warren Susman has described as a fundamental shift in antebellum culture: the growing division between Puritan character and American personality. In the new culture of personality, Susman argues, every American would be expected to play "the role of a performing self."[6]

In Whitman's case, however, the performance was largely rhetorical in that it explicitly argued for an audience to complete the performer's personality. Because the poet committed himself to the principle of election, because his identity was made evident in the audience's affection for his words, the creation of that identity necessarily involved his convincing us to value his work. Among its various speech acts, *Leaves of Grass* regularly deploys the persuasive rhetoric at the heart of democratic capitalism: the poet sells his readers on their role in forming his representative personality. To be a celebrity, for Whitman, was to possess a political identity: the poet who reached the people, whose voice won their praise, could truly be said to represent them in a democratic society. Positioned between a respect for public opinion and the rising interest in personality, Whitman developed a poetics that used the figure of public attention to legitimate his individual expression. As with Marshall's celebrity, he knew that the audience's image was central to sustaining his identity as the authentically American bard. He would use his poems to project a fictive celebrity until true admirers materialized.

THE CAMPAIGN FOR PERSONALITY

Antebellum Americans were remarkably enthusiastic about the emergent notion of personality. As if it were a recent phenomenon, today's commentators often censure the public's interest in stars, grumbling about audiences that identify with actors or actresses rather than appreciating their dramatic skills. The attraction to personality dates back several centuries, and similar to our own time, critics grew alarmed at the number of readers who seemed to follow an author's exploits more than they valued his or her work. Perhaps the most significant of these authors was Lord Byron, whose literary fame arose in part from his scandalous and engaging personality. Byron fueled the rumors of his debauchery and bravado in poems that called attention to his own sensational experience. As Ghislaine McDayter explains, "What set Byron apart from previous poets or literary critics was that he was in the business of selling not just poetry, but himself—and thus his fame depended as much on his personal as on his poetic charms."[7] Sir Walter Scott commented that Byron wrote as "an actual living man expressing his own sentiments, thoughts, hopes, and fears."[8] In making this judgment, Scott meant to dismiss Byron's work, but his opinion was not widespread. The public found the "actual living man" irresistibly fascinating. Five biographies of Byron were published the year after his death.[9]

Whitman eagerly participated in the culture's new interest in personality. Keeping in step with the popularity of portrait galleries, daguerreotypes, memoirs, and biographies, newspapers and magazines began to follow the lives of the renowned. From 1853 to 1859, for example, the *Pittsfield Sun* regularly kept its readers abreast of Bayard Taylor's activities: his arrival from China, his opinion of the Russian crown jewels, his marriage in Saxony, and the success of his lectures in the West. Whitman was particularly attracted to the new profiles of individuals that offered glimpses into their private lives. Not only did he save these articles, he annotated them heavily. Reading an article titled "Egotism" in *Graham's,* he marked the passages recounting Wordsworth's confident self-absorption in both his private and public affairs. Whitman's extensive notes on Shelley register little about his intellect or verse. They focus almost exclusively on the poet's personal self. On a sheet titled "Notes on Shelley," he copied out that Shelley had a tall, slight figure and that he "screamed loud in talking when enthusiastic." He also recorded that Shelley was "generous, benevolent, pure early riser—in winter evenings lay on the rug before the fire and slept curled round, like a cat." "Fed simply," he added, "liked bread and raisins."[10]

In a remarkably ambitious project, Susman reviewed over two hundred self-improvement manuals, pamphlets, and essays from the nineteenth and twentieth centuries to understand changing conceptions of the self. He found that nineteenth-century Americans were devoted to the concept of character, which they associated with *"citizenship, duty, democracy, work, building, golden deeds, outdoor life, conquest, honor, reputation, morals, manners, integrity,* and above all, *manhood."* With the rise of the twentieth century, cultural attention shifted from discourse about character to discourse about personality. "From the beginning," Susman writes, "the adjectives most frequently associated with personality suggest a very different concept from that of character: *fascinating, stunning, attractive, magnetic, glowing, masterful, creative, dominant, forceful."* Along with P. T. Barnum, Mathew Brady, and Fanny Fern, Whitman recognized the advent of a culture organized around the cultivation (and consumption) of personality, though as Susman remarks, he was unusually perceptive in understanding its rising significance.[11] In lexicon as well as manner, he anticipated the broad cultural shifts that would occur a half century later. With the exception of the words *stunning* and *creative,* Whitman used a version of each of these key personality terms in his poetry and prose, often using them to describe the poet's special powers. A country would know its poets not by their capacity to tell truths, please the senses, or instruct readers in morality. A country would know its poets by observing their impact on others. *Attractive, magnetic, masterful,* Whitman's poet wields an affective kind of power. His personality is visible in the reaction of the crowd.

As he explained near the end of his life, the concept first dawned on Whitman in the early 1850s. At the age of thirty-one he was overtaken by a desire so sharply defined that over the next two years it came to dominate everything else: "This was a feeling or ambition to articulate and faithfully express in literary or poetic form, and uncompromisingly, my own physical, emotional, moral, intellectual, and aesthetic Personality, in the midst of, and tallying, the momentous spirit and facts of its immediate days, and of current America—and to exploit that Personality, identified with place and date, in a far more candid and comprehensive sense than any hitherto poem or book" (*WPP,* 658). For Whitman, this ambition would become a desire to understand and proclaim the importance of personality itself. In one of the many pocket-sized notebooks he carried with him, he broke the concept into five distinct parts—pride, self-esteem, self-appreciation, egotism, and elevatedness.[12] The importance of personality announces itself in the opening pages of the 1855 edition of *Leaves of Grass* with the frontispiece photograph putting forward the author—later described as "Walt Whitman, an American, one of the roughs, a kosmos"—as its primary subject of interest (48). As with Byron, the poet's charismatic, even scandalous temperament came to recommend his poems. When Whitman comments in "So Long!" that we should regard *Leaves of Grass* as a man rather than a book, he not only alludes to the trope of the talking book. He offers the poems as his performance of a self (*WPP*, 611).

Personality emerges in the early editions of *Leaves of Grass* as one of the poet's most distinctive and durable concerns, and he is remarkably confident that this interest places him at the vanguard of history. In the *Inscriptions* sequence, he describes himself as a "Chanter of Personality," a poet whose respect for individuals allows him to outline "what is yet to be" and to "project the history of the future" ("To a Historian," *WPP*, 167). In "Song of the Broad Axe" he celebrates the "power of personality" as being vital to the nation's growth (*WPP*, 334). He amplifies the theme in the 1860 work "Poem of Joys" which, in its original version, directly associated the power of performers with the joys of democratic individualism:

> O the orator's joys!
> To inflate the chest—to roll the thunder of the voice out from the
>   ribs and throat,
> To make the people rage, weep, hate, desire, with yourself,
> To lead America—to quell America with a great tongue.
>
> O the joy of a manly self-hood!
>
> Personality—to be servile to none—to defer to none—not to any
>   tyrant, known or unknown,
> To walk with erect carriage, a step springy and elastic,
> To look with calm gaze, or with a flashing eye,
> To speak with a full and sonorous voice, out of a broad chest,
> To confront with your personality all the other personalities of
>   the earth. (*LG* 1860, 268)

With its emphasis on masculinity and confrontation, the poem fuses ante-bellum notions of character with a revolutionary emphasis on personality. Like Beecher, who wanted to "bring his personality to bear upon" his congregation, Whitman's orator exercises considerable control over his audience, making "the people rage, weep, hate, desire." In its mounting series of infinitives, the poem conveys the deliberate successive actions of this powerful man.

Whitman's sense of personality fits into the general constellation of beliefs that made him a champion of Jacksonian democracy. He frequently invokes the concept to move readers toward realizing their own latent power, asking them to recognize in his own masculine self an example of their potential individuality. Whitman explained his reasoning in "A Backwards Glance O'er Travel'd Roads." He wrote *Leaves of Grass* because democracies had historically been jeopardized by "powerful personalities." He hoped the book would help form a great nation by helping to create multitudes of great individuals (*WPP*, 668). The poet balanced his desire to create a union of personalities with an equally strong concern for ensemble. In "Starting from Paumanok," he announces, "I will effuse egotism and show it underlying all, and I will be the bard of personality," but he quickly follows this stanza with the declaration that "I will not make poems with reference to parts / But I will make poems, songs, thoughts, with reference to ensemble" (*WPP*, 183). As he describes it in "One's Self I Sing," the "simple separate person" is a necessary foil to "the word Democratic, the word En-Masse" (*WPP*, 165). The personality forms a natural complement to the group.

Although he associated it with a defiant individualism, Whitman believed that personalities ultimately required external confirmation of themselves. A personality's power was validated by a successful performance, by an audience that actually felt the emotion and desire he wanted them to feel. The democratic Whitman explains that his egotism teaches readers their own capacity for selfhood, that his pride in the end has a significantly civic purpose. But this "bard of personality" required the ensemble's support in order to be a personality himself. The fullness of the orator's voice, the thunderous sounds emerging from his ribs and throat, are contingent on the people who have gathered around him. A reflection of both a nation and a self, the personality is a collaborative achievement; the power of the many is not just realized in the charismatic individual: they give that individual a public stature.

The importance Whitman placed on the success of his persona is evident in a notebook written before the first edition of *Leaves of Grass*. The notebook contains many lines and images that would appear in the poems he eventually titled "Song of Myself," "The Sleepers," and "Faces." In the midst of these early drafts and experiments, Whitman's mood seems to change. He becomes quite personal, confessing his ultimate reliance on others' opinions of his personality: "I should think poorly of myself if I should be even a few days with any community either of sane or insane people, and not make them convinced, whether they acknowledged it or not, of my truth, my sympathy, and my dignity.—I should be certain enough that those attributes were not in me."[13] The sentiment conflicts with Whitman's declarations that the poet "is complete in himself" and that "nothing, not God, is greater to one than one's-self is" (*LG* 1855, 9, 82). Writing purely for himself, Whitman admits that he is so preoccupied with social judgments that he would pay little attention to a community's competence when it determined his temperament and identity. Even sympathy, the prized capacity to imagine the lives of others, appears as a publicly determined quality. Whether "sane or insane," the people would ratify the most prominent elements of Whitman's personality.

The notebook suggests that the poet's hunger for approval periodically led him to a type of Sartrean hell where he seemed condemned to require his reflection in other people's thoughts. In its acceptance that an unfit public might determine personal value, the passage recalls the strong denunciations of celebrity culture that came from Dickinson and Poe. In contrast, Whitman seems resigned to living with an ambiguously public self, a representative man who requires the external confirmations of an unreliable popular will. It is possible to see in the statement a buoyant confidence and faith that the poet will prevail over every community, but more important there is a nagging uncertainty about the relationship between public and private selves. Whitman envisions personality as an exercise in persuasion. He seems to steel himself for the task of campaigning for his personality.

In a more personal and unguarded manner, the notebook offers a unique perspective on Whitman's thinking at the end of the 1855 Preface: the country determines the poet's literary value, its affection grants legitimacy. The origins of this insecurity are worth considering, however speculatively and briefly. Stephen Railton has argued that such sentiments

stem from Whitman's inability to face his own erotic desires. He maintains that the poet's overt courting of popularity served to screen his
repressed homosexuality. While Whitman may have consciously believed
"he was addressing a mass audience that would absorb him affectionately," he was actually seeking "a specific audience—an audience of men
who, like himself, had unacknowledged homoerotic longings."[14] Although he concedes that the issue is problematic, Railton concludes that
Whitman's driving concern for acceptance can be explained as a form of
sexual repression that was displaced onto the reader and the nation at
large. We need not limit this repression to homosexual desire. Public
performance in *Leaves of Grass* can acquire an erotic intensity that sub-
stitutes for multiple kinds of sexual contact. In "Song of Myself," the poet
feels himself convulsing as if he had climaxed as he sits in the audience
listening to the soprano's aria.

The need for acceptance may also have been fueled by Whitman's
youth. The poet had seen his family's fortunes decline precipitously from
what he regarded as a wealthy, heroic past, and he spent his early years
shuttling between rural Long Island and Brooklyn as his father searched
for new economic opportunities. As he tells us in "There Was a Child Went
Forth," objects, people, and sensations deeply impressed themselves on
him, causing everything from apple blossoms to crowded streets to come
into his being. The poem presents this as a passive occurrence, but at times
it took on a willful, calculating force. As a young reporter at the *New York
Aurora*, Whitman quickly adopted the costumes and affectations of Manhattan. A daguerreotype from the 1840s shows him dressed in a gray frock
coat and highly fashionable hat. Although it does not capture the bouton-
niere he usually wore in his lapel, the image features the cane he carried to
announce himself a stylish young man. Whitman was so enamored with
the outfit that he wrote about it in the paper: "[W]e took our cane, (a heavy,
dark, beautifully polished, hook ended one,) and our hat, (a plain, neat
fashionable one, from Banta's, 130 Chatham street, which we got gratis, on
the strength of giving him this puff,) and sauntered forth to have a stroll
down Broadway to the Battery . . . on we went, swinging our stick, (the
before mentioned dark and polished one,) in our right hand—and with our
left hand tastily thrust in its appropriate pocket, in our frock coat, (a gray
one)."[15] The article puts Whitman on display, and his use of the editorial
we—at once forceful and collaborative—suggests an early attempt to fold

his audience into that persona. If Whitman, as Thayer described him, was a "poseur of truly colossal proportions," it was because he was eager to be noticed and admired. The proof of his identity would be its credibility to others. This was not a simple question of vanity. To borrow from the media theorist Georg Franck, Whitman presaged the arrival of "the economy of attention" that governs Western societies today. Attentive to the world around him, he despaired at the thought of his not figuring largely in public consciousness.[16]

POETRY AND POPULARITY

Whitman's desire for an external confirmation of his character was matched by a culture that emphasized public systems of value. Antebellum writing was filled with puffery and civic pride, as changes in print capitalism produced an increasingly crowded and competitive marketplace. The development of the cylinder press not only made printing less expensive, it also made mass circulation possible. Exploiting these technological advances, the penny press made large readerships a sign of preeminence and authority. James Gordon Bennett regularly trumpeted the circulation figures of the *New York Herald*, citing them as an index of his paper's democratic constituency.[17] Having edited at least five newspapers and written for many more, having seen his novel, *Franklin Evans*, sell twenty thousand copies in pamphlet form, Whitman was well aware of the place of hype in the political and publishing worlds (*EPF*, 124). His insistence on popularity builds on the practice of many antebellum publishers who made a book's reception a significant part of its appeal. "TEN THOUSAND COPIES SOLD IN TWO WEEKS!" bellowed an early advertisement for *Uncle Tom's Cabin*. The 1853 collection *Leaves from Fanny's Portfolio* (whose title may have influenced Whitman himself) was presented to the public under the banner "FANNY FERN'S BOOK, 6,000 COPIES ORDERED IN ADVANCE OF PUBLICATION!" As Brodhead points out, the popularity of these books became "the basis of their market identity."[18]

Poets were unlikely to enjoy similar commercial power, but there were enough examples of sparkling success to nurture an ambition such as Whitman's. In 1851, American newspapers were quick to celebrate the arrival of Martin Tupper, the British poet whose *Proverbial Philosophy* (1838) had enjoyed tremendous popularity over the previous decade. (Henry James would later compare Whitman's long poetic line to Tupper's

Philosophy as evidence of an essentially prosaic mind straining to lift itself into poetry.) Tupper's U.S. tour involved public lectures, celebratory dinners, visits with dignitaries, and an evening at Millard Fillmore's White House.[19] A handful of American poets also attracted significant attention. Despite long periods of creative inactivity, Fitz-Greene Halleck was a staple of the New York literary scene in the 1830s, and his collected works went through multiple editions.[20] John Greenleaf Whittier published more than two hundred poems by the age of twenty-five, but it was his commitment to writing a stridently abolitionist verse that earned him a national reputation in the 1830s and 1840s. Whittier's *Snow-Bound,* a series of poems about an isolated New England family, sold over twenty thousand copies when it was first published in 1866. Whittier carefully tended to his growing reputation, expressing his preference for immediate notoriety over posthumous fame.[21] With their shared Quaker backgrounds, interest in the working class, and political activism, Whitman had good reason to hope that the famous poet might support *Leaves of Grass* when he sent him a complementary copy in 1855. As legend has it, Whittier was so offended by the volume that he threw it into his fireplace.[22]

William Cullen Bryant and James Russell Lowell struggled to find audiences for their early works, but their busy public lives gave their poems wide exposure and respect. Barbara Packer notes that Bryant's first volume of poems, published in 1821, did not sell enough copies to pay the cost of publication, but with the help of special illustrated editions, his reputation steadily increased over the next decades.[23] Bryant's position as editor of the New York *Evening Post* made him one of the most institutionally powerful poets of his age, and he immersed himself in politics, eventually becoming a founding voice of the Republican Party. (It was Bryant who introduced Abraham Lincoln's famous speech at Cooper Union.) Boosted by Washington Irving, praised by Poe, Bryant's poems attracted an international following. Whitman became friends with Bryant while editing the *Daily Eagle,* and he frequently joined the older poet on long walks through Manhattan. (Whitman's journalistic sketches of Long Island, "Letters from Paumanok," appeared in the *Evening Post* in 1851.) By the end of the Civil War, Bryant's reputation had become so marketable that publishers sought the rights simply to name him as an adviser to their books—among them, a history of the United States, an anthology of American verse, and a new edition of Shakespeare.[24]

Whitman's lifelong rivalry with James Russell Lowell makes him an unusual model for literary fame, for as William Pannapacker has shown, the Boston Brahmin enjoyed the kind of economic and political capital that consistently eluded the more avant-garde Brooklynite.[25] Lowell had emerged in 1848 as a major American poet when, in a single year, he published four books of poems to widespread acclaim: *The Biglow Papers, Poems: Second Series; A Fable for Critics,* and *The Vision of Sir Launfal.* Lowell's Yankee didacticism received praise from like-minded writers throughout the country, and his association with New England culture and probity was so strong that many admirers wrote him wishing that their own states and villages were as intellectually vigorous and morally righteous as Boston seemed to be. As Whitman prepared the first edition of *Leaves of Grass,* Lowell was quickly climbing the ladder of both academic and popular respectability. His 1855 lectures on English poetry at the Lowell Institute in Boston were so well received (they earned effusive praise from Charles Sumner and Lydia Huntley Sigourney) that he commenced on the kind of lecture tour that Whitman would soon envision for himself. Traveling as far west as Madison, Wisconsin, Lowell found lecturing to be tedious and uncomfortable, though the experience netted him six hundred dollars in profits and, as he commented privately, "*tremendous* puffs in the local papers." Like Whittier, Lowell's abolitionist activities regularly brought his poems before the public eye, and like Bryant, he commanded tremendous institutional power. In addition to teaching at Harvard, he served as the editor of the *Atlantic* and the *North American Review.*[26]

Undoubtedly the most loved and celebrated American poet of the nineteenth century was Henry Wadsworth Longfellow, a friend of both Lowell and Bryant and perhaps the only Fireside poet whose reputation seems ascendant today. Whitman had printed excerpts from Longfellow's *Evangeline* in the pages of the *Daily Eagle,* comparing its sorrowful conclusion to "a solemn-psalm, the essence of whose deep religious music still lives on in your soul, and becomes a part of you."[27] A professor of modern languages at Harvard, a scholar distinguished by his knowledge of foreign cultures and literatures, Longfellow had managed to reach the people in a way that Whitman never did. Readers throughout the country memorized poems such as "Excelsior" and "A Psalm of Life," taking comfort in their Victorian stoicism and calm. Combining a heartbreaking narrative with an infectious rhythm, "The Wreck of the Hesperus" quickly found a popular audience when Longfellow published it as a broadside. With his genteel Yankee reserve, he neither trumpeted his sales nor declared his triumphs as some of his New York counterparts did. Ticknor and Fields' advance notice of *The Song of Hiawatha* simply described it as "A PROMISED LITERARY TREAT." But Longfellow, who had consulted with N. P. Willis early in his career about how to increase his sales, was well aware of his growing fame and reputation.[28] In 1857, he privately tallied the number of volumes he had sold since his first publication less than two decades before:

Hyperion (1839)	14,550
Voices of the Night (1839)	43,500
The Spanish Student (1843)	38,400
The Belfrey of Bruges (1845)	38,300
Evangeline (1847)	35,850
The Seaside and the Fireside (1849–50)	30,000
The Song of Hiawatha (1855)	50,000

The numbers convey a truly remarkable readership and make Whitman's inflated sales figures seem downright modest. For Longfellow, the success would keep coming. Later in 1857, the poet's historical romance, *The Courtship of Miles Standish,* sold twenty-five thousand copies in just two months, while the British edition sold ten thousand copies on the first day of its release.[29]

Longfellow's fame extended beyond his astonishing book sales. He was recognized for his deep commitment to the Union, stance against slavery, and populist appeal. Despite the fact that many of his best-known works were based on European forms (*Hiawatha* was actually based on a Finnish national epic), he was respected on both sides of the Atlantic as *the* poetic representative of the United States. Longfellow's famous Cambridge home, Craigie House, had been the headquarters of General Washington during the War for Independence, and he was deemed a worthy keeper of that heritage, a poet who had the gravitas of a national institution. The publication of "Paul Revere's Ride" as part of *Tales of a Wayside Inn* (1863) only burnished this statesmanlike reputation. In 1847, Whitman's *Daily Eagle* had twice promoted an engraving being sold in New York of the U.S. Senate.[30] The artist had populated the Senate chamber and galleries with about a hundred illustrious Americans from different time periods, most of them politicians and cabinet officers, but a few from other walks of life: John James Audubon, Dolly Madison and, as the paper noted, two distinguished poets—Longfellow and Bryant.

However much he desired it, Whitman's work was not suited to the kind of critical and popular acceptance that Longfellow enjoyed, for *Leaves of Grass* addressed democratic ideals far more than democratic taste. Though he had clearly admired him in the 1840s and 1850s, Whitman's final assessment of the Boston poet was withering. "Longfellow was no revolutionarie: never traveled new paths: of course never broke new paths." He was "the expresser of common themes—of the little songs of the masses," and for this reason, Whitman predicted that he would always maintain "a popular conventional pertinancy" (*WWC*, 3:24). As we will see in the final chapter, this description conveys the position Whitman would adopt at the end of his life when he viewed public neglect, rather than popularity, as the mark of his groundbreaking achievement. By any standard, *Leaves of Grass* would have struggled to be a popular text. Dispensing with traditional forms and line length, rejecting rhyme as a monarchical ornament, the book challenged the public's sense of what American poetry should and could be. In contrast to Halleck's "Marco Bozzaris" or Poe's "The Raven," Whitman's poems were not easy to memorize and recite. As formal and genteel as the Fireside poets could be, their poems emerged out of recognizable literary and popular modes: the sonnet, the ode, the ballad, the extended narrative poem. One of Longfellow's greatest strengths was his ability to create memorable, mythic, almost novelistic characters: the wandering Cajun beauty Evangeline, the doomed and heroic Hiawatha. Whitman tried to encompass a panorama of social types, but in his effort to contain everyone, he gave antebellum readers few characters with whom they could fully identify. (The first Whitman poem to appear in an anthology was "Come Up from the Fields Father," which reflects on a tragedy so common—a family learns of a son's fatal injury during the Civil War—that it required little characterization to appeal to general readers.[31])

While Longfellow's poems were reinforcing Puritan concepts of moral character, Whitman was forming a new poetics based on the coming world of personality. To nineteenth-century Americans accustomed to the values of duty, honor, work, reputation, integrity, and masculinity, Longfellow provided an exquisitely accomplished and interesting poetry.

"The Village Blacksmith," for example, celebrates an American artisan whose story is meant to be both moving and inspiring. The poem opens with the smithy working at his anvil; his "brawny arms" and "flaming forge" excite the children and are as reliable as the church bell. We learn that in spite of suffering his wife's death, the blacksmith has remained pious, steadfast, and kind, a father fulfilling his duties to his family, village, and God:

> Toiling,—rejoicing,—sorrowing,
>   Onward through life he goes;
> Each morning sees some task begin,
>   Each evening sees it close;
> Something attempted, something done,
>   Has earned a night's repose.

At the poem's end, Longfellow lifts his blacksmith into a larger, universal realm, thanking his "worthy friend" for the lesson he has taught: "Thus at the flaming forge of life / Our fortunes must be wrought." The "measured beat" of the blacksmith's forge becomes a model for the poet's art.[32]

For Whitman, a truly democratic poetry involved more than lessons from the heroic working class. "The expression of the American poet is to be transcendent and new," he wrote in the 1855 Preface to *Leaves of Grass*. "It is to be indirect and not direct or descriptive or epic" (8). The principle of indirection led Whitman to eschew the history and context through which readers recognize both literary and moral character. Section 12 of "Song of Myself" presents a scene of male labor comparable to Longfellow's, but the poet emerges as an observer rather than a moralist:

> The butcher-boy puts off his killing-clothes, or sharpens his
>   knife at the stall in the market,
> I loiter enjoying his repartee and his shuffle and breakdown.
>
> Blacksmiths with grimed and hairy chests environ the anvil,
> Each has his main-sledge .... they are all out .... there is great
>   heat in the fire.
>
> From the cinder-strewed threshold I follow their movements,
> The lithe sheer of their waists plays even with their massive
>   arms,

> Overhand the hammers roll—overhand so slow—overhand so
>   sure,
> They do not hasten, each man hits in his place.
>   (*LG* 1855, 34–35; Whitman's ellipses)

The section reveals the abiding importance of personality even when Whitman puts others on display. What draws the poet to these workers is their mastery, their magnetism, their self-possession, their physical and erotic force. The butcher boy performs his "shuffle and breakdown" without regard for its significance. In comparison to Longfellow, who inserts himself into the poem as the blacksmith's moral interpreter, Whitman simply watches the performance. He presents the blacksmiths as personalities with no history or context; their meaning lies in their bodies' impact on the loitering appreciative audience. The "measured beat" of Longfellow's verse is replaced by a poetic line determined by breath and the repetition of phrase and syntax: "Overhand the hammers roll—overhand so slow—overhand so sure." The verse does not mimic the labor, as a popular audience might expect. The repetition slows and orders the line, so we see the action emphatically take place.

Although his poems suggest otherwise, Whitman was not as steady and self-possessed as the workers he observed. He grappled with the lack of audience throughout his life, nursing the desire to have it ratify his poetic identity. Whitman's description of Longfellow as the creator of "little songs of the masses" reveals the gap that would eventually open in his understanding of popularity. When he predicted that Longfellow would always have a "popular conventional pertinancy," Whitman, of course, was speaking pejoratively. As we will see in chapter 5, by the end of his life Whitman had come to see himself as an aesthetic revolutionary whose achievements were evident in his lack of acclaim. This position belied the poet's early efforts to imagine, cultivate, and even feign his own popularity. The mass of antebellum Americans did not acknowledge Whitman's power, but meeting his ambitions in 1855 may have been an impossible task. He wanted to be celebrated for encouraging readers to ignore much of what they had been taught, for coaxing them to see their lives and world differently. He wanted the people to absorb him affectionately even as he sought to transform the medium by which he reached them. The metaphor of absorption is significant, for it implied a slow, almost unconscious process by which his personality would become as-similated into the public mind. He would saturate the country like water a piece of cloth, pervading its consciousness until their values were mutual and shared, until poet and audience ceased to have an autonomous exis-tence. Whitman did not dream of conventional fame—reputation, emi-nence, respect, prestige. He wanted the country's attention to be expan-sive, benevolent, and vitalizing.

Whitman expressed these desires in the language of popular sov-ereignty. His interest in popular opinion emerges in *Leaves of Grass* as a fusion of publicity and personality, the adaptation of republican virtue to a climate of democratic individualism. In thinking about the political import of fame, Whitman was drawing upon his eighteenth-century predecessors. Republicanism conventionally demanded the individual's subordination to the common good, and thus celebrating oneself in a republic would be acceptable only if that celebration made the poet's ambition a sign of his republican commitments. A writer's dedication to the people would be most evident in the degree to which his fellow citizens recognized his work as their own, in the ways in which his virtue was paradoxically manifest in public celebrations of his self. The poet who received his country's ap-proval, who emerged as a national personality, would become a metarepre-sentative of the public sphere itself.

REPRESENTATION AND CELEBRITY:
THE LEGACY OF TOM PAINE

An important precursor to Whitman's vision of literary personality was the radical Thomas Paine. Like the poet, Paine displayed deep respect for the power of public opinion to validate an individual's writing, and he helps us see that Whitman's construction of a representative voice owes as much to the forms of American political culture as it does to the themes of Emersonian romanticism. Over sixty years before the publication of *Leaves of Grass,* Paine was developing a rhetoric based on the premise that in a country founded on the principles of popular sovereignty, fame was an important expression of cultural power. Celebrated writers, by virtue of the attention they garnered, could truly claim to represent the people in their work.

For two writers so profoundly concerned with the civic import of renown, Whitman's reverence for Paine occurred against the backdrop of the United States' near-total rejection of his work. The poet was first exposed to Paine during his youth, and as he told Traubel, his father "had been an acceptor of Paine" at a time when he was "much vilified" (*WWC*, 3:139). As a young man Whitman had vowed to "do public justice" to Paine's much maligned reputation (*WWC*, 2:205–6). Throughout his last years, the poet frequently remarked upon the awful gap between Paine's contribution to the American Revolution and his fall into disrepute, for he was acutely troubled by Paine's status as one of America's "unpopulars" (*WWC*, 2:135).

In an 1877 lecture he gave in Philadelphia on the 140th anniversary of the revolutionary's birth, Whitman reminded the audience that Paine was largely responsible for the Union's independence, freedom from religious tyranny, and radical devotion to human rights. Hoping to dispel the many rumors about the old revolutionary's drunkenness and vulgarity, he insisted on Paine's "noble personality" and pointed to the philosophical calm with which he died. The reputation Paine commanded in the 1770s and 1780s had been ruined in posterity, and Whitman charged America with failing to protect its founders' eminence and prestige: "America [must] learn to better dwell on her choicest possession, the legacy of her good and faithful men—that she well preserve their fame, if unquestion'd—or, if need be, that she fail not to dissipate what clouds have intruded on that fame, and burnish it newer, truer and brighter, continually (*WPP*, 799)."

Paine's popularity had evaporated with the publication of *The Age of Reason* (1794–95), and Whitman ruminated about how a man who had "served the embryo Union with most precious service" could be afflicted with "foul and foolish fictions" in death (*WPP*, 799). "Did History ever more thoroughly victimize a man?" he asked Traubel. "Paine himself did signal lasting work—work to which our people have been disgracefully oblivious" (*WWC*, 1:79). In Whitman's understanding, a "polite circle" of partisan elites had turned the celebrated author of *Common Sense* (1776) and *Rights of Man* (1791–92) into a drunken infidel rather than a beloved representative. As he saw his own celebrity rising in 1892, the poet grew angry about Paine's ill-repute: "Poor Paine! Poor Paine! His fame or mal-fame is the work of three or four howling preachers—damn 'em!" (*WWC*, 9:374).

Paine's great service to the nation hinged on his popularity, for without his large readership, his writings would have had minor political consequence. Paine himself addressed his renown in the second volume of *Rights of Man,* in which he defended the French Revolution by explaining the success of republicanism in America. In 1776 he had written, "No man is a true republican worthy of that name that will not give up his single voice to that of the republic," and as if to prove his political resolve, he embraced the colonial practice of publishing his works either anonymously or with a pseudonym.[33] By the 1790s, Paine was known throughout the Anglo-American world, and not only did he sign his name to *Rights of Man,* he also reflected on how he "arrive[d] at an eminence in political literature" that even "aristocracy" had been unable "to rival."[34] Perhaps feeling that these claims to distinction were ostentatious and dangerously unrepublican, he relegated the details of his authorial past to a footnote that extended in the first American edition to nearly ninety lines.

The footnote emerges as a fascinating attempt to fuse the representative potential of celebrity with the conventions of republican discourse. The note begins by emphasizing Paine's candor and impartiality in making political judgments. "I did not at my first setting out in public life, nearly seventeen years ago, turn my thoughts to subjects of government from motives of interest" (219). Paine argues that it was his stern independence, his disregard for both praise and censure, that helped him gain "the ear and confidence of America" (220). "I thought I saw an opportunity, in which I thought I could do some good, and I followed exactly what my heart dictated. I neither read books, nor studied other people's opinions. I thought for myself" (219). Paine constructs himself as a model republican, a citizen-author whose devotion to reason and the public good has led the people to ratify his texts as the voice of popular opinion. Whitman would later echo this statement in "Song of Myself," encouraging readers to filter books and expert opinions in thinking for themselves (*LG* 1855, 26).

At the center of his portrait of virtue and eminence, Paine places the history of *Common Sense* and its remarkable reception in the colonies. Arguing that "monarchy and aristocracy were frauds and impositions upon mankind," he explains that when he published *Common Sense,* "the success it met with was beyond anything since the invention of printing" (219). To this remark he adds an ingenious stroke of self-renunciation: "I gave the copyright up to every state in the union, and the demand ran to not less than one hundred thousand copies" (220). As distinct from his many rivals and enemies, the author owes his public character to his public acceptance, and he thus enjoys a "range in political writing beyond, perhaps, what any man ever possessed in any country" (219). Readers of Burke's *Reflections on the Revolution in France* (1790) may recall the author's exhaustive attempts to root his political voice in the learning of the ancien régime: the Latin quotations from Juvenal and Terrence, the comparison of Richard Price to the witches in *Macbeth,* the portrait of Marie Antoinette as the dignified Lucretia. Paine mocks this learning and defiantly roots his text in expressions of popular opinion. He integrates into his representative personality two seemingly opposite rhetorical stances: the virtue of selflessness and the power of celebrity.

A comparison to Emerson is quite revealing, for despite his gestures toward self-reliance, Paine suggests that his authority ultimately derives from the crowd. The vast citizenry to which he appeals surfaces most frequently in Emerson's writings as an insidious threat to the complete or representative individual. "Society is everywhere in conspiracy against its members," he comments in "Self-Reliance," an essay that treats the populace as a passive beast with no will of its own. As Emerson writes, "the sour faces of the multitude, like their sweet faces, have no deep cause, but are put on and off as the wind blows and the newspaper directs" (264). With his emphasis on the public's mindless instability, Emerson offers the type of cultural reproach employed by other antebellum critics of celebrity. The world's opinion seems subject to the same volatility that marks both Fortune and fame.

A more revealing portrait of representation and popularity emerges from Emerson's essay "Napoleon; or, The Man of the World" from *Representative Men* (1850). In Napoleon Emerson faced an eminent and powerful individual who commanded a tremendous following, and thus while in "Self-Reliance" he had criticized the newspaper for its control over the populace, he now focused on the part it played in Napoleon's representativeness. "Napoleon is thoroughly modern," Emerson comments, "and, at the highest point of his fortunes, has the very spirit of the newspapers. . . . The man in the street finds in him the qualities and powers of other men in the street" (728). "A man of Napoleon's stamp," he continues, "almost ceases to have a private speech and opinion" and "is so largely receptive, and is so placed, that he comes to be a bureau for all the intelligence, wit, and power of the age and country" (729). As "an organ and a leader" of the "industrious masses," Napoleon is a remarkable example of how Emerson envisioned the representative's relation to the populace: "Bonaparte was the idol of common men, because he had in transcendent degree the qualities and powers of common men" (736, 729).

The essay depicts Napoleon's command over the public as being essential to his cultural power. Napoleon's "grand weapon," Emerson explains, "namely the millions whom he directed, he owed to the representative character which clothed him" (736). On first glance, the statement suggests the logic we'd find in something by Paine or Whitman, but Emerson's thinking requires a closer look. Napoleon's power comes from his popularity, and his popularity comes from his representative character. Emerson's statement does not answer the crucial question about the origins of that representativeness: who or what actually clothes the leader in his representative dress? Individuals might diffuse their power through the populace, and the populace certainly can come to recognize itself in them; in Emerson's estimation, however, neither transaction can account for a man's or woman's representativeness.

Despite an active interest in Napoleon's popularity, Emerson's anatomy of his character does not include the public. "The times, his constitution, and his early circumstances, combined to develop this pattern democrat," Emerson writes, without considering the public's influence at all (730). The next paragraph continues this line of inquiry by presenting Napoleon as a creature of destiny rather than the public will: "Nature must have far the greatest share in every success, and so in his. Such a man was wanted, and such a man was born" (731). The passivity of this demand is quite revealing, for elections in Emerson are decided by vertical rather than horizontal powers. Napoleon does not campaign to be the people's representative; he is passively chosen by Nature to portray the whole or complete man.

Emerson's thinking corresponds with his notion that representation is an essentially pictorial phenomenon. The people see a magnified version of themselves in the representative individual; what they do not expect is that *they* can make that individual representative, that they have some voice in who speaks for them collectively. Whitman made precisely this point later in his career, charging Emerson's circle with being unpatriotic for disliking American crowds. Written on stationery from the United States Department of Justice and titled "On Emerson and the New

England Set," the comment emphasizes the transcendentalists' dislike for the *sounds* of American democracy:

> Life in its grand turbulence in the United States with all its mul-
> titudinous noise & practical business & politics, and vehement
> and oceanic crowds rushing to and from the trains and voices as
> of squads and regiments in armies endlessly gesticulating and
> talking in every key, especially the loud ones, is painful to them,
> grating upon their ears, their nerves and they shun and abuse it.
> They teach and maintain in their writings a proper demeanor, &
> seriously condemn laughing. They secretly (and not always se-
> cretly) despise the idea of patriotism and think it fine to sub-
> stitute some other ism in its place.[35]

According to Whitman, Emerson's notion of representation avoids the verbal turbulence that he was trying to associate with American democracy.

The poet's catalogues overtly attest to his interest in visually *depicting* the country. But when Whitman turns to the problem of *speaking*
for the nation, he places significant power in the people themselves. The
1855 poem "A Song for Occupations" makes this practice abundantly
clear. Imagining his readers as a group of physical laborers and artisans,
Whitman reminds them that they are the source of the government's
power:

> The sum of all known value and respect I add up in you whoever
>   you are;
> The President is up there in the White House for you . . . . it is
>   not you who are here for him,
> The Secretaries act in their bureaus for you . . . . not you here for
>   them. (*LG* 1855, 91–92; Whitman's ellipses)

The passage subsumes the people's official representatives to their common origin in the reader. As both the source and sum of public authority,
Whitman's audience becomes the Republic's most important ratifying
agent.

This assertion of popular sovereignty would be neither exceptional
nor noteworthy if not for the next stanza's expansion of these principles to
the realm of culture and history:

> All doctrines, all politics and civilization exurge from you,
> All sculpture and monuments and anything inscribed anywhere
>   are tallied in you,
> The gist of histories and statistics as far back as the records
>   reach is in you this hour—and myths and tales the same;
> If you were not breathing and walking here where would they
>   all be?
> The most renowned poems would be ashes . . . . orations and
>   plays would be vacuums. (*LG* 1855, 92; Whitman's ellipsis)

Although the poet respects these various cultural achievements, he insists that his readers understand their own collective power. "It is not they who give the life," he comments, "it is you who give the life" (*LG* 1855, 91). Lawrence Levine has pointed out that in contrast to the twentieth-century practice of preserving and revering artistic productions, nineteenth-century Americans tended to alter the works of people such as Shakespeare and Mozart to fit them into their own cultural needs and desires.[36] Whitman makes this attitude a central part of his poetic, situating the origins of his art in the audience's response. Even the "most renowned poems would be ashes" without their public foundation.

What Whitman proposed as an American aesthetic, Paine had already defined in *Rights of Man* as a powerfully new republican rhetoric. Moving from the "strategy of personal abstraction" found in works such as *Common Sense*, he used his notoriety, his recognizability, as the base of his political commitments.[37] In contrast to many of his contemporaries, he seized on the dynamics of print culture not to divest his personality in a wholly public expression but to endow himself with a distinctly representative personality. Against Burke's elaborate citations, the second volume of *Rights of Man* taunts Paine's opponents with the power indicated by the forty to fifty thousand copies the first volume sold in the British Isles: "If Mr. Burke, or any person on his side the question, will produce an answer to *Rights of Man*, that shall extend to an half, or even to a fourth part of the number of copies to which *Rights of Man* extended, I will reply to his work. But until this be done, I shall so far take the sense of the public for my guide (and the world knows I am not a flatterer) that what they do not think worth while to read, is not worth mine to answer" (155). In suggesting that readers determine what is "worth while" or relevant, Paine situates cultural authority in the behavior and sensibility of the community at large. In Paine's rhetoric, the relevance of an author is registered in the dissemination of his work because the community can endorse political positions through its consumption of pamphlets and books. In a democratic republic of letters in which writings are circulated throughout the community, the voices most representative of public opinion would be the ones most widely received. The highly concentrated civic voice Paine achieves in *Rights of Man* amounts to a form of rhetorical celebrity in which fame and acceptance become strategically useful as signs of political relevance and legitimacy.

Like his radical predecessor, Whitman predicated his public identity on the audience's power to celebrate his work. Although he never approached Paine's commercial success, he firmly believed that even the semblance of popularity would help him realize his extraordinary ambitions. The poet's relevance would be most evident in images of his acceptance, for fame, like representation, did not signify the embodiment of an abstract ideal as much as the value of circulation in a meritocracy. This thinking pervades an announcement for the 1856 edition of *Leaves of Grass* distributed through the publishing firm Fowler & Wells. Trying to create the sensation that Whitman was fast becoming one of the country's favorite poets, the announcement moves beyond a simple description of the book's price, size, and publication date. It makes a broad case for the poet's legitimacy. Like the banners for Fern's and Stowe's books that trumpeted their popularity, the advertisement rests Whitman's claims to be a national poet on the real and fabricated success of the 1855 edition:

> It is evident that the American people will give a hearing to any man who has it in him to reward attention. Walt Whitman's poems, the now famous "Leaves of Grass," would scarcely have been thought likely to become speedily popular. . . . Yet the "Leaves of Grass" found purchasers, appreciators, and admirers. The first edition of a thousand copies rapidly disappeared, and we now have the pleasure of announcing that a second edition, with amendments and additions, is about to be issued. . . .
>
> Walt Whitman has thus become a fixed fact. His message has been found worthy of regard. The emphatic commendation of America's greatest critic has been ratified by the public, and

henceforth the "Leaves of Grass" must receive respectful mention, wherever Americans are reckoning up those of their country's productions which could have sprung into existence
nowhere but in America.[38]

Appearing in *Life Illustrated*, Fowler & Wells's in-house newspaper, the
passage shrewdly turns the public into the culture's most compelling
authority. Whitman's "message" is "worthy of regard" because the people
have selected it to occupy their attention; their interest has granted him
"respectful mention" as a distinctly national text. The announcement
functions by the same logic that Whitman found in *Rights of Man*, in
which Paine suggested that readers had determined what texts were worth
his answering.

The 1856 edition of *Leaves of Grass* made much of Emerson's support.
It printed Emerson's July 24, 1855, letter in an appendix and garishly
displayed his ringing endorsement on its spine: *I greet you at the beginning
of a great career. R W Emerson.* Emerson's position in the 1856 edition
attests to a tension in Whitman between his desire for artistic acceptance
and his desire for popularity. The tension would persist throughout Whitman's career and would later surface in his relationship to Abraham
Lincoln. But despite the publicity he garnered from his impressive associations and endorsements, fame for Whitman would suggest his deep
immersion in democracy. The gold-leaf lettering emphasized the triumphant nature of Emerson's puff, but the advertisement subsumes his real
critical assessment to a lie about the book's popularity. Like the poet,
Emerson's judgments are "ratified" by the people, authenticated by the
expression of popular opinion through the marketplace. The "American
people will give a hearing to any man who has it in him to reward attention." The announcement elevates Whitman's fantasies about celebrity
over Emerson's genuine support; it affirms his commitment to being
recognized as a democratically sanctioned personality.

CELEBRITY AS A COLLABORATIVE FORM AND PROCESS

As distinct from the Emersonian hero, the celebrity is a social construct, a
figure whose very identity lies in the community's embrace. Celebrity may
come to strong individuals, but it is more than a form of exalted individualism. Peter Briggs emphasizes the public's significance in creating the

renowned: "Celebrity is finally a collaborative social form and process, a sort of dance, a coming together of attitudes, aspirations, and behaviors on the part of the celebrity with patterns of expectation and response on the part of an audience. In other words, the phenomena which constitute celebrity depend heavily upon the mental habits of all concerned, and public gestures associated with celebrity which, taken in isolation and out of social context, might appear bizarre or simply unaccountable are in fact parts of a shared idiom."[39] Whitman was not the only antebellum figure for whom the "shared idiom" of celebrity took on a particularly political cast. Personalities as diverse as Stowe, Barnum, and the Hutchinson Family Singers each experienced celebrity as a kind of political identity, one in which the public either validated their beliefs or viewed them as expressions of national character. The social forms associated with antebellum fame—the newspaper profiles, the daguerreotypist's gallery, the throngs of curious well-wishers—all suggest a collaboration between antebellum Americans and the people who occupied their attention.

For a would-be representative, a man without popularity, the task of intimating that fame was complex. As a poet he learned to structure the illusion of collaboration into the poems themselves, foregrounding their social context. At times Whitman implies that his poems have been called forth by an audience, that they owe their existence to external demand. "O take my hand Walt Whitman!" a speaker calls at the beginning of "Salut au Monde!" (WPP, 287), and as the poet wanders across the earth, he responds to the various prompts of this nameless interrogator: "What do you hear Walt Whitman?" (WPP, 288), "What do you see Walt Whitman? Who are they you salute, and that one after another salute you?" (WPP, 289). "The Wound Dresser" relies on a similar structure in narrating the poet's hospital experiences during the war. Whitman imagines himself as a beloved old patriarch who is sought after by young men and women eager to hear his story. "Come tell us old man," they affectionately approach him, the imagined address turning the poem into a publicly requested reminiscence (WPP, 442).

More commonly, Whitman helped create his audience through the apostrophe, his direct address to readers. Throughout Leaves of Grass the poet directs dozens of apostrophes to named and unnamed individuals, invoking historians, singers, prairie boys, and "you whoever you are." At times he depicts himself addressing large crowds—an army, an audience, buyers at a slave auction. In "A Broadway Pageant," he directs his thoughts to "Superb-faced Manhattan! / Comrade Americanos!" (*WPP*, 384). "Pioneers! O Pioneers" begins "Come my tan-faced children, / Follow well in order" (*WPP*, 371). Scholars have tended to focus on the apostrophe's importance in establishing the immediacy of Whitman's voice. As Tenny Nathanson has argued, the apostrophe both underscores and undermines the poet's presence.[40] It positions the poet alongside the reader, endowing the text with himself. The apostrophe is equally significant in bringing the audience into Whitman's poems, making it both present and complicit in his poetic identity. When Whitman invokes his comrade Americans, when he orders "Fall behind me States!" he creates the impression of a shared but fictive performance involving the poet and his readers ("By Blue Ontario's Shore," *WPP*, 479). Both are authenticated through their implied relationship with the other.

Among the customs and rites that make up Whitman's democratic version of celebrity, the act of identification occupies a central position. The poet immerses himself in the populations around him, creating a kind of representative identity. The 1855 poem eventually titled "Song of the Answerer" endows the poet with an exquisite combination of personal charisma and public stature:

> He walks with perfect ease in the capitol,
> He walks among the Congress . . . . and one representative says
> to another, Here is our equal appearing and new.
>
> Then the mechanics take him for a mechanic,
> And the soldiers suppose him to be a captain . . . . and the sailors
> that he has followed the sea,
> And the authors take him for an author . . . . and the artists for
> an artist,
> And the laborers perceive he could labor with them and love them;
> No matter what the work is, that he is one to follow it or has
> followed it,
> No matter what the nation, that he might find his brothers and
> sisters there. (*LG* 1855, 131; Whitman's ellipses)

According to Susman, the culture of personality is organized around the essentially antinomian vision of following not "a higher law but a higher self." This vision is "tempered by the suggestion that the self ought to be presented to society in such a way as to make oneself stand out from the crowd, and at the same time appeal—by fascination, magnetism, attractiveness—to it."[41] "Song of the Answerer" exhibits this sense of personality as if it were a textbook on the subject. The poet's personality is confirmed by the claims that various individuals make on it. In the passage above, Whitman's familiar parallelism reinforces his difference from the people who identify with him. The poet demonstrates his uniqueness by establishing a pattern of equation—"the authors take him for an author . . . . and the artists for an artist"—and then subtly departing from it— "And the laborers perceive he could labor with them and love them." The people's recognition testifies to Whitman's singular importance; they produce his celebrity along with him.

Readers have long struggled with the poet's persona in *Leaves of Grass*, questioning the degree to which it is autobiographical or fictional. Is the figure of "Walt Whitman" an actual man, or is it a mythic construct? Whitman provided plenty of clues to suggest that the answer lay somewhere in between. The subject becomes particularly murky around the poet's ability to elicit the interest and affection of strangers. William Douglas O'Connor emphasized precisely this aspect of Whitman's personality in *The Good Gray Poet*, the promotional pamphlet he published in 1866. O'Connor and his wife, Ellen, had been good friends to the poet in Washington, DC. Not only did he visit the family frequently, he lived with them for five months in 1863. When the poet lost his position at the Bureau of Indian Affairs, allegedly because of the licentious nature of *Leaves of Grass*, O'Connor published an impassioned defense of the book and its creator. In a near echo of "Song of the Answerer," he underscored the poet's ability to arouse the affection of common people. The passage is not well known, so I quote at length:

> I have seen singular evidence of the mysterious quality which
> not only guards him, but draws to him with intuition, rapid as
> light, simple and rude people, as to their natural mate and
> friend. I remember, as I passed the White House with him one
> evening, the startled feeling with which I saw a soldier on guard
> there—a stranger to us both, and with something in his action
> that curiously proved that he was a stranger—suddenly bring his

musket to the "present" in military salute to him, quickly min-
gling with this respect due to his colonel, a gesture of greeting
with the right hand as to a comrade, grinning, meanwhile, good
fellow, with shy, spontaneous affection and deference, his ruddy,
broad face glowing in the flare of the lampions. I remember, on
another occasion, as I crossed the street with him, the driver of a
street-car, a stranger, stopping the conveyance, and inviting him
to get on and ride with him. Adventures of this kind are frequent, and "I took a fancy to you," or "You look like one of my
style," is the common explanation he gets upon their occurrence. It would be impossible to exaggerate the personal adhe-
sion and strong, simple affection given him, in numerous
instances on sight, by multitudes of plain persons, sailors, mechanics, drivers, soldiers, farmers, seamstresses, old people of
the past generation, mothers of families—those powerful, unlet-
tered persons, among whom, as he says in his book, he has gone
freely, and who never in most cases even suspect as an author
him whom they love as a man, and who loves them in return.[42]

The passage substantiates the claims Whitman had been making in
Leaves of Grass, attesting to the poet's capacity to draw his countrymen's
love. Like the Answerer, he appears as a comrade to the sailors, mechanics, and drivers who all see him as one of their own. O'Connor's
effort to capture Whitman's charisma highlights the sudden intuitive response he arouses in the people about town. As "rapid as light," the
Washingtonians recognize the poet as a natural companion; "You look
like one of my style" becomes a characteristic refrain. When the soldier
greets him with "spontaneous affection and deference," he signifies the
poet's singularly personal power. Whitman is both in the crowd and apart
from it, an antinomian republican, a celebrity of the common folk.

It is difficult to know the extent to which Whitman's image making influenced O'Connor's account. He surely had read "Song of the Answerer,"
and like many of Whitman's devotees, he probably consulted with the poet
as he was writing the pamphlet. What we know for certain is that Whitman
clearly valued and amplified the kind of responses O'Connor described. In
the same notebook in which he expressed a hope that others would confirm his personality, Whitman imagined the Poet at the center of a raucous,

euphoric celebrity. The passage is breathtaking in its conception of fame as the fulfillment of aesthetic, political, and erotic desires:

> I think ten million supple-wristed gods are always hiding beauty in the world—burying it every where in every thing—and most of all in spots that men and women do not think of and never look—as Death and Poverty and Wickedness—Cache! And Cache again! all over the earth, and in the heavens that swathe the earth and in the waters of the sea—They do their jobs well; these journeymen divine. Only from the Poet they can hide nothing and would not if they could.—I reckon he is Boss of those gods: and the work they do is done for him; and all they have concealed, they have concealed for his sake.—Him they attend indoors and outdoors—They run ahead when he walks, and lift their cunning covers and signify him with pointed stretched arms. Their President and their Pet! I see them lead him now.—I see his large, slow gait—his face illuminated like the face of an arm-bound child. Onward he moves with the gay procession and the laughing pioneers and the wild trilling bugles of joy.[43]

Whitman would later rework this material for "The Sleepers," eliminating the distancing effect of "the Poet" and softening some of the paragraph's erotic energy. While the poem retains the scene's dreamlike quality as a "gay gang of blackguards" leads the poet "with mirthshouting music and wildflapping pennants of joy," the revisions can make it difficult to see that what the Poet is discovering are hidden caches of beauty (*LG* 1855, 107). The notebook explores the theme quite directly, and over the course of multiple drafts, it consistently turns the apprehension of beauty into a kind of erotic, social acclaim. The "ten million supple-wristed gods" are integral to the Poet's vision of the cosmos, acceptance of death, and capacity to perceive beauty in all things. They engage the Poet in a game of hide-and-seek in which he uncovers the beauty concealed to everyone but him. The Poet emerges from the parade as both a president and an infant—a man elected to great power and a child borne by the preceding gods. The passage lends credence to the theory that Whitman sought in celebrity the erotic fulfillment he was unable to achieve personally. Discerning beauty becomes less a mode of individual perception than a strange celebratory assembly, with the gods lifting their cunning covers (the pun on bed sheets is unmistakable) and signifying their Poet, President, and Pet.

Whitman recorded this scene on the last page of the notebook and then later crossed it out. He seems to have continued the scene on the first page of a subsequent notebook that turns to the impact of this large, slow-gaited man. The gleeful fantasy that marked the previous entry now becomes a mandate for the Poet's singular power:

> In his presence all the Presidents and governors and kings of
> the world bend their hearts . . . . When he appears, Presidents
> and Governors descend into the crowd, capitalists and bankers
> are cheap with all their golden eagles. The learnedest professors
> and the authors of the most renowned books are baffled of their
> art . . . . , having come to a great fact in the orchard of nature cov-
> ered with flowers and fruit, where the best of themselves is but a
> [left blank] feebly pushing through the February ground.[44]

The passage is both more grandiose and less extraordinary than the vision that preceded it. In what some might call a puerile daydream, Whitman reveals the tangled forces driving his understanding of fame. Official representatives from around the globe—presidents, generals, kings—all join in the Poet's celebration, all become part of the crowd. He unleashes his commitment to democracy upon all professions and trades, subsuming these recognized cultural authorities to the Poet's superior presence. And yet, that leveling spirit comes attached to an aggressive, conquering desire. Out of a scene of sexual and aesthetic ecstasy comes a vision of cultural power, an antic megalomania that transforms the populist procession into a glorification of the self. The Poet's charismatic personality is evident in the people's immediate deference; he becomes their representative because they "bend their hearts" to him. The Poet draws everyone into the crowd and simultaneously stands apart from them.

Amid this web of imagined pleasures and feats, we see Whitman thinking about how personality is realized in public interest and support. *Leaves of Grass* anchors this relationship in its portrait of the poet as a man whose potential election by the people will extend the promise of constitutional democracy. Writing about the U.S. Constitution, the historian Edmund S. Morgan has explained that representation is a fiction that creates both "the people" and their spokesmen. With Madison as their guide, the framers had invented the notion of a sovereign people in order to "secure popular consent to a governing aristocracy."[45] As Brian Seitz has suggested, the phenomenon of representation is creative and transformative. It has no originating consciousness. "The discursive and practical mechanisms of political representation produce this political subject at the same time that they produce a representative for it."[46] Representation simultaneously establishes the citizen and the delegate, each identity contingent on the other. The many readers of *Rights of Man* become a politically powerful and identifiable group when Paine is recognized as their spokesman.

Whitman offers a strikingly literal rendition of the illusory quality of political representation. Whatever his complex personal motives, he invents himself as the authentic representative of a fictional populace. The followers described in *Leaves of Grass* serve as models by which the audience can recognize itself. While the many supporters bear little relation to the material world, their image is meant to influence the reception of the flesh-and-blood bard. They not only assign the poet his public identity, they also assign his genuine readers an identity as well. Readers of *Leaves of Grass* are already constituted as part of the celebratory mass; the role they occupy is that of euphoric enthusiastic fans.

As he grew disappointed with the book's poor sales and impact, Whitman turned to the future for its support, extending his election over generations. If the "proof of a poet" was to be "sternly deferr'd," then he would direct his address to a time when that proof had already come true (*LGV,* 204). To a certain extent, the tactic suggested a retreat to traditional associations of fame with immortality, the idea that earned through time, fame would reward its recipients with a kind of eternal, universal life. This version of fame had been motivating poets from Petrarch to Keats. Although Whitman would eventually adopt the idea himself, the early editions of *Leaves of Grass* persist in their commitment to a democratic understanding of popularity. Whitman's address to future admirers was less a departure from his aesthetic than a new way of staking his claim to a present-day representativeness. In poems such as "Poets to Come," "Crossing Brooklyn Ferry," and "The Wound Dresser," Whitman gathers his readers outside the confines of time, meeting them in the transcendent space of his personality. The great city, he says in "Song of the Broad Axe," is the place where slavery ceases to exist, presidents serve the people, and men and women walk together in open public procession. He begins his description of this utopian democracy by referring to its warm regard for poets: "Where the city stands with the brawniest breed of orators and bards, / Where the city stands that is belov'd by these, and loves them in return and understands them" (*WPP*, 335).

Whitman's appeals to his readers, both as individuals and en masse, create what communications researchers call a "model of contagion" in which an array of carefully selected crowd scenes produce the impression of an expansive interactive event.[47] Television frequently uses this technique to minimize the audience's awareness that the medium is transforming an actual historical occasion into a passively received spectacle. On New Year's Eve, for example, many broadcasts will report on the celebrations in an array of American and international cities. The series of cascading images both simulates and performs the viewer's identification with the crowds in those cities, and many viewers will join in the countdown to midnight as they see it on their screen. To use an anachronism, Whitman is like the television producer assembling these images in New York. He presents us with scattered groups of admirers, hoping that we will regard them as a kind of synecdoche for broader celebrations of his work. Whitman's appeals to the future serve as invitations to all of his readers—regardless of their position in history; he draws them into a crowd of liberated citizens.

What made Whitman's poetic exceptional among those of his contemporaries was how he imagined this audience in terms of publicity. The poet's address to his readers symbolically performs the relationship he desires with them. As we will see in chapter 4, Whitman's interest in the crowd did not diminish his attentions to individual readers, with whom he presumed an unparalleled intimacy. Even the most intimate discourse in *Leaves of Grass* tends to draw readers into a broader zone of publicity where we are asked to observe, admire, and reflect on the poet's whispered entreaties.

A distinction with Longfellow and Lowell can be quite revealing here. James H. Justus has argued that an important trope for each poet was the fireside, the symbolic center of family life and the domestic space in which they imagined their works being read. "My fires light up the hearths and hearts of men," Longfellow's January announces in "The Poet's Calendar." In "A Winter-Evening Hymn to My Fire," his paean to the New England hearth, Lowell depicts the fireside as the scene of hope, memory, and the "homely faith" and wisdom of the English muse.[48] Kirsten Silva Gruesz has shown that Longfellow did much to nurture this association in his collection *The Seaside and the Fireside*. Presenting himself as both a man and a talking book, he positioned himself at the reader's hearth: "I hope, as no unwelcome guest, / At your warm fireside, when the lamps are lighted, / To have my place reserved among the rest." Seated at the fireside, the poet is a steadfast image of domestic prudence and order, a patriarch dispensing wisdom to his intimates. For all of his renown, Longfellow was remarkably uncomfortable appearing before crowds, and he never appeared on the lecture circuit that was so personally and financially important to his friends Emerson, Dickens, and Holmes. The Whiggish politics that emerge from Longfellow's poems are grounded in his masculine reclamation of the hearth.[49]

The image of the fireside was so important to Whitman's contemporaries that it was regularly incorporated into the titles of books of poetry, fiction, and essays: among them, we might include Dexter King's *Fireside Poetical Readings* (1843), Maria Edgeworth's *Fireside Story Book* (1854), C. M. Kirkland's *Autumn Hours and Fireside Reading* (1854), and Lowell's *Fireside Travels* (1864). Editors on both sides of the Atlantic quickly picked up on the trope, and as the century progressed, they used it in popular anthologies and miscellanies: *The Fireside Companion* (1850), *The New York Fireside Companion* (1869), *The Fireside Library* (1876), and Henry T. Coates's blockbuster collection *The Fireside Encyclopaedia of Poetry*, which went through multiple editions after first appearing in 1881. The hearth became the site of American reading, the place in which writers and publishers imagined themselves communing with their readers.

The word *fireside* does not appear in Whitman's collected works, and its absence reveals the difference between a poetics based on personality and one based on character.[50] Rather than address its readers at the home's symbolic center, *Leaves of Grass* works to usher them out of doors, to bring them into the public arena where they can be remade and transformed. Even sexual acts, like the fellatio described in "Song of Myself," tend to occur outside or in rooms with open windows and views. "Unscrew the locks from the doors!" Whitman writes, "Unscrew the doors themselves from the jambs!" (*LG* 1855, 48). The preference for outdoor settings indicates the extent to which he imagined his voice as a public performance. The bonhomie Lowell associates with his fireside intimates becomes in Whitman a fleeting passion for an anonymous passerby. The Fireside poet advances his character, his ethos, his venerable position in the household and society at large. Whitman would periodically give himself a similar role, but by and large, he was much more interested in the performative aspects of personality. What was the personality's impact on its audience? How did it transform isolated individuals into an identifiable community? How did that community naturally coalesce around others who became personalities themselves? How did the poet's utterance serve to shape the material world? Longfellow's poems might enter the parlors of American families, his voice appearing as a respected, treasured guest. But he himself did not expect that trope to translate into his making a personal visit. Whitman, on the other hand, had every expectation that the magnetic reception he projected in *Leaves of Grass* would eventually come to pass, that his performance would result in a reciprocal affection between the poet and his country.

In "Song of the Open Road" the poet encourages readers to join the "delicious burdens" he carries with him wherever he goes. Throughout the poem he assumes an army of followers, urging them to march with him in public procession: "Now if a thousand perfect men were to appear it would not amaze me, / Now if a thousand beautiful forms of women appear'd it would not astonish me" (*WPP*, 300). Such images momentarily erase the differences between the spectator and the participant. "Allons!" he cries to his imaginary admirers before finally imploring his readers to enter into the kind of affectionate relation he described in the 1855 Preface:

> I give you my love more precious than money,
> I give you myself before preaching or law;
> Will you give me yourself? will you come travel with me?
> Shall we stick by each other as long as we live? (*WPP*, 307)

Whitman confesses that his power lies in his and his followers' "presence," but the poem is particularly significant in bringing the followers into being. The model of contagion operates quite successfully, with Whitman urging readers to join in this army of admirers, to become a part of the relentless crowd as it passes from fiction into reality. Who can resist identifying with the thousand perfect men and women? Who would not see themselves as part of that welcoming, transformative procession?

The martial tone of "Song of the Open Road" reminds us of the urgency behind Whitman's construction of personality. The poem invites readers to participate in a world in which selves are buoyed by rituals of acceptance and celebration. Susman writes that the problem of personality emerges out of the problem of how to present oneself in a market society; the self, like a commodity, must attract the attention of others. "We live now constantly in a crowd, how can we distinguish ourselves from others in that crowd?" The crowd, he explains, begets the need for personality.[51] Whitman reverses this dynamic, working from the notion that it is the individual who needs the crowd to collaborate on his personality. As he indicated in the early notebook entry, sympathy, truth, and dignity were not self-evident qualities; they were contingent on the community's acceptance that they exist. If the community did not acknowledge these traits, he wrote, "I should be certain enough that those attributes were not in me." The performative self is the rhetorical self because the performance must be convincing for the personality to exist.

The sentiment forms the basis for Whitman's evangelical efforts to convince us that in celebrating the poet, we learn to celebrate ourselves. By following the lives of people such as Whitman, we learn to acquire our fifteen minutes of fame. The 1860 poem "To a Pupil" invites readers to partake in Whitman's civic fantasy. The poem instructs a student how to capture the crowd's attention and love, presuming that Whitman has already achieved that personality himself, that his stature as a poet has been validated publicly:

> Is reform needed? Is it through you?
> The greater the reform needed, the greater the PERSONALITY you
>   need to accomplish it.
>
> You! Do you not see how it would serve to have eyes, blood,
>   complexion, clean and sweet?
> Do you not see how it would serve to have such a body and Soul,
>   that when you enter the crowd, an atmosphere of desire and
>   command enters with you, and everyone is impressed with
>   your personality?
>
> O the magnet! the flesh over and over!
> Go, mon cher! if need be, give up all else, and commence to-day

> to inure yourself to pluck, reality, self-esteem, definiteness,
>   elevatedness,
>   Rest not till you rivet and publish yourself of your own
>   personality. (*LG* 1860, 400)

The poem suggests that personality is published out of the self, and yet it is the publication of that self as well. It is both a product and a process, the impression and the state of impressing oneself on the crowd. Whitman promises his pupils precisely what the book has told us are the qualities we will find in him: magnetism, irresistibility, a command of everyone's desire. In the nascent world of American celebrity, such attributes expressed the public impact of the celebrated self. Like the poet, Whitman's pupils will find proof of their personalities when they attract the crowd, when they are absorbed as affectionately as they too desire.

CHAPTER THREE

Publicity

SAYING BIG THINGS ABOUT HIMSELF

IN AUGUST 1888, Whitman's health was in serious decline, and his
nightly meetings with Horace Traubel took on a new sense of urgency.
Although they focused on planning a final edition of *Leaves of Grass,* the two
friends closed almost every evening with Traubel reading from a pile of
editorial correspondence the poet had received over the years. The experience left Whitman feeling overlooked and unwanted by the nation's most
prominent literary magazines, though as Traubel pointed out, a majority of
the letters plainly announced their authors' admiration and support.
Among the letters was an 1884 message from Sam Walter Foss, who
professed the "great inspiration" he had received from *Leaves of Grass.* The
young editor of a Massachusetts newspaper, Foss had recommended the
book to his readers, for as he wrote Whitman, "it makes a new era in
American literature, and is to stand out more and more prominently, as
time advances, as the distinctively American book" (*WWC,* 2:227).

Revisiting Foss's compliment did little to lift Whitman's mood, but as
we can see in Traubel's account of the exchange, it prompted the poet to
recall his own notorious efforts to promote *Leaves of Grass:*

> I said: "He makes a big claim for you." "Yes, so he does—but
> will anybody believe him? When I say such things about myself

the world looks on and calls me crazy!" He seemed to be a good
bit amused with his own fancy, adding: "Time was when I had to
say big things about myself in order to be honest with the
world—in order to keep in a good frame of mind until the world
caught up. A man has sometimes to whistle very loud to keep a
stiff upper lip." "When the cries and the silences are all against
him?" "Yes—then: the cries and silences: that's just it." (*WWC*,
2:227)

The conversation offers a revealing glimpse into Whitman's lifelong engagement with publicity. Though he displays some of the bitterness that
was familiar to him in old age, he maintains a deep conviction that in
promoting his book, his actions had been both necessary and just. Speaking over thirty years after the 1855 edition, he gives Traubel a series of
explanations, as if no single response would suffice.

The poet's most conspicuous concern is how the tension between
sanity and insanity suffused his promotional work. On one hand, the
world was calling Whitman crazy for advertising and believing in the
magnitude of his book. On the other, he deemed those advertisements
necessary to the protection of his own mental health. He would "keep in a
good frame of mind" by publicly exulting in *Leaves of Grass*, and the
prevalence of his claims would somehow make the accomplishment
seem more substantial and real. Amid his half articulated explanations,
he acknowledges that trying to inject *Leaves of Grass* into public consciousness demanded a good deal of bravado, a willingness to talk about himself
as he wished others would. As the point evolves through conversation, the
poet did not whistle in the dark, but rather whistled in the midst of
criticism and indifference. The self-promotions compete against the problems of being at once notorious and anonymous.

What makes the response particularly puzzling is the apparent ease
with which Whitman was heartened by his own pronouncements. Sub-
stituting his own celebratory claims for the world's disappointing reaction, he views publicity as both a psychological cover and a therapeutic aid,
a form of self-delusion that allows him to continue his revolutionary
project. Whitman not only wrote his own press releases: he took comfort
in knowing that they were there, that they had entered the public sphere
where they seemingly confirmed his poetic achievement. The previous

chapter explored how Whitman's respect for the public's legitimizing powers shaped his conception of personality. Here, we see a new aspect to his persona as the celebrated American bard. The poet distributes a set of enabling fictions, engaging the public as if it were a mere extension of his personal desire. No matter how twisted the logic may be, it was the publication of Whitman's assertions that helped sustain his belief in his own aesthetic worth.

The strangeness of these comments indicates a man who had perhaps so internalized the values of fame and celebrity that even the most fabricated evidence had consequence to him. There seems to have been no midlevel of acceptance with which he would be pleased. Literary success meant the kind of messianic, populist acclaim that would place him in a pantheon of national greats. As "Song of the Answerer" tells us, there is only one Poet, one Answerer, in *Leaves of Grass,* and all other writers are simply singers following in his wake. For these reasons, Whitman viewed publicity as an unremitting all-out campaign. It might soothe his insecurities, but more important, it might remedy the situation from which they arose. Whether saying "big things" about himself or "whistl[ing] very loud," he hoped his expression would counter and transform the culture's reception of his work. He would be "honest with the world . . . until the world caught up," publicizing what he hoped was true of *Leaves of Grass* until admirers such as Foss could make their own pronouncements. The guile of Whitman's self-reviews and his early exaggeration of the book's commercial sales make this notion of honesty inadvertently comic. Whitman assumes an expedient exchange between traditional notions of integrity and the rhetorical value of public support. In order to claim a representative voice, he would strategically engage in misrepresentation. He would distort and manipulate public opinion because he valued and respected it. The poet did not regard this practice as being conflicted or contradictory. He imagined publicity as a dialectical process; by responding to the "cries and silences," his self-promotions might alter critical consciousness and foster progressive notions of literary value. As a radically American poet, he would produce an array of illusions until "the world caught up," until the nation, that is, learned to absorb him as affectionately as his fantasies had instructed.

In combating a hostile or indifferent audience, Whitman joined such contemporaries as P. T. Barnum, Robert Bonner, and Park Benjamin, who each seized on publicity as a prerequisite for renown. While Dickinson scorned the practice of pursuing fame, describing publication itself as an "auction of the mind," Whitman was immersed in the photographs, newspaper reviews, and commercial advertisements that helped antebellum Americans create their version of celebrity. Far from undervaluing ethereal poetic gifts, publicity gave the work of poets a public existence.

Readers have often chuckled at Whitman's legendary efforts to "puff" *Leaves of Grass,* but there has been little attempt to understand how publicity suffused his work. Though he heard something more piercing than a whistle, Henry James was among the first to remark on this aspect of Whitman's poetics in his 1865 review of *Drum Taps.* Writing in the *Nation,* James focused not on Whitman's extratextual promotion of his books but on the impact publicity had clearly exerted on the poems. "Mr. Whitman," he wrote, "is very fond of blowing his own trumpet, and he has made very explicit claims for his book." To the poet's claim in "Shut Not Your Doors" that his book was distinct from any other, that it would bring the nation what it needed most but lacked, James offered the dismissive pronouncement: "These are great pretensions."[1]

James objected to the pretense of Whitman's publicity, his efforts to achieve recognition by suggesting his immersion in civic life, but publicity for the poet was never simply a means to an end. It was neither the undesirable nor necessary evil about which so many of Whitman's and our own contemporaries complain.[2] Publicity was a legitimating discourse, both a condition for public speech and the uniquely defining quality such speech would possess. It was the belief system that allowed poets to claim that they brought the country what it "needed most" but lacked. Paying particular attention to "Song of Myself," this chapter examines how Whitman fashioned a poetics of hype, a poetry that consistently sells its value to a public it already claims to represent. Learning from early advertisers who aimed to boost their products' sales, he directed his efforts toward the point at which legitimacy could arise from renown.

AMERICAN PUBLICITY

In April 1854, the *New York Times* reported that "the policy of advertising had been pronounced good by all business men," but because the costs were extensive, many were unable to gain its advantages. The trick, the *Times* explained, was learning how to advertise "in a sly way, so as to get its benefits without incurring the cost." Advertising on the sly had become a veritable New York art, and the paper listed numerous ways in which its readers could promote themselves cheaply. To businessmen it recommended a variety of strategies, most involving the feeding of reporters with flattery, information, and expensive meals. To authors, however, the *Times* suggested a more elaborate path because an author who was too solicitous would appear foolish and desperate. It would be suicidal for a young writer to turn up in a newsroom with book in hand, so the *Times* advised that, before their books were published, authors should cultivate the friendship of the city's key critics and then mention their work only after several meetings about town. Authors who were able to secure a third person to make those introductions or to praise their books directly would make a better impression. "Be modest to appearances," the paper counseled, "but remember if you do not blow your own trumpet, it is hardly probable that any one else will."[3]

Fifteen months later, Whitman would open *Leaves of Grass* by blowing his trumpet harder and more clearly than perhaps any poet before him. Throwing the semblance of modesty aside, he directly addressed the public with a statement of his cultural worth. Perhaps surprising in a work so dedicated to democracy, he began "Song of Myself" with a prediction in the form of a command: "I celebrate myself / And what I assume, you shall assume." The conventional interpretation of these lines has been that they express the poet's democratic individualism and that the third line, with its rising combination of iambs and anapests, provides a melodious reason for the bold assertion of power: "For every atom belonging to me as good belongs to you" (*LG* 1885, 25). Whitman, the argument follows, invites readers to participate in the making of a collective American self. They are to see themselves magnified in his egotistical voice, for they are undeniably made of the same flesh—a fact that is supposed to secure their assent because it gives them comfort and hope.[4] Betsy Erkkila spoke for many when she wrote in 1988 that "these opening lines immediately engage the reader as a participant in the action of the poem, which is simultaneously about the creation of a democratic poem and the creation of a democratic self/nation/world."[5]

Such analyses carry a good deal of weight, for they view the poem within the critical parameters Whitman established in his 1855 Preface: namely, that the poem will inspire, nourish, and uplift its readers as they discover their own selves. Focusing on this theme too narrowly, however, can leave the impression that "Song of Myself" is primarily about the creation of someone else's power. What we see in the poem's opening lines is a remarkable faith in hype, a faith that readers, once introduced to the poet's example, will blow his trumpet as well. Whitman celebrates himself and expects others to do the same. He draws us into his advertisement by couching it in the language of our empowerment. While other writers may have followed the *Times*'s jaded advice by indirectly seeking the favor of critics, the poet boldly promotes himself, cultivating and engaging his audience in the creation of a celebrated American bard. At once democratic and manipulative, genuine and bombastic, the opening of "Song of Myself" is a good introduction to the promotional lessons Whitman absorbed from the culture around him: how to integrate his readers into his self-representation, grounding his hype in a consubstantial link that vested them with his swagger and self-confidence; how to advertise openly, assuming that as long as he said big things about himself, others would follow suit; how to advertise on the sly, not by toadying up to critics, but by posing as one himself; and finally, how to advertise lyrically, drawing on his age's promotional energy to create a new kind of verse.

Whitman's sense of publicity was rooted in the shifting, sometimes contradictory forces that marked antebellum advertising. Scholars have long recognized the 1830s and 1840s as decades crucial to the association of American political institutions with laissez-faire capitalism. Economic developments during the Jacksonian era gave birth to the vibrant popular culture of cities such as New York and Philadelphia.[6] Concurrent with these social changes was the emergence of advertising as a powerful and pervasive influence in American society. During these decades, drummers first made their way into the countryside, combining salesmanship, public relations, and a good degree of theatricality in promoting brand awareness and loyalty.[7] More significantly to Whitman, urban advertisers began to make use of signs, banners, handbills, posters, and eye-catching typography in selling patent medicines, entertainment, magazines, and newspapers. Commercial language appeared on buildings, windows, clothing, sandwich boards, and horse-drawn wagons and trucks.[8] The proliferation of printed advertisements was not confined to the East Coast. In 1855, Chicago's *Daily Democratic Press*—both a newspaper and a printing house—boasted of its capacity to print 345,000 sheets of paper a day, making it an ideal supplier of cards, extras, handbills, and posters for businesses throughout the Northwest.[9]

Reviewing this material, one sees a culture beginning to fathom the promise of a new technology and discourse. American newspapers had included advertisements since the eighteenth century, but it was with the rise of the penny press that they began to take an interest in teaching businesses how to manage and profit from publicity. In 1854, the *Brooklyn Daily Eagle* titled an editorial "A Few Reasons why People should Advertize in the Eagle." Not only did the paper enjoy a tremendously loyal and diverse readership, the piece argued, it was particularly popular with women readers, who were "the patrons of most kinds of business in the fancy line." The editorial reminded businesses that the *Eagle*'s policy was to give new advertisements its most coveted space, publishing them "side by side with our telegraphic dispatches and most important and interesting news."[10] As newspapers plugged their capacity to reach and influence consumers, advertising agencies emerged to navigate this uncharted terrain. In 1841, Volney Palmer established the first American advertising company in Philadelphia, and over the next decades, new agencies arose to sell commercial space in magazines and newspapers across the country. Initially, these agencies did little more than buy advertising space in bulk and then sell it to individual businesses, but in the 1850s, they began to develop and design content. The Globe Advertising Agency of Boston promoted itself as a full-service company with international reach. According to an 1859 broadside, the agency wrote copy and prepared a variety of "advertising arrangements," including notices in "the best papers in every section of The United States, The Canadas and Eastern Provinces, England, Ireland, Scotland, &c." Advertisements were sold in four-line blocks, with businesses paying a dollar and fifty cents per newspaper for a six-month run.[11]

For Whitman, the explosion of commercial print was clearly something to celebrate. In *Life Illustrated,* he described his fellow newspaperman Robert Bonner as "the hero of unheard-of and tremendous advertising, who fires cannon, fills page upon page of newspapers, and—if he could—would placard the very walls of paradise with hifalutin handbills, to sell that gorgeous and unprecedented sheet, the New York *Ledger.*"[12] As Ezra Greenspan has pointed out, Whitman's enthusiasm for Bonner sometimes waned, and he worried that the "monotonous nonsense" in his paper could cloud over "really valuable article[s]." At other times, however, he described Bonner as "one of the greatest men of the day" for offering such an important example about "the benefits of advertising."[13]

No one seemed to benefit more from advertising or to be more strongly identified with its values than P. T. Barnum. As *Printer's Ink* eulogized him in 1891, the great showman stood as "one of the shining examples of success attained through judicious advertising."[14] Though some in the profession viewed him as an embarrassing (and thus, inconvenient) patriarch, Barnum had proudly advocated the importance of advertising throughout his career. "I was aware of the great power of the public press and used it to the extent of my ability," he wrote in his 1855 autobiography, *The Life of P. T. Barnum*.[15] Several decades later he returned to the theme, this time acknowledging his wider (and, indeed, shrewder) sense of publicity: "I thoroughly understood the art of advertising, not merely by means of printers' ink, which I have always freely used, and to which I confess myself so much indebted for my success, but by turning every possible circumstance to my account. It was my monomania to make the Museum the town wonder and town talk. I often seized upon an opportunity by instinct, even before I had a very definite conception as to how it should be used, and it seemed, somehow, to mature itself and serve my purpose."[16]

In his effort to create a sensation, to attract both wonder and talk, Barnum learned to play on the public's collective sense of itself. In an often-repeated example, he once attracted a sizeable crowd by hiring a man to move a series of bricks between four Broadway street corners. Every hour, the man stopped this puzzling routine and silently walked to the American Museum and entered its doors. The onlookers followed, with about a dozen each time becoming paying customers. The promotion ended three days later when the police complained that the crowds had grown so large that they were dangerously obstructing the sidewalks.[17] Publicity was evolving into a performance in which the public played a vital, though at times unwitting, role.

Under Barnum's encouragement, advertising became a spectacle unto itself, an all-encompassing effort to transform individuals into a public of spectators and consumers. The success of such events signaled a broader shift in cultural orientation than the advent of a new business practice. Barnum had clearly mastered the art of the "sly advertisement" that the *New York Times* described in 1854. Shortly after Whitman published the first edition of *Leaves of Grass*, the *Eagle* reflected on Barnum's latest stunt, a nationwide beauty contest to be held at his museum. "Newspapers cannot avoid affording gratuitous advertising to Barnum," the paper grumbled. "He is one of the institutions of the country and his proceedings are as much a part of our social history as the doings of Congress are of our political life."[18] As Jennifer Wicke has argued, Barnum effectively "authored" advertising by turning a set of new but fragmented commercial techniques into a coherent cultural discourse.[19] The pioneer ad man George P. Rowell pointed toward a similar kind of impact when he wrote in 1871 that Barnum created "a new way of reading the world through advertisements."[20]

The rise of advertising is indicative of how antebellum Americans were coming to view publicity. The concept had been vital to eighteenth-century republicans who associated it with the ways in which print culture made issues and opinions public and therefore political. The proliferation of signs, placards, handbills, broadsides, and other forms of advertising participated in the general redefinition of publicity's cultural role. Jurgen Habermas has written that in the 1830s the press was transformed from "a forum of rational-critical debate" into "a commercial business."[21] As market forces expanded, the critical forms of publicity became used for manipulative, commercial purposes. Publicity came to designate not the kind of scrutiny that watched over the public sphere but what Richard Salmon has described as an "asymmetrical form of social display." The shift in meaning, Salmon explains, lies in the difference between being "constituted by" or "represented before a public."[22] In 1791, the value of publicity led the authors of *The Federalist Papers* to write under the pseudonym "Publius." In 1842, it led Barnum to distribute fake editorials to the New York press as a way of bringing a museum exhibit into "public notice."[23]

From a historical perspective, such definitions of publicity seem meaningfully distinct, and they can certainly chart the broad transformations taking place. In the antebellum period, however, the political and promotional aspects of publicity were intertwined. Publicity could express a commitment to the public sphere, a faith in Jacksonian democracy, or an interest in drawing attention to an individual or event. It could also suggest each of these things at the same time. As a newspaper editor, Whitman was accustomed to composing a front page organized into columns of advertisements for such things as watches, jewelry, books, stationery, and saloons—all alongside his own announcements for the stories, features, and political opinions readers could find on the inside pages.

A good index of publicity's multiple meanings is the almost habitual deference antebellum advertisers expressed to the reading public. With a formality that would soon be challenged by assumptions of personal intimacy, businesses addressed their language to an abstract public, the recognized foundation of civic and commercial life. "FAMILY PATENT MEDICINES, AND PERFUMERY AGENCY STORE," an advertisement in Whitman's *Eagle* read. "The public in general, and the inhabitants of Brooklyn in particular, are respectfully informed that a store of the above description has been opened . . . where most of the Patent Medicines of any celebrity will be found."[24] When a popular magician shifted his performances from Tripler Hall to the Astor Place Opera House in 1851, an advertisement in the *New York Daily Times* began "Prof. Anderson begs to thank the public of New-York and its vicinity for the unprecedented support with which they have crowned his first appearance in America." And when the National Miniature Gallery hoped to draw customers to its Broadway studio, it launched its nearly one hundred lines of copy, most of which listed the names of the famous men and women whose portraits could be seen on display, with the surprisingly formulaic sentence: "The attention of the public is requested to this establishment, for the production of Photographs on SILVER, IVORY, GLASS, and PAPER."[25] Although clearly commercial in orientation, these advertisements—and the many others like them —were rooted in a republican sensibility that affirmed the public as an abstract, legitimizing force. In bold and capital letters, advertisers displayed themselves before the public as if it were a powerful anonymous patron.

At its most basic level, this hybrid sense of publicity could lead to a crude association of commerce with democratic nationalism. Barnum frequently capitalized on the connection, decorating his museum and advertisements with American flags and patriotic symbols. As Terence Whalen points out, Barnum instinctively knew that "the social meaning of any event . . . was not given from the start but could instead be created or manipulated through the emergent mass media."[26] He learned early in his career that appeals to patriotism were particularly effective. Barnum first rose to prominence when he exhibited Joice Heth, an elderly African American woman, as the 161-year-old former nursemaid to George Washington. The publicity surrounding Heth trumpeted her age and presidential connection, envisioning the public as a peculiar combination of spectators and citizens. As one advertisement shamelessly proclaimed, Joice Heth "was the first person *who put clothes on the unconscious infant* who was destined in after days to lead our heroic fathers to glory, to victory, to freedom." The advertisement, in Barnum's words, contained a "closer appeal to both patriotism and curiosity."[27] Whitman found national holidays to be especially fertile occasions for publicity. Readers have long understood the poet's effort to publish the first edition of *Leaves of Grass* on July 4, 1855, as an expression of democratic nationalism, but it was of course a promotional decision as well. The date became a platform for Whitman, contributing to the legend of his personality. He returned to the strategy in 1876 when he printed a special centennial edition of the poems. As Whitman grew older, these efforts began to pay off, for by the 1880s many Americans knew him as the poet of Abraham Lincoln.

Whitman's differences from Barnum are ultimately more revealing than their similarities. Unlike the showman, Whitman primarily addressed his readers more as citizens than consumers, and he viewed the literary market as another opportunity for the nation to realize the cultural promise of democracy. This does not mean, as we will see shortly, that he did not promote the poet as a kind of magically restorative commodity, but his vision of publicity was ultimately less mercantile and more complex than Barnum's. Even as *Leaves of Grass* looked forward to new forms of commercial display, it hearkened back to the models set forth by its eighteenth-century predecessors. In his 1867 review, James scolded the poet for suggesting that "the shortest and most economical way for the public to embrace its idols—for the nation to realize its genius" was in his own person.[28] Despite the dismissive tone, James understood this aspect of Whitman's poems quite well. By promoting himself in the language of popular sovereignty, he suggested that his talents were representative of the American populace. Whitman's experience with the press had taught him to associate virtue with print culture, and like many publishers, he presented his work as serving a critical function in the Republic. Publicity for a writer could simultaneously be a celebration of individual talent and an affirmation of the community.

These themes emerge quite prominently in the packaging of Whitman's first major publication, the 1842 temperance novel *Franklin Evans; or, The Inebriate.*[29] Appearing in the *New World* newspaper in a series of extra numbers titled "Books for the People," the novel proved to be Whitman's most commercially successful work, selling close to twenty thousand copies. Told in the first person, the novel offers the melodramatic tale of a young man, Franklin Evans, whose addiction to alcohol leads to his near ruin. Evans's exploits in New York gin houses and brothels lead him down a path in which he neglects his wife, commits robbery, and spends time in jail. When Evans travels south to Virginia, he drunkenly marries a mulatto woman who quickly becomes the object of his hatred. She eventually kills herself in jail after murdering a perceived rival. Like much reformist literature, *Franklin Evans* manages to titillate and scold at the same time. After his journey through the underbelly of American society, Evans is able to turn his life around by pledging to abstain from all forms of alcohol, including beer and wine.

Whitman would later denounce *Franklin Evans* as "damned rot—rot of the worst sort" (*WWC*, 1:93). And at one time or another, he claimed to have written the novel under the influence of port, gin, or whiskey. However, working with his publisher Park Benjamin gave the young writer valuable exposure to the political dimensions of publicity. The text of the newspaper edition of the novel is literally wrapped in patriotism, as the inside back cover features an advertisement for "DOCTOR RUSH'S INFAMOUS HEALTH PILLS." Because Rush was a signer of the Declaration of Independence, the advertisement proclaims, his "fame is interwoven with the history of his country, and his virtues of benevolence embalmed in the hearts of all who venerate the memory of a great man." "No one," it continues, "will be so hardy as to doubt Dr. Rush's skill in his profession, or his ability to compound a medicine suited to the various maladies which afflict the human race." Like Barnum's promotion of Joice Heth, the advertisement grounds its commercial concerns in filiopietism.

Benjamin's announcement of the series struck a similar political chord. "Books for the People," he wrote, was designed to issue "the most popular, instructive and entertaining works of the day, in a convenient form, and at so cheap a rate as to come within the means of every individual in the country." "How many thousands have been debarred the pleasure of reading a new work because of its high price," he asked, and "how

immense the revolution which breaks down the barrier between the people and that which tends to satisfy their intellectual wants!" Benjamin
specifically marketed the series as an agent of perpetual revolution, link-
ing both its price and its politics with an all-encompassing faith in democratic nationalism. The announcement culminated in the introduction of
Whitman as simply "a Popular American Author," a man whose sensibilities and politics had already attracted the public's admiration. The byline
subsumes the author's identity to the image of his reception, for who
better to author a "book for the people" than someone whose only distinguishing characteristic was that he was widely admired? Fusing hype with
republicanism, Benjamin transformed the author into a selfless and democratic star.

Whitman had satirized Benjamin in the pages of the *New York Aurora*
only months before, calling him "one of the most vain pragmatical nin-
compoops in creation" and claiming that his name was "inseparably interwoven with Bamboozle."[30] However, when it came to writing an introduction for *Franklin Evans,* he echoed the publisher's rhetoric. The poet who
had published "Ambition" earlier that year, who had suggested that "lofty
aspirations" would ultimately pierce the soul, now presented a dramatically different view. Writing under the guise of popularity, he channeled
his desire for fame through the idiom of commercial populism:

> Can I hope that my story will do good? I entertain that hope. Is-
> sued in the cheap and popular form you see, and wafted by every
> mail to all parts of this vast republic; the facilities which its pub-
> lisher possesses, giving him the power of diffusing it more
> widely than any other establishment in the United States; the
> mighty and deep public opinion which, as a tide bears a ship
> upon its bosom, ever welcomes anything favorable to the Tem-
> perance Reform; its being written for the mass, though the
> writer hopes, not without some claim upon the approval of the
> more fastidious; and, as much as anything else, the fact that it is
> as a pioneer in this department of literature—all these will give
> *The Inebriate,* I feel confident, a more than ordinary share of pa-
> tronage. (*EPF,* 126–27)

The passage is one of Whitman's first and most self-conscious attempts to define his voice in relation to public opinion. In imagining the

public as his patron, he presents his book's success as the fulfillment of American democracy, an electoral exercise in which the cause of reform would be buoyed by his work's popularity. If the proof of a writer is that his country absorbs him as affectionately as he has absorbed it, *Franklin Evans* begins by insinuating that such absorption had already occurred. Celebrity becomes a manifestation not of vanity but of the popular will.

By the time he wrote *Leaves of Grass*, Whitman had learned to characterize his poetic voice by pointing to his unique relationship to readers. "The greatest poet hardly knows pettiness or triviality. If he breathes into any thing that was before thought small it dilates with the grandeur and life of the universe," he writes in the 1855 Preface (9). "[T]he others are as good as he, only he sees it and they do not." In "A Song for Occupations," he tells us, "I own publicly who you are, if nobody else owns . . . . and see and hear you, and what you give and take" (*LG* 1855, 88; Whitman's ellipsis). It is amusing to see Whitman make similarly inflated claims when he returned to editing newspapers in 1858. Writing in the *Brooklyn Times,* he praised the journalist as "the most self-reliant, the most contented and the most useful of mortals," claiming that his power and influence came from the community's perceiving his text to be "an organ of public opinion." As in his poems, Whitman promoted the paper to the public, representing it before them even as he vigorously proclaimed that it was constituted by them. A great benefit of the journalist's profession, he tells his readers, is "the silent veneration of the public who regard the terrible 'We' as a semi-omniscient and omnipotent being."[31]

On one level this was Whitman's familiar penchant for grandiosity finding new outlets of expression. The temperance novelist, the poet, and the editor all assert their exceptional relation to readers, a relation that stands apart from other cultural figures. The passages complement the vision we previously explored of presidents, bankers, authors, and professors descending into the crowd as they acknowledge the poet's superiority. In each case, the author is noticed above the public he affectionately celebrates and absorbs. Whitman's hybrid application of publicity is predicated on a more commercial vision of the public sphere than the rational dialogues Habermas saw in the late eighteenth century, one in which different voices competed for widespread attention. Throwing out earlier concerns about virtue as the cornerstone of government, the Constitution's framers had placed the representation of public opinion at the center of political life, and by the 1830s, Alexis de Tocqueville would argue that this opinion wielded a greater authority in America than monarchs in Europe did. "Faith in public opinion," he predicted, "will become a species of religion there, and the majority its ministering prophet."[32] Because of its almost uniform deference to the majority's will, de Tocqueville found the country's intellectual climate to be homogenous and stifling. But this common devotion to public opinion also had the effect of creating an increasingly combative and competitive culture. With different voices, parties, and discourses vying for cultural prominence, the public's attention came to matter as much as public opinion itself. When a photographer solicited the public's attention, his unmistakable message was *Come to my studio—not someone else's.*

In this market environment, exposure to the public was perhaps as valuable as acceptance. Barnum profited by exploiting the press to keep his exhibits in the public mind. When interest in Joice Heth began to wane, he secretly planted letters in newspapers charging that she was a hoax, not a genuine person but an automaton. Customers paid to see Heth again so that they themselves could determine whether she was a woman or a machine. When spectators were disappointed in his exhibit of the Feejee mermaid in 1842, he again published their complaints, keeping the subject of mermaids, hoaxes, and the American Museum in popular consciousness. Whether for Barnum or Whitman, controversy created a layer of public signification to an event—the meaning of which was only provisionally determined by its original participants. Although he did not enjoy Barnum's success, Whitman frequently created the illusion that *Leaves of Grass* was the subject of intense disagreement. Saying big things about himself became a way of both soothing the soul and holding the public's attention, a way to redress and remedy the cries and silences. Later in his career, Whitman skillfully created controversies about his reputation to increase his public profile. Before the war, he often responded to the clamor of his world as if he were vying for the scrutiny of an audience immersed in other things. In 1860, he published the third edition of *Leaves of Grass.* In this year of seismic shifts in the American political landscape, he must have been keenly aware of the difficulty of appearing culturally significant. He included with the volume a pamphlet titled *Imprints,* which contained nearly every review the book had received since 1855—the positive, the negative, the congratulatory, and the belligerent. The pamphlet's effect was to suggest that amid the commotion of a nation falling apart, an important contentious argument was brewing over a new American poet. While several poems in the 1860 edition hint at the poet's waning commitment to being the nation's bard, the pamphlet effectively reiterates his determination to promote himself as the man who would fill that role.

MAKING AN AUDIENCE

David Marshall has written that the "celebrity . . . is by definition a fundamentally intertextual sign."[33] Celebrities, he explains, require an array of interpretive writings that make them intelligible to the community as famous or public individuals. People cannot declare themselves celebrities without the aid of corroborating signs—whether reviews and commercials on television or photographs and gossip in magazines. Whitman did not have the extensive apparatus that the famous use today, but he early on recognized the value of deploying satellite texts to fashion a public personality. A good example lies in the many items he brought to bear on the 1856 edition of *Leaves of Grass:* an afterword containing a private letter from Emerson and the poet's essay-length response, copies of previous reviews, extracts from various literary essays (published well before *Leaves of Grass*) that might cast those reviews in a favorable light and, on the cover, Emerson's gold-emblazoned endorsement. When taken as a whole, the volume remarkably anticipates the experience of watching a film with the aid of a studio press kit. The elaborate web of texts collaborates with Whitman in realizing his representativeness. Not only do the materials reinforce the poet's pronouncements, but in their attention to *Leaves of Grass,* they emphatically certify his relevance.

Of Whitman's many self-advertisements, surely the most notorious are the three anonymous reviews of *Leaves of Grass* that he wrote for the *American Phrenological Journal,* the *United States Review,* and the *Brooklyn Daily Times.* Published in the autumn of 1855, the reviews make little effort to disguise the poet's voice, and they openly echo the book's Preface. We would expect a series of self-reviews to champion an author's accomplishment. In Whitman's case, they also display an interesting concern for pedagogy, clarifying for readers some of the mysteries in *Leaves of Grass.* One review offers a guide to "Song of Myself" that not only summarizes the opening narrative but also translates some of the poem's more challenging stanzas.[34] Another review compares Whitman to Tennyson as a way of reflecting on his innovative poetics. Explaining that only "second-rate poems" immediately gratify their audience, the piece excuses "the chilly and unpleasant shudders" that would surely accompany a first reading of *Leaves of Grass*.[35] Whitman fabricates this critical discourse as a way of both promoting his work and teaching readers how to recognize its achievement. The two objectives work together in that the pedagogical instruction serves to substantiate the manufactured image.

The self-reviews make *Leaves of Grass* seem a part of popular consciousness only months after its release. Hoping to create this impression in 1856, Whitman resorted to making up figures about the book's commercial sales. He boasted in his letter to Emerson that the first volume had sold a thousand copies and that he expected "in a few years . . . the average annual call" to be "ten or twenty thousand copies—more quite likely" (*WPP*, 1326–27). With the book only recently in print, the self-reviews could not include such outlandish statements, and they focus instead on predicting the poet's reception. "He is to prove either the most lamentable of failures," Whitman wrote in one review, "or the most glorious of triumphs, in the known history of literature."[36]

This confidence in the poet's ability to garner public attention surfaces again in the critique published in the *United States Review*. Under the guise of a supporter, Whitman linked the book's necessity to its creation of scandal and controversy. The poet's great virtues, he argued, will shock and provoke America's conformist society: "You have come in good time, Walt Whitman! In opinions, in manners, in costumes, in books, in the aims and occupancy of life, in associates, in poems, conformity to all unnatural and tainted customs passes without remark, while perfect naturalness, health, faith, self-reliance, and all primal expressions of the manliest love and friendship, subject one to the stare and controversy of the world."[37] The paragraph modifies the sentiment that closed the 1855 Preface. Whitman does not predict affection as much as he emphasizes his ability to create public interest: the revolutionary poet—the one who dares to represent his nation—will be the one most subject to the world's scrutiny and dissension. The review epitomizes the poet's efforts to *make* an audience that would nourish his reputation. This public, on one hand, was a figurative "world" fervently debating the poet's egotism and vulgarity. On the other, it was the crowd of actual readers who might come to *Leaves of Grass* inspired by such fabrications.

Whitman found a surprising precedent for these practices in Wordsworth. Theater managers and publishers often paid newspapers to print the positive reviews they submitted, and to showmen such as Barnum, the practice was customary and expected.[38] Evidence suggests, however, that Whitman had formulated some of these ideas in relation to the British poet. From different pen and pencil marks, it is clear that he several times studied an essay about the poet in *Graham's* titled "Egotism, as Manifested in the Works and Lives of Great and Small Men." He admired the essay so much, in fact, that at one point he wrote on the cover "This article contains *good stuff*," which he punctuated by drawing all five fingers of a pointing hand. Of the many passages Whitman underlined, one was a paragraph concerning Wordsworth's egotism and his efforts to overcome indifference to his work. Wordsworth, the author writes, took "the task upon himself, and in his prefaces glorified his own powers and works in a spirit of unhesitating self-reliance."[39] The passage sheds light on Whitman's own use of prose to glorify and explain his poetic powers. Like Wordsworth, he explicated his principal themes and concerns to prepare his readers for the challenging poems ahead. Beyond its tactical advice, the passage gripped Whitman's imagination, and its reasoning is echoed in the first two editions of *Leaves of Grass*. In 1855 he wrote, "The cleanest expression is that which finds no sphere worthy of itself and makes one" (13). The following year in "By Blue Ontario's Shore," he incorporated the idea into one of his self-characterizations: "I myself make the only growth by which I can be appreciated" (*WPP*, 469). The essay seems to have given Whitman a philosophical justification for his synthetic construction of celebrity.

Particularly when adapted to the American Republic, Wordsworth's thinking suggests that representative poets must earn the nation's approval by first teaching it how to value them. In the critical excerpts Whitman selected to reprint in the 1856 *Leaves of Grass*, Wordsworth is cited specifically for his ability to forge an appreciative audience: "Poetry . . . must become the exponent of a new spirit through new forms. Such is demanded by authority greater than all the critics of Europe and America, the common sense and common instinct of the people. The new forms are not to be judged by the old models, but are to be judged by themselves. Wordsworth truly said that every original first-rate poet must himself make the taste through which he is to be fully appreciated."

Ezra Greenspan has pointed out that the passage became one of Whitman's favorites, and it spoke quite clearly to his concerns.[40] While second-rate poets might enjoy a genteel or comfortable following, the truly original writer had to rely on the type of self-promotion that would make his gifts discernible to audiences rooted in the past. However, when the author cites "the common sense and common instinct of the people," he describes a poetics that is ultimately more compatible with Whitman than Wordsworth. As poems such as "To You" and "Song of Occupations" attest, Whitman attributed all power and meaning to his reading public. Wordsworth's interest in the people arose from his literary and pastoral concerns. As he explains it in the preface to *Lyrical Ballads,* he chose to write about the "humble and rustic life"—not because rural people were the source of sociopolitical authority, but because their language was more philosophical and permanent than that of poets.[41]

Positioned between Barnum and Wordsworth, between what we might describe as commercial and romantic populism, Whitman understood antebellum publicity in significantly political terms. While Wordsworth saw the need to make his audience, Whitman saw the need to persuade them. He would have to define *Leaves of Grass* as a public event in a way that Wordsworth did not anticipate. Like Barnum, he would promulgate his fictional claims in order to foster his publicity. As a groundbreaking American poet, he would promote the strength of his audience as a way of bringing them into being; in his fame they would recognize a representative version of themselves.

THE POETICS OF HYPE

Thus far we've addressed advertising as a general cultural orientation, seeing in its broad gestures and tone a stimulating environment for Whitman's self-promotions. As advertising was emerging as a newly recognizable discourse, its practitioners were envisioning a kind of writing that was at once persuasive, informative, and in some cases lyrical. Nineteenth-century newspaper advertisements descended from the shipping and commercial notices that appeared in newspapers and gazettes throughout the colonies. These notices were more a record of a merchant's activities than an appeal to consumers, and the bulk of antebellum advertising retained their predecessors' uniform, sober quality. Bound into columns by heavy black lines, arranged by category, the advertisements' principal agenda was to convey information. Some businesses tried to be visually innovative within this format, using the text to create icons or shapes that would catch the reader's eye. An 1860 advertisement for Mrs. Sherman's Excelsior Skirts took the shape of a corseted skirt, the text creating the image as if it were the prose version of a Renaissance pattern poem. But as was typical of many antebellum advertisements, the copy was repetitive, disorganized, and unimaginative.[42]

Amid the awkward attempts to overcome restrictive typography and space, advertisers employed repetition as their chief rhetorical device. Bonner famously promoted the writers appearing in his *New York Ledger* by repeating the same short message until he filled an entire column in the *New York Herald*. A more prevalent (and affordable) tactic was the use of repetition to make a coherent and memorable text. When Root's Daguerreotype Gallery promoted its Washington, DC, business in May 1855, it distributed leaflets that connected the gallery's name with the personal value of a portrait:

> If strangers would procure a *faithful and beautiful*
>   Portrait of loved ones at home,   Go to Root's.
> Would parents make a valued gift to a child,   Go to Root's.
> Would a child behold a parent's face in after years,   Go to Root's.
> In fine, do you wish a superior "Sun Painting,"
>   life-like, And artistic in whatever style,   Go to Root's.[43]

However crudely, the lines directly address the consumer, appealing to a variety of familial bonds. Root's does not presume an intimate relationship with its customers. It does not claim, for example, to play an integral role in developing the American family, as later companies would. Rather, it raises awareness of the gallery's services by invoking the customers' affection and longing.

As a genre, the best advertisements are lyrically persuasive; they manage to impart the desirability of a service, attraction, or commodity in language that is innovative enough to be memorable but not so innovative that it might complicate, challenge, or offend. (This is one of many places in which advertising and poetry sharply diverge.) An increasing number of advertisers tried to develop texts that were both playful and informative. A magazine advertisement for R. H. Macy's captures the embryonic quality of advertising copy before the Civil War:

> SPRING RIBBONS now Opening every day.
> SPRING FLOWERS just received from Paris.
> JUST RECEIVED, an invoice of Linen Handkerchiefs.
> JUST RECEIVED, an invoice of New Lace Goods.
> JUST RECEIVED, an invoice of Hosiery and Gloves.
> JUST RECEIVED, Spring Styles Housekeeping Dry Goods.
> LADIES' CORSETS, 6s., 7s., and 10s., Good Styles.
> LADIES' KID GLOVES, 63c., all colors and sizes
> ALL KINDS EMBROIDERIES, very cheap, to close.
> OUR GREAT SALE is still on the
> INCREASE. Ladies please call.[44]

In this 1859 advertisement, the text is clearly reaching for a lyric quality that it can neither sustain nor fully possess. The opening of spring ribbons, the flowers from Paris, the sonic repetitions in "just received" and "invoice," even the parallel listing of commodities all seem a fragment of a potentially coherent voice. As if the merchant were afraid that the lovely, almost inspired repetition was crowding out his wares, the advertisement collapses into a heap of colors, sizes, and prices. The business of prose quickly takes over, the lineation is abandoned, and the text bluntly concludes, "We sell good Goods, R. H. Macy."

Sensing the need for a more distinctive approach, many businesses began to cast their advertisements in rhyme. Verse advertisements appeared in a variety of media from handbills to magazines and newspapers. With a usually forced sense of meter, they described their products and themselves in an amusing, catchy manner. A Boston merchant announced,

> None with SALOM can compare,
> His store is quite a Fancy Fair.
> 'Tis much larger, yes by far,
> Than any other Toy Bazaar.[45]

The use of rhyme came with the advantage that the advertisement was easily memorized and mildly entertaining. Some advertisers wrote their copy according to popular songs, appealing to consumers with an already ratified tune and meter. They sold their products, one might say, in a preapproved format. Grover and Baker's Sewing Machines and Co-Star's Vermin Exterminators both set their text to the tune of "Yankee Doodle Dandy" with memorably comic results ("As spring approaches / Ants and roaches / From their holes come out").[46]

Rhyme and publicity became so strongly identified that when the publisher James Fields addressed a group of authors, politicians, and publishers in 1855, it seemed perfectly appropriate to include a sample of his verse. What better way to celebrate the benefits of advertising than in balladic meter and rhyme?

> How slow and sure they set their types!
> How small editions ran!
> Then fifty thousand never sold—
> Before the sale began.
> For how could they, poor plodding souls,
> Be either swift or wise,
> Who never learned the mighty art
> Of how to advertise.[47]

For some, the prevalence of commercial verse threatened to blur the distinctions between poetry and advertising. When the *Brooklyn Daily Eagle* attacked Longfellow's *Hiawatha* for its monotonous trochees, it complained of its "jog-trot, jingle, jingle, jingle, jingle, from beginning to end."[48] In the background of this already nasty comparison to carriage bells was perhaps the worst insult one could give nineteenth-century poets: to call them jinglers, writers who composed the kind of pleasing, artificial verse one might find in advertising copy. As advertisers appropriated rhyme, repetition, and parallelism, as they published acrostics honoring the names of businesses and their products, it became unclear precisely who or what was a poet. The Boston toy merchant Salom played with this confusion, announcing in his advertisement,

> SALOM'S A POET!
> And that you may know it
> Takes this method to show it

—though he comically balked at comparing himself to Shakespeare.[49]

It would be misleading to argue that Whitman rejected rhyme in response to the advertising copy around him. The 1855 Preface describes the "gaggery and gilt" of rhyme as a monarchical ornament, one fit for a society that thrived on luxuriant dependency (*LG 1855*, 10). The argument against rhyme and traditional meter clearly had political overtones for Whitman, and as a number of scholars have shown, the earliest evidence we have of his breaking into free verse comes from a notebook in which he declares, "I am the poet of slaves, and of the masters of slaves."[50] At the same time, however, the rhyme that had played a predominant role in literary history had ironically become the superficial jingle of nineteenth-century commerce. As Sean Francis has argued, Whitman was clearly aware of the "pejorative influence of the unknown versifiers writing their reams of advertising verse," and in one of his self-reviews, he distinguished his work from the "modern successions of jinglers and snivelers and fops."[51] Informed by the Bible, he built his open poetic line around a mounting series of parallel phrases and oppositions—creating a poetry that reflected the energy and expanse of democratic capitalism and yet resisted the surface amusements of commercial writing.

Stripped of its rhyme and jingle, the rhetoric of advertising prominently appears in "Starting from Paumanok," one of the 1856 platform poems in which Whitman celebrates the poet's cultural work. The poem follows the poet as he addresses various audiences, boasting of his intentions and all that his voice encompasses. Lawrence Buell has written that Whitman's catalogues "express the boundless fecundity of nature and human life, and thereby his own 'leaves' as well."[52] In the penultimate stanza of "Starting from Paumanok," the catalogue becomes a promotional device, one that invites readers to visualize the fecund world represented in *Leaves of Grass*:

> See, steamers steaming through my poems,
> See, in my poems immigrants continually coming and landing,
> See, in arriere, the wigwam, the trail, the hunter's hut, the flat-
>   boat, the maize leaf, the claim, the rude fence, and the
>   backwoods village. (*WPP*, 187)

Whitman conjures a wide expanse, drawing upon his Adamic ability to bring these scenes into consciousness by naming them. Creating a world that is at once historical and visionary, the poem employs the direct address and anaphora of antebellum publicity. The poet's repetition of *See* (used eighteen times in the thirteen-line stanza) recalls the way advertisers addressed their audience with recurrent commands. Like the owners of Root's, Whitman instructs his readers how to think about and value his commodity. He hypes *Leaves of Grass* in the manner of a huckster, vigorously announcing what the public will discover within his book.

After visiting Manhattan in 1857, the Russian traveler Aleksandr Lakier commented, "No one better than the American can depict in an advertisement the beauty and sweetness of the most ordinary things."[53] Like antebellum New York, a city bursting with commercial placards, signposts, and handbills, "Starting from Paumanok" is immersed in the rich potential of advertisements to help us see the world anew. What Whitman is ultimately selling, however, is a vision of the poet at the center of American democracy. The poem culminates in a rousing command to see the poet as he is embraced by a future society:

> See, ploughmen ploughing farms—see, miners digging mines—
>   see, the numberless factories,
> See, mechanics busy at their benches with tools—see from
>   among them: superior judges, philosophs, Presidents,
>   emerge, drest in working dresses,
> See, lounging through the shops and fields of the States, me
>   well-belov'd, close-held by day and night,
> Hear the loud echoes of my songs there—read the hints come at
>   last. (*WPP*, 187–88)

Whitman's catalogue intensifies as he moves from the opening scenic objects to the kinds of superior individuals he hopes his book will generate. He creates this swelling energy by breaking his line into a series of shorter commands, all initiated and drawn together by the imperative to see. The line slows and relaxes with an image of the poet as he is affectionately woven into his country. While some appealed to a sense of nationalism, gender, and family, most antebellum advertisements had an abstract sense of the public as an anonymous monolithic force. Whitman anticipates a kind of publicity that is remarkably precise and individuated. He places *Leaves of Grass* among an array of social types and individuals and then folds them into a vision of his rising prominence. The stanza informs us that among the many treasures readers will find inside Whitman's book is our admiration for him.

"Starting from Paumanok" creates a lyric that is built on the performative aspects of advertising. It suggests an image of the poet—"See, projected through time, / For me an audience interminable"—and invites us to participate in making that image come true: "Hear the loud echoes of my songs there." Just as it was necessary to make a voice representative, the public's presence was necessary to transform promotion into publicity. Without the Broadway spectators following Barnum's brick movers, the act itself would have been socially and commercially meaningless. The principal task of the drummer was to encourage customers to recognize his performance of their relationship. "Starting from Paumanok" asks readers to see themselves as part of a vast historical process, successive generations stretching into a perpetual American community that emanates from the poet.

OUTBIDDING THE OLD CAUTIOUS HUCKSTERS

The performative aspects of advertising were particularly important to lecturers who traveled from town to town. Lecturers had to gather their audiences through the medium of newsprint, making the newspapers and handbills that carried their announcements a primary site of publicity. Usually focused on a series of events, the best of these advertisements built a sense of momentum and opportunity. Lecturers promised to connect their audiences to the knowledge and expanse of the larger world. The advertisement had to marshal the excitement of a performance, turning the reader into a potential spectator and participant.

Despite their growing interest in attracting famous speakers, lyceum-based lecture series were remarkably straightforward when announcing their events. With their roots in republican self-improvement, lyceums included only the most basic information about speakers, halls, and sponsoring committees in their newspaper advertisements. In the decade before the Civil War, advertisements for New York lectures by Emerson, Holmes, and Taylor were gentlemanly and subdued, despite wide interest in these men's activities. Even a benefit lecture for "The John Brown Fund" at Cooper Institute in 1859 came without heated rhetoric. "DR. GEORGE B. CHEEVER, WENDELL PHILIPS, AND PROF. HIRMAN MATTISON Will speak at the COOPER INSTITUTE, in aid of the FUND for the benefit of JOHN BROWN'S FAMILY, on THURSDAY EVENING."[54] The only hint of promotion was the promise that while admission was twenty-five cents, purchasers of the one-dollar tickets would receive a photograph of the militant abolitionist.

Itinerant lecturers had to promote themselves more energetically. Arriving in town without the aid of sponsoring committees, they created and managed their own publicity. Lyceum speakers were often packaged in a course of lectures, and patrons were encouraged to buy a subscription that included five or six individuals. Itinerant lecturers provided their own series, offering several different lectures in the course of their stay. The so-called popular lecture mixed education and entertainment, and from chemists to phrenologists, the theme that runs through these advertisements is how new and original the material will be. Formerly the U.S. consul at Cairo, George Gliddon traveled the country lecturing on the pyramids and other archaeological discoveries. As one might expect, Gliddon's advertisements emphasized both his authority as a speaker and the exciting nature of his topic. An 1851 broadside from Washington, DC, announced that he would disclose "EGYPT'S REVELATIONS" in a program of lectures that would be illustrated with a "moving panorama." Gliddon's vast archaeological collection featured many "*discoveries,* far in advance of publication."[55] Five years earlier, Whitman's *Brooklyn Daily Eagle* had championed Gliddon as a lecturer, commenting, "There had been nothing in this city half as entertaining in the shape of popular lectures for years, as these discourses about old times, in Egypt."[56]

A more energized rhetoric pervades a broadside for a series of Civil War lectures in Fitchburg, Massachusetts, that promised to engage its audience with realistic, up-to-date information. "GRAND HISTORIC MIRROR OF THE AMERICAN WAR!" the advertisement trumpets: "**The most exciting topic of the times.**" The broadside vies for attention with a vigorous dose of superlatives, boasts, and font types. The lecture would be illustrated with "**Startling Dioramic Accompaniments!** . . . on a scale of magnificence never before attempted." For the price of fifteen cents, spectators would be treated to an event of "UNRIVALLED SPLENDOR AND ACCURACY." At turns patriotic and sensational, the advertisement turns the Civil War into a stirring spectacle for "all who love the SACRED CAUSE OF FREEDOM" and thus would want to learn about the principal and latest military events.[57] Reminiscent of the iterative *See* in "Starting from Paumanok," the advertisement emphasizes its visual accompaniments.

The most marketable aspect of a lecture was its proven popularity. The speaker who advertised his lecture on "the newly discovered Science of PSYCHOLOGY" in the *New York Times* reminded readers that experiments in the field engaged "a large share of the public attention."[58] When the Brooklyn Institute promoted its 1852 lecture program, the organizers stepped out of their traditional republican character to pronounce that the "series of truly intellectual entertainments" would surpass "in interest, attractiveness and utility, every series of popular lectures heretofore enjoyed by this community." Heralding the series' importance, they added that a "very numerous and brilliant audience will attend," thus making an immediate and full subscription expedient.[59] Even the Hutchinson Family Singers, symbols of New England virtue and liberalism, not only boasted of their popularity but feigned it as well. Their journals record their frequent efforts to "paper" different towns and villages in preparation for upcoming concerts. In Saco, Maine, they distributed advertisements suggesting that their performances had been pleasing audiences along the eastern seaboard: "[T]hey will introduce a variety of New and Popular Solos, Trios & Quartetts which have received the applause of the most fashionable and popular audiences in New York, Boston, and the principal places in New England." And yet, at this point, the singers had never performed in what was clearly the most impressive of these sites, New York City.[60]

Whitman strongly identified with itinerant lecturers and periodically entertained the idea of becoming one himself. As C. Carroll Hollis has demonstrated, the literary style of *Leaves of Grass* owes much to nineteenth-century oratory. Hollis observed that Whitman's interest in the lecture made him one of the first poets to exploit the erosion in English between the singular and plural forms of *you*. Using lines he had initially written for lectures, he simultaneously addressed a private and public audience, recognizing readers as individuals while drawing them into a larger group.[61] The form of address is central to poems such as "Song of the Open Road," which not only encourage readers to see themselves as part of a building movement but actively sell them on its benefits. Whitman admired the performative aspects of the lecture and the immediacy of the crowd's response. What he learned from advertisements was that he could structure that response into the poem itself, effortlessly folding the audience into his public address. Although he ostensibly asks readers to join in his reverie, the poem leaves little question about how the audience will react. We will assume what he assumes because, as he puts it in "Song of Myself," he is "around, tenacious, acquisitive, tireless . . . . and can never be shaken away" (*LG* 1855, 31; Whitman's ellipsis).

Readers can follow a loosely defined narrative in "Song of Myself" in which the poet gathers and addresses the crowd from which he emerges. In what would later become section 38, the poet imagines himself being crucified and then resurrected as "one of an average unending procession" that travels North American roads (*LG* 1855, 69). Within four lines, however, Whitman transforms this parade of sympathetic republicans into a crowd of student-admirers. "Eleves I salute you, / I see the approach of your numberless gangs . . . . I see you understand yourselves and me" (*LG* 1855, 69; Whitman's ellipsis). Two sections later, he appears as a peddler hawking his new vision of the cosmos. "Outbidding at the start the old cautious hucksters," the poet-orator puts everything at risk in competing against the religious teachings of centuries before (*LG* 1855, 71). He is a teacher and a promoter, a salesman eager to assemble an audience and proclaim his distinctiveness.

These statements occur at an important moment in the poem as Whitman begins to emphasize the poet's verbal performance rather than the voices contained within him. The poem's early sections are filled with examples of the poet's immersion in the people and his consequent capacity to speak for them. "These are the thoughts of all men in all ages and lands," he tells us, "If they are not yours as much as mine they are nothing or next to nothing" (*LG* 1855, 41). "Through me many long dumb voices," he declares, "Voices of the interminable generations of slaves, / Voices of prostitutes and deformed persons . . . / Voices indecent by me clarified and transfigured" (*LG* 1855, 48). The poet becomes a medium for a newly representative publicity in which he speaks for those who, having been marginalized by society, have come to disregard themselves. In *Federalist* No. 10, James Madison defined the republican representative as one who would "refine and enlarge the public view."[62] He would virtually represent his constituents rather than actually convey their words. "Song of Myself" gives the poet a similar responsibility, for he seeks precisely both to purify and to broaden the public view, making it large enough to include voices traditionally prohibited. At the same time, the poet does not let those voices speak for themselves, but rather he clarifies and transfigures them

into his visionary eloquence. A radical democrat, a republican representative, and a master of civic publicity, the poet is constituted by the people
even as he distinguishes himself as a separate vocal entity.

Midway through "Song of Myself," the poet-representative begins to
shade into the poet-orator. In what would become section 42, he plainly
announces himself a lecturer and promulgates his voice with the confidence of one who expects to be heard: ". . . . A call in the midst of the
crowd, / My own voice, orotund, sweeping, and final" (LG 1855, 73; Whitman's ellipsis). If before the poet had vied for attention with the hucksters
who preceded him, here he exhibits absolute confidence in his address.
Moving from the general to the specific, from context to description and
effect, the two-line stanza suggests a voice that works by fiat rather than
process, a voice that is broad, bombastic, and final. The power Whitman
grants the poet-orator becomes increasingly evident as the poem pro-
gresses. Some fifty lines later, he turns to the centripetal and centrifugal
gang and addresses them "like a man leaving charges before a journey"
(LG 1855, 75). By the end of "Song of Myself," the poet has so effectively
assembled human and natural admirers that he can now address his
readers as if they were reluctant to depart. "It is time to explain myself,"
he says in what would become section 44, "let us stand up. / What is
known I strip away . . . . I launch all men and women forward with me into
the unknown" (LG 1855, 76; Whitman's ellipsis). Pointing to a "plain
public road," he tells one follower, "Not I, not any one else can travel that
road for you, / You must travel it for yourself" (LG 1855, 80). Even when
describing his own perception of beauty, Whitman uses a metaphor of
social approbation. Referring to an array of impressions—among them
singing birds, underbrush, and a woman's face on a train—he positions
the poet at the center of fanatical affection:

> My lovers suffocate me!
> Crowding my lips, and thick in the pores of my skin,
> Jostling me through streets and public halls . . . . coming naked
> to me at night. (LG 1855, 78; Whitman's ellipsis)

Whitman created a similar vision in the early drafts of "The Sleepers,"
turning the apprehension of beauty into greetings from ecstatic admirers.
In both poems, the poet not only loves beauty, he seems to command its
loving return; his presence organizes the world into an overeager crowd.

The image of the lecturer in "Song of Myself" encompasses two distinct notions of publicity. On one hand, the poem regularly highlights its civic qualities, emphasizing its immersion in the community as if that were a condition for the kind of national audience Whitman expected for *Leaves of Grass*. At the same time, Whitman filters his concern for the audience through his desire for its acclaim. He demonstrates how his voice is constituted by the public before turning it into a form of social display. The organizers of the Brooklyn lyceum had trumpeted their 1852 series by celebrating the "very numerous and brilliant audience" it expected to attend the events; the audience itself became an attraction. "Song of Myself" performs its publicity, treating readers as a legitimating force and an awestruck crowd. They become the subject of the poem and the poem's principal advocates—observers and participants in the performance of *Leaves of Grass*.

I SHALL BE GOOD HEALTH TO YOU

The most significant antebellum advertisements, and the ones that most influenced Whitman, came from the burgeoning trade in patent medicines. The 1830s and 1840s saw an explosion in the number of bitters, elixirs, and fever drops available to consumers as well as the emergence of several genuinely national brands such as Wright's Indian Vegetable Pills. The medicines appealed to the antiauthoritarian spirit of the age, offering a commodity that seemed to liberate consumers from doctors and other elite experts.[63] Announcements for medicines like Pinkham's Liver Pills and Berentham's Vegetable Supplements provided the chief source of revenue for antebellum newspapers, though many companies developed pamphlets and street signs that also promoted their wares.[64] In contrast to the sober utility with which lyceum organizers approached their publicity, distributors of patent medicines worked to instill in consumers a pressing need for their product. Rather than rely on the simple transmission of information, the advertisements were full of hyperbole and swagger. They created an intensely persuasive style that suggested the kind of promise and unparalleled originality that Whitman celebrated in *Leaves of Grass*.

An 1855 issue of the *Pittsfield Sun* demonstrates the spectacular quality of these medicinal advertisements quite well. On January 25, the Young Men's Association of Lee, Massachusetts, advertised the final two speakers in its series. After detailing the date, time, and location of each lecture, the advertisement promoted the event with the strikingly passive statement: "It is proposed to sustain these Lectures by the sale of Tickets. A liberal encouragement is hoped for." A list of stores selling tickets followed. Directly beneath this text came an announcement for Durno's Catarrh Snuff, a medicine designed to alleviate excess mucus. The text boldly presumes the energy of a rhetorical performance.

> **A Deficiency Supplied in Medi**cal Science.—The best remedy in
> the world for Sore Eyes, Deafness, Cold in the Head, Nervous
> Headache, Bronchitis, and the very worst forms for Catarrh, is
> *unquestionably* DURNO'S CATARRH SNUFF. Its fame has spread far
> and near, in consequence of being sent *free* of expense by mail,
> on receipt of thirty-one cents in stamps or specie.[65]

The advertisement begins by expressing the inadequacy not just of other products but of the medical profession itself. Durno's has arrived to meet an intellectual and cultural shortcoming; its unique value is evident in its fame and popularity. While the medicine's many applications give it a kind of ubiquity in the marketplace, its makers cultivated a distinct identity by emphasizing its singular source: "Prepared *only* at the Depot of Durno's Family Medicines" in Albany, New York. A pointing hand marks the lecture and the medical advertisements, both of which squeeze into the *Sun*'s narrow column. However, the owners of Durno's snuff promise consumers a dynamic relationship with their product that the lyceum committee does not.

The patent medicine industry flourished in Brooklyn during the 1840s and 1850s. As Whitman walked the city's streets, he passed numerous shops selling a variety of pills, ointments, elixirs, and syrups. At the corner of Prospect and Pearl, a family patent medicines store opened in 1846. A branch of a New York company, the Health Agency, could be found at 5 Market Street. The offices of Whitman's *Daily Eagle,* situated at 30 Fulton Street, were in the midst of a thriving medicinal business. At 175 Fulton Street, Mrs. M. Hayes sold "the largest and Best Selected Stock of all the Popular Patent Medicines, both Foreign and Domestic." At 139, there was another branch of the Health Agency which, by 1855, had been taken over by Mrs. Hayes. At 126, Clapp & Townsend produced their Compound Extract of Sarsaparilla, "[t]he Most Extraordinary Medicine in the World." At 101 1/2 there was yet another Health Agency store. Not only did all of these companies regularly advertise in the *Daily Eagle,* they produced broadsides and handbills testifying to their products' miraculous cures. Similar to Whitman's own promotional pamphlets, Clapp & Townsend distributed a free paper almanac that described the medicine's discovery and offered pages of testimonials to its wondrous success.

"Song of Myself" directly invokes the language of patent medicine advertising in describing the poet's astonishing impact. During Whitman's editorship, *The Brooklyn Daily Eagle* ran dozens of announcements for "THE GREATEST DISCOVERY OF THE NINETEENTH CENTURY!—*STRONG & OSGOOD'S VEGETABLE PHYSIANTHROPIC PILLS.*" As the advertisement proclaims, the pills' ability to cleanse and purify the "vitiated state of the blood" had gained it "a celebrity unparalleled in the annals of medicine."[66] The penultimate stanza of "Song of Myself" assigns the poet the same therapeutic qualities:

> You will hardly know who I am or what I mean,
> But I shall be good health to you nevertheless,
> And filter and fibre your blood. (*LG* 1855, 86)

Like Strong & Osgood's vegetable pills, the poet attains his celebrity in cleansing the blood of its impurities. He will be a source of renewal and strength. The assertion was quite common among Brooklyn-based medicines. Published just blocks from the Eagle building, Townsend's almanac claimed that their Sarsaparilla "creates *New, Rich, and Pure Blood,* and consequently invigorates the system." The Compound "purifies the whole system and strengthens the person." It contains "a power possessed by no other medicine."[67]

"Song of Myself" may very well have been challenging its readers by offering to heal them through poetry rather than pills. Whitman, we might say, was outbidding his medicinal counterparts, implicitly pressing the question *To whom would you entrust your health? The poet Walt Whitman, who lies underneath your boots, or the hucksters who work their trade on Fulton Street?* Though it cannot be triggered by a substance, the transformation the poet promises has both bodily and spiritual results. Its effect goes beyond anything a liver pill might accomplish. Whatever playful challenge we might construe in these lines, however, Whitman does not undermine these advertisements as much as he acknowledges and absorbs them. With their shortened lines and deliberate pacing, the poem's final stanzas create a mood of calm acceptance as they confidently prepare readers for the task of re-creating themselves. Invoking the claims of patent medicine advertisers would make sense in this context, for the industry was quite effective in associating its products with a kind of messianic renewal and change. Medicine advertisements did not simply address the disorders of cholera, constipation, and scrofula. They promised to give consumers a dramatically new kind of life. The owners of Brant's Indian Medicines—"THE MOST ACTIVE AND EFFICACIOUS PURIFIER OF BLOOD IN THE WORLD"—claimed to give nothing short of a resurrected self: "THEY THAT WERE DYING YET LIVE, THEY THAT WERE SICK ARE HEALED. They that were LAME WALK. They that were UTTERLY HELPLESS AND WERE GIVEN UP AS SUCH BY ALL, HAVE BEEN RESTORED, AND RAISED, AS if it were from the GRAVE, TO LIFE AND HEALTH."[68]

Whitman's civic evangelism was firmly grounded in the republican lyceum, but his sense of promotion shares much in common with the patent medicine industry and its revolutionary impact on advertising. Building on a foundational trope in American cultural history, early advertisers publicized their products by associating them with conversion: take this pill, drink this tonic, and regardless of what ails you, a wondrous change will occur. Without sacrificing its concern for the body, Whitman returns such language to its spiritual roots in announcing the impact of his teachings. If we stop with the poet for a day and night, we will possess the origin of all poems; we will learn to see things independently, to read without the spectres in books, to listen to all sides and filter them from ourselves (LG 1855, 26). The poet guides us to this independence and wants us to know that in his company we can find a more fulfilling life. Near the end of "Song of Myself," he claims to have awakened us to a more genuine existence:

> Long enough have you dreamed contemptible dreams,
> Now I wash the gum from your eyes,
> You must habit yourself to the dazzle of the light and of every
> moment of your life. (LG 1855, 81)

Whitman redefines the poet's relationship to the reader in much the same way that early advertisers invented a relation between consumers and products. Borrowing from Foucault, Wicke comments that Barnum's advertisements clearly "defined a group of subjects," namely "modern consumers," who found themselves "articulated by their relationship to this discourse."[69] What gave advertising such a strong position in antebellum culture is that it began to define its audience as subjects who occupied a unique position in regard to it. People were no longer pedestrians or readers; they were spectators, consumers, witnesses, and bodies in need of healing. Advertising offered individuals a public image of themselves, a commercial vision of their vibrant health and personality. "Publicity speaks in the future tense," John Berger explains, "and yet the achievement of this future is endlessly deferred." We judge publicity "not by the real fulfillment of its promises, but by the relevance of its fantasies to those of the spectator-buyer." As a newly emergent discourse, antebellum advertising appealed to democratic ideals, positing the historical person against the visionary self, the individual transfigured with perfect body and blood. As Berger notes, publicity's "essential application is not to reality but to daydreams."[70]

With its roots in patent medicine advertising, Whitman's publicity anticipates the commercial claims of a media-saturated age. An endless variety of products echo the poet's promise to uncover our true sense of self and to lead us consumers to a deeper, more satisfying experience. Consuming *Leaves of Grass* will guarantee self-fulfillment, independence, and the kind of charismatic individuality that will make us the center of every crowd. Such consumption will bring an ecstatic appreciation of our bodies, the pleasures of desiring and being desired. However superficially, the makers of Toyota cars, Budweiser beer, and Special K cereal all seem to agree with the author of *Leaves of Grass* that what they offer will result in our deeper happiness and newly discovered harmonious relation to the world.

Recognizing the promotional tenor of Whitman's evangelism can deepen our appreciation for such well-known passages as the parable of the twenty-ninth bather. Eventually organized into section 11, the passage demonstrates the kind of conversion Whitman hopes to effect in his readers. Inspired by the twenty-eight men cavorting in the water outside her home, a wealthy woman imaginatively joins them, leaving the confines of her mansion and frolicking in the erotic waters:

Where are you off to, lady? for I see you,
You splash in the water there, yet stay stock still in your room.

> Dancing and laughing along the beach came the twenty-ninth
>   bather,
> The rest did not see her, but she saw them and loved them.
>   (*LG* 1855, 34)

Some have suggested that the portrait of erotic loneliness serves as a screen for the poet's own longings and desires, and as we have seen, publicity for Whitman clearly had a profoundly erotic appeal.[71] The woman may also be a model of Whitman's reader, the decorous individual who is tempted from the house by the poet's compelling visions. No matter how imaginative it is, the woman's contact with Whitman dramatically awakens her sense of adventure, self-fulfillment, and sexual desire. From the poem's beginning, he has associated the insides of homes with decorum, perfume, intoxication, and restraint. The parable participates in the larger effort to link a new set of values with the public world of Whitman's embrace. The bather's isolation and lack of fulfillment make her an effective advertisement for why we need *Leaves of Grass:* she is promised the same sexuality, self-knowledge, and sense of personal power that he promises all of his readers. The twenty-ninth bather emerges as a prototype for the poet's consumers: her desires become eroticized as they become associated with his personality.

It is tempting to argue that "Song of Myself" appropriates the language of advertising in an effort to criticize and undermine commercial culture. Just as he tries to persuade the twenty-ninth bather to leave her riches behind, the poet conveys his distaste for possessions and the gathering and spending of money. "I am less the reminder of property or qualities," he says later in the poem, "and more the reminder of life" (*LG* 1855, 47). He has little patience for a society filled with the walking dead, with zombies who rush through Manhattan with dimes on their eyes and brains in their bellies (*LG* 1855, 73). But despite this distrust of commercialism, Whitman remains committed to the principles behind publicity and promotion. Advertising itself was not a narrow-minded practice; what mattered was *what* one advertised and hoped to achieve: to save the nation through the formation of strong individuals or to earn piles of money by tricking thousands of spectators into seeing a bogus mermaid? Whitman's aspirations may have been all he needed to justify his absorption in publicity, but for twenty-first-century readers, his relentless grandiosity may raise more questions than answers. The force with which he sells the image of himself and democracy can lead us to forget that he is ultimately promoting the value of a single poet and his poems.

Whitman unwittingly articulates the historical appeal of consumer capitalism. As both an advertisement and a commodity, the celebrated poet becomes a key to public unity. Not only does he invite us to find our individuality through his book, he promises that in the end, our many divisions will be swept into his colossal unifying force. Tuckahoe, congressman, prostitute, fugitive, all have access to the poet of *Leaves of Grass*. Lauren Berlant has argued that the most politically marginalized groups in the United States have been encouraged to discover their identity, as well as a larger sense of community, through the purchase of commodities.[72] Surely that participation has been meaningful to consumers, but it raises the problem of whether consumption can be a form of political power. Despite Whitman's misgivings about capitalism, "Song of Myself" participates in a long historical process in which consumption would become a primary means of casually participating in public life. Whitman would have been disappointed with those results and the limited perspectives they have produced. At the same time, we might ask whether the poet's insistent publicity threatens to obscure his democratic goals.

Once we see in Whitman's poet a nexus of increasingly prevalent cultural forces—namely, promotion, advertisement, and celebrity—the bravado of his claims makes startling, if not terrifying, sense. He signals a social transformation that no single person can resist, for his is the power to turn the private individual into a public being. Although he nominally directs his address to the weak and the faltering, he pursues his readers in "Song of Myself" with hegemonic intensity:

> I dilate you with tremendous breath . . . . I buoy you up;
> Every room of the house do I fill with an armed force . . . . lovers
> of me, bafflers of graves:
> Sleep! I and they keep guard all night;
> Not doubt, not decease shall dare to lay finger upon you,
> I have embraced you, and henceforth possess you to myself,
> And when you rise in the morning you will find what I tell you is
> so. (*LG* 1855, 71; Whitman's ellipses)

Brant's Indian medicines claimed that their product had helped the sick rise from the grave, offering a literal version of the transformation metaphor that would later underlie countless advertising campaigns. Whitman promises a similar resurrection for each of us. He will invade our homes, converting us into one of his unified celebrants. In Whitman's publicity, we shall come to share an eternal public life, for not only will we celebrate him, we shall identify that act as a celebration of ourselves. When we rise in the morning, we will find that what he has told us is so.

There is an obvious manipulativeness to these claims that recalls Quentin Anderson's discussion of Whitman as an "imperial self." Anderson coined the term in 1971 when analyzing the tendency of writers such as Whitman, Emerson, and Henry James to substitute the individual imagination for the social and physical world. The imperial self elides the stubbornness of history in creating a vision so large and comprehensive that it converts all others into images of itself. Anderson argues that writers such as Whitman rarely lead us to any form of agency but encourage "us to use our sensibilities to incorporate the whole, to take the whole into consciousness."[73] From mashed firemen to weeping mothers to lovesick slaves, Whitman converts the elements of the historical world into signs of his comprehensive mastery. What they signify is not material fact but the poet's astonishing range.

Anderson focuses on the philosophical and aesthetic dimensions of this practice, what we might understand as an American reformulation of romantic correspondence. The phrase *imperial self* invites us to think about these writers in the sociopolitical context that Anderson himself does not explore. Passing from *Leaves of Grass* into the material world, the imperial self proves to be coercive and calculating. Whitman's resistance to history quickly becomes a willingness to manipulate the organs of public opinion and democracy. We have seen the poet mislead the public in his self-reviews, trying to counterfeit the material world to suit his promotional purposes. The poet's vision of storming our homes to save us from despair suggests a similar impatience with resistance and dissent. To some, the image of armed force may recall the poet's previous hint that he would protect a runaway slave from captors. To others, the image may seem awfully close to democracy at gunpoint. Ultimately, however, the vehicle of Whitman's commando metaphor is perhaps less ominous than the discursive power it is meant to express. Despite his many democratic qualifiers, the poet envisions himself occupying our very selves, and once unveiled, his promise of publicity may prove to be a threat. Poetry has not filled the rooms of American homes by force, but publicity and advertisement have.

Whitman puts great stock in his ability to follow readers wherever they go, his language relentlessly assuring them that his thoughts are also their own. Representing himself as a pervasive rhetorical power, Whitman offers a remarkable allegory for advertising's efficacy and growth:

> I teach straying from me, yet who can stray from me?
> I follow you whoever you are from the present hour;
> My words itch at your ears till you understand them.
>   (*LG* 1855, 81)

In his widely read tract "The Art of Money Getting," Barnum had championed the ways in which commerce allowed merchants to "transcend" their bodies, to establish a "commercial persona," as Adams explains, "in markets far beyond" their physical selves.[74] Whitman's claims reflect a similar enthusiasm for the ways in which a rhetorical presence could be established through the publicity of the poems. Readers cannot stray from Whitman because, as a disembodied advertisement for himself, he knows no space or time. His power lies in the fact that he circulates among the fancy houses, the tawdry sickrooms, the beds of husbands and wives. What Adams sees in Barnum applies equally well to Whitman: in all these places, he does not sell a product as much as the value of his fame.

Whitman's ubiquity results in his faith that his readers will come to identify their thinking with his. The poet's words itch at our ears, coaxing us to see ourselves in his public image. Of all the rhetorical tropes, "Song of Myself" depends most on identification with the poet embracing our identities and asking that we do the same with him. Whitman's self-advertisements have the goal not of bringing riches but of enacting his publicity:

> I do not say these things for a dollar, or to fill up the time while I
>   wait for a boat;
> It is you talking just as much as myself . . . . I act as the tongue of
>   you,
> It was tied in your mouth . . . . in mine it begins to be loosened.
>   (*LG* 1855, 81–82; Whitman's ellipses)

The passage folds together the speaker and his audience, the representative and his citizens, the would-be celebrity and his fans. The poet's relation to his readers comes to resemble the advertiser's to the consumer, for both the reader and consumer are remade in the image of the commodity. Jacques Derrida has described public opinion as "the silhouette of a phantom" because like a ghost it is both everywhere and nowhere. Public opinion never speaks for itself, he continues, but rather, "one cites it, one makes it speak, [one] ventriloquizes it."[75] Acting as their tongue, Whitman both conjures and ventriloquizes his readers in "Song of Myself," explaining how to receive him. We shall assume what the poet assumes, for he is inside our thoughts, inescapable. We shall assume what he assumes, for we are the fiction he maintains in making his critical publicity manipulative.

"Song of Myself" is the prime and most important example of Whitman's invoking the language of promotion to cloud and mystify his present state. The strategy endowed the poet's persona with the burgeoning possibility antebellum Americans found so exciting and attractive. As the poem works toward its close, Whitman offers us a vision of his celebrity. He blurs the lines between the people he has affectionately absorbed and those who have absorbed him:

> The young mechanic is closest to me . . . . he knows me pretty
>   well,
> The woodman that takes his axe and jug with him shall take me
>   with him all day,
> The farmboy ploughing in the field feels good at the sound of
>   my voice,
> In vessels that sail my words must sail . . . . I go with fishermen
>   and seamen, and love them,
> My face rubs to the hunter's face when he lies down alone in his
>   blanket,
> The driver thinking of me does not mind the jolt of his wagon,
> The young mother and old mother shall comprehend me,
> The girl and the wife rest the needle a moment and forget where
>   they are,
> They and all would resume what I have told them.
>   (*LG* 1855, 82; Whitman's ellipses)

The passage remarkably moves between an array of tenses, weaving confirmations of the poet's significance with professions that such a state will solidify and grow. Mixing observation with command and the indicative with the imperative mood, Whitman promises his uncommitted readers the satisfaction he asserts that others already have. The paradox drives to the heart of Whitman's poetics of hype, the poetics of saying "big things" about oneself until the world can catch up. Although Whitman did not admit it to Traubel on that August afternoon, the loud whistles and big talk came long before the cries and silences had greeted *Leaves of Grass*.

CHAPTER FOUR

Intimacies

SHOWING THE WHOLE ANIMAL

WHITMAN'S FONDNESS FOR PUBLICITY was so well known that even in death he was vulnerable to charges of garishly courting the spotlight. A year after he died in 1892, the poet's admirers published *In Re Walt Whitman,* a commemorative book meant to proclaim his unique contribution to the world. The book was edited by Whitman's literary executors: Horace Traubel, Thomas Harned, a Philadelphia lawyer, and R. M. Bucke, the Canadian physician who would later describe Whitman as having a finer moral consciousness than that of either Jesus or the Buddha. Gathering a wide variety of materials, the volume began the awesome task of committing the poet to text, of commemorating the magnificence of his personality after it had left the earth. The focus on personality was important because for men such as Traubel and Bucke, editing the volume was a semireligious task, and Bucke in particular came to regard himself as playing the role of Paul to Whitman's Christ.[1] The volume's medical reports, autopsy notes, and exhaustive recollections all serve to present the poet as being as much a religious icon as a literary innovator.

The spiritual value of the collection was not evident to all of its readers. William Kennedy, Whitman's friend and biographer, later suggested that in its relentless attention to the deceased poet, the book had little

value. He compared the volume to a barker announcing an exhibit outside a museum or circus tent:

> Of the big volume *In Re Walt Whitman* (Philadelphia, 1893) not
> so much good can be said. There is too much of it: its thirty arti-
> cles, including Symonds's long poem, Love and Death, sorely
> tried the patience of the indifferent public. Even the Whit-
> maniacs find rather grewsome [*sic*] its horrible verbatim report
> of the autopsy, the physicians' note-books, the long prosy trans-
> lated articles, and, above all, the repellent personal egotism of
> the old, broken-down, dying bard himself. To the anti-
> Whitmanite it is very much like this: "Gentlemen, walk up and
> view the greatest poet on earth. We've captured him here in Phil-
> adelphia. We'll give you his dimension in inches, cut him open
> and show his anatomy; and we've got a phonographic report of
> his talk. We show the whole animal, gentlemen."[2]

In Kennedy's description, Whitman emerges as a figure shrouded in
hype, what some might see as the revolting culmination of a half century's worth of practice. Whitman the icon becomes Whitman the freak
show, the "greatest poet on earth" captured and exhibited as if he were
Barnum's Feejee mermaid. What made the volume especially "grew-
some" to Kennedy was how indecorously intimate its portrait of Whitman
was. In delivering "the whole animal," the editors had put the poet on
display; as in an autopsy, they had opened him up to public view. While
the editors may have regarded their work as a testament to Whitman's
divinity, the volume had produced a bizarre portrait of the animal poet
and his corpse.

Kennedy's response is instructive, for in its grotesque and exaggerated way, the volume encouraged the same association of intimacy and
publicity that had informed Whitman's writing since 1855. The poet began his career welcoming every inch and organ of human flesh and ended
it worrying about the influence of constipation on his work.[3] Throughout
his career, he seemed set on making spectacles out of his seemingly
private existence. As Kennedy suggests, *In Re Walt Whitman* celebrated
and commemorated the poet by offering readers graphic access to his
bodily self, creating a scientific but also privileged glimpse into the most

personal aspects of his life. The volume is a strikingly literal version of the figures of intimacy that Whitman had employed to characterize his relations with his audience. In the 1860 poem "So Long," he described the act of reading as a distinctly private embrace in which the printed page comes alive as the bearer of a human voice:

> This is no book,
> Who touches this, touches a man.
> (Is it night? Are we here alone?)
> It is I you hold, and who holds you,
> I spring from the pages into your arms—decease calls me forth.
>   (*LG* 1860, 455)

In Re Walt Whitman dispenses with the metaphor by emphasizing not the textual body nor the image of that body, but the guts and organs themselves. While Whitman had promised to spring from the pages into his readers' open arms, the published autopsy and medical reports accentuate the visceral capacity of that embrace; they create a kind of phrenological monody asserting that the poet's body was indeed as significant as he had claimed.

The volume's intense focus on Whitman's physical character emanates from the editors' devotional approach to their work. The almost sacramental attention to Whitman's body endows it with a decidedly Christic significance, the editors seeming to anoint the corpse with medical data rather than biblical aloes and myrrh. In its wearily comic way, however, Kennedy's response also raises the question of celebrity. The Whitmaniacs to whom he refers are the precursors of our present-day fans, followers distinguished by their exuberant devotion to a star. Like their Beatlemaniac descendants, they were drawn to emblems and expressions of intimacy, seizing on an array of personal items as important devotional relics. In 1885, a group of working-class men began to meet in Bolton, England, to share their enthusiasm for democracy and *Leaves of Grass*. Known as both the Eagle Street College and the Bolton Whitman Fellowship, the group established deep emotional ties to the American poet. They proudly included as part of their collection a lock of Whitman's hair, a broken fountain pen he *might* have used, a cup and saucer he was confirmed to have used, and his deceased canary, stuffed, mounted, and ready for display.[4]

The excesses that Kennedy associated with *In Re Walt Whitman* speak to the conflation of intimacy and publicity that emanates from figures of celebrity. The volume exposes Whitman for largely promotional ends, attempting to secure the public's attention through the reverent exhibition of his corpse. Although in the editors' case this unarticulated strategy had largely failed, its central theme had already inspired the devotion of Whitman's followers and friends. "The greatest poet on earth" had helped himself achieve that Barnumesque epithet by carefully hinting at and revealing a seemingly authentic self. Alongside the public forms of address that were so important to *Leaves of Grass,* he wrote poems courting individual readers, claiming to speak alone to them in the middle of the night. In other poems, he described himself as confessing personal sorrows, disclosing secrets not to the public at large but to a sympathetic lover. Kennedy's description of *In Re Walt Whitman* is a fitting expression of the poet as celebrity, for since the earliest editions of *Leaves of Grass,* Whitman had been constructing his public persona by rhetorically invoking his privacy.

The previous chapter explored the ways in which Whitman understood publicity as both the state of being constituted by the public and the means by which one might be represented before it. At times a deeply political quality and, at others, a form of commercial display, publicity involved an array of widely visible activities—the performance of identities, the passing of handbills, the summoning of crowds. Since the eighteenth century, however, public life had also begun to depend on and claim the domestic sphere. The reading of colonial newspapers, for example, had established the home as an important setting for the imagining of civic communities. As commercial culture grew in the nineteenth century, publicity pressed its way further into the home, turning the parlor, study, and bedroom into sites of both consumption and communal identity. Beatriz Colomina explains publicity's expanding domain: "It no longer has so much to do with a public space, in the traditional sense of a public forum, a square, or the crowd that gathers around a speaker in such a place, but with the audience that each medium of publication reaches, independent of the place the audience might actually be occupying. But, of course, the fact that (for the most part) this audience is indeed at home is not without consequence. The private is, in this sense, now more public than the public."[5] Publicity, Colomina argues, is not just about one's performance in front of a crowd; rather it is the ability to fashion a virtual crowd through the reaching of private individuals. The public is effectively created by publicity and the various sites in which the desire for consumption occurs. The new forms of promotion that arose from health products in the 1840s explicitly attached themselves to the personal body. As Jackson Lears has commented, advertisements re-flected a broader cultural fascination with making the private public.[6]

The promotional value of intimacy enhanced the growth of ante-bellum celebrity culture. The intensive focus on personality—in the press, in publishing, in daguerreotyping, on the stage—addressed a public eager for information about renowned individuals and their private lives. The popularity of a work such as Fanny Fern's *Ruth Hall* clearly demonstrated the ways in which the biographies of well-known writers coincided with the appeal of their literary work. Detailing Ruth's heartless family and struggle with poverty after her husband died, the semiautobiographical novel served to personalize and therefore publicize the story of how a popular columnist had overcome considerable tragedy in rising to fortune and fame. The book's blunt depiction of Fern's real-life brother, the much-feted author and editor N. P. Willis, gave it even wider commercial appeal. *Ruth Hall* was just one of dozens of midcentury texts that offered sensa-tional exposés of Anglo-American celebrities, a list that includes Willis's own writings and social observations. The phenomenon captures what Baker describes as a central feature of antebellum fame: "Its traffic in style and secrets was also a trade in personality, a commercial enterprise dedi-cated to packaging inner experience and private relations for broad public consumption. Faced with a world whose progress seemed to be spiraling increasingly toward dispersion and atomization, antebellum Americans were inclined to freight this market for intimacy with mounting value, even as they worried about publicity's impact on the familiar relations of home and family."[7] While widely recognized as a threat, the relations between publicity and intimacy grew in strength. This transformation not only changed the ways in which celebrities were presented before the public, it also altered the experience of public life—both for those whose lives were now open to popular scrutiny and for those who enjoyed their seemingly privileged glimpses into the private world of the renowned.

The rhetoric of intimacy in *Leaves of Grass* enhances and conveys the poet's persona. In the penultimate poem of the Calamus cluster, later titled "Here the Frailest Leaves of Me," intimacy and publicity become strategically intertwined:

> Here my last words, and the most baffling,
> Here the frailest leaves of me, and yet my strongest-lasting,
> Here I shade down and hide my thoughts—I do not expose
>   them,
> And yet they expose me more than all my other poems.
>   (*LG* 1860, 377)

A preliminary reading of the poem would emphasize Whitman's statement that the Calamus cluster had exposed him more than he had intended. Writing the poems to "shade down and hide" his thoughts, he is puzzled by the knowledge that his concealments have been in vain. The work of art foils both repression and intentionality. In the context of this avowedly personal sequence, however, the poet's hiding from attention ensures the other poems' authenticity. The poem encourages us to conclude that Calamus offers a truer, more sincere portrait of Whitman than that of any other work in *Leaves of Grass*. What readers encounter in Calamus is the real poet, the real man, the genuine self that exists beyond the ambitious impresario.

But even as it asserts its authenticity, the poem is as rhetorically savvy and publicity driven as any of Whitman's platform poems. The opening lines essentially preface the rest of the poem, introducing its message with a kind of drumroll assertion of significance: "Here my last words, and the most baffling, / Here the frailest leaves of me, and yet my strongest-lasting." The repetition underscores the uniqueness of the Calamus sequence and its mysterious revelations. The poem constructs a private, intimate world even as it dismantles that world in favor of promoting itself to the public at large. In the context of Calamus, the poem enacts a rather coy dance with its readers, describing the cluster as the profoundly personal expression of a man who has become disenchanted with his fame—a fame that Whitman did not yet possess. In promoting its intimacy, the poem underscores the privileged, magical nature of the communication between an audience and its alleged literary star.

Charles L. Ponce de Leon writes that with the end of the nineteenth century came a gradual consolidation of the reportorial techniques used to illuminate a person's "real self." These techniques originated in the

1850s as urban Americans assumed that "all self-presentation in the public sphere was, to one degree or another, artificial and unreliable as a guide to a person's real self." Newspapers and their readers consequently oriented their attention toward the genuine individual who emerged from behind the public artifice. "To glimpse a person's real self," Ponce de Leon explains, "it was necessary to see her in private, when she dropped her front and refrained from the contrived, mannered self-presentation that she adopted in the public sphere."[8] Trying to avoid the hagiography of earlier eras, journalists began to interview the famous in domestic settings and publish profiles exploring what made them interesting and unique. These techniques resulted in a set of journalistic conventions that gradually became institutionalized over the first decades of the twentieth century. It is with the birth of this human-interest journalism that Ponce de Leon detects the creation of an identifiable celebrity class.

The film critic Richard Schickel sees a similar trajectory in an analysis that begins with the rise of Hollywood in the 1920s. Schickel argues that a central staple of the public relations industry has been to cultivate an "illusion of intimacy" between stars and their fans. Stars have become ubiquitous in the cultural landscape at the same time that their scripted confessions and televised interviews have made them appear increasingly personal and accessible to spectators around the world.[9] Celebrities, Schickel concludes, have become "intimate strangers" because they inspire feelings of both identification and familiarity. No longer the passive victims of opportunistic journalists, celebrities and their handlers have developed sophisticated methods for suggesting a more personal relation with supporters, a seemingly private, nonmediated connection with the many individuals who admire them. Anyone who has ever flipped through the pages of *People* or watched an "up close and personal" interview on television has experienced the careful construction of intimacy for promotional purposes.

Although developed to explain a very different set of historical and aesthetic circumstances, Schickel's ideas can help illuminate *Leaves of Grass*. The culture of celebrity was of course neither as organized nor as pervasive in antebellum America as it would later become. Nonetheless, its rudimentary forms and rites were clearly taking shape as Whitman attended the theater, edited newspapers, strolled on Broadway, and fantasized about the public's devotion to his work. In the inchoate, carnivallike atmosphere of antebellum New York, Whitman cultivated an illusion of intimacy that took two distinct but related forms. One emphasized the poet's personality, suggesting that the poems offered a privileged, unintended glimpse into the private struggles of a renowned public man; he concealed himself in order to find himself inexplicably exposed. Before he developed this strategy, however, Whitman had focused on championing his own empathic insight into the people around him. If a poet's popularity were ultimately an expression of his democratic commitment, if his fame were an index of his being commensurate with his readers, then he would need to publicize his unrivaled ability to enter into their lives.

SYMPATHY

In the 1856 work "Poem of You, Whoever You Are" (later titled simply "To You"), Whitman addressed readers whom he feared had been "walking the walks of dreams," going about their daily lives in unconscious mockery of themselves (*WPP*, 375). Having little sense of their individual worth, they lived in the "supposed realities" that Emerson had described in "The American Scholar" as "the *divided* or social state" (54). They neither saw each other nor saw themselves with any degree of clarity. The situation was ripe for Whitman's evangelistic energies, and by the poem's end, he frees his audience from the fetters that have bound them, singing their grandeur and coaching them to "claim [their] own at any hazard" (*WPP*, 377). What precipitates this release is the poet's inviting his readers to exchange their limited vision of themselves for his vision of their glories. Out of the matrix of social identity, he alone can see the readers' "true soul and body." To the poet and only the poet, "They stand forth out of affairs, out of commerce, shops, work, farms, clothes, the house, buying, selling, eating, drinking, suffering, dying." His extraordinarily penetrating vision is able to "dissipate" the "mockeries" that have stood for the self (*WPP*, 375–76).

Whitman's concern for his readers may have been genuine, but in the end the poem is less about their condition than his own power to aid them. (As the title suggests, the poem never gets beyond a rather generic impression of who that audience is.) The poet commits himself to seeing his readers with a more relentless and intimate vision than anyone who has previously observed them:

I pursue you where none else has pursued you,
Silence, the desk, the flippant expression, the night, the
   accustom'd routine, if these conceal you from others or from
   yourself, they do not conceal you from me. (*WPP*, 376)

Undeterred by their defenses, unfazed by their weakness, Whitman does not rest in his effort to see his readers' true and glorious selves. The theme is familiar enough to students of *Leaves of Grass* who are accustomed to the poet's designs on others' souls. In reaching its audience, the poem also underscores the value of the author's seeing beyond the confines of the social world.

"Poem of You" is a paean to the corrective powers of intimacy, particularly as they appear in the form of Walt Whitman. He is the one who moves beyond the barriers, sees through the unreality, and pushes the superficialities aside. Ascribed to and initiated by him, our intimacy with the poet is plainly meant to remedy the delusions of social life. Nineteenth-century Americans viewed intimacy as having an important moralizing effect, and many scholars have pointed to the relations between domestic virtue and sentimental readership.[10] Whitman echoes his contemporaries in offering personal attachment as an antidote to the self-alienation and moral ambiguity that arose with democratic capitalism.

The poet's most intimate and sympathetic gestures, however, cannot be divorced from their promotional tenor. Whitman masculinizes the conventionally domestic and female intimacy in reorienting it toward the public sphere. Filtering his thoughts through the language of popular sovereignty, he professes his attributes with the logic of an advertisement: *You can know the reality of my intimacy,* he says, *by imagining its miraculous effects, and hereafter that quality will be integral to your perception of what I give you and who I am.* Whitman emerges from the poem as both an advertisement and a commodity, his persona becoming the site at which intimacy and publicity merge. No matter how artificial their origins, tropes of identification are central to the illusion of intimacy, for they allow both the famous and their fans to move beyond their marked social differences in constructing a seemingly affectionate bond in which each purports to be fulfilled through the other. Whitman purrs his way through the poem's second stanza:

Whoever you are, now I place my hand upon you, that you be
   my poem,
I whisper with my lips close to your ear,
I have loved many women and men, but I love none better than
   you. (*WPP*, 375)

The sentiment behind the last line has been repeated so many times, and
in so many different rhetorical contexts, that we may very well break out
in laughter reading it. The illusion of intimacy does more than express the
poet's democratic commitments and more than broadly enact his fantasies of popular acceptance. In "Poem of You," it takes on a persuasive,
wooing function as if Whitman had returned home to tell his reader-
partner that his various liaisons were ultimately about him or her.

   Whitman's sympathy was his poetic counterpart to the culture's general—though by no means unanimous—enthusiasm for sentiment. D. H.
Lawrence famously mocked the poet's self-professed sympathy, pointing
to how he merged with his subjects and claimed their wounds as his own
rather than genuinely *feel with* them and their condition.[11] Lawrence's
opinions were not shared by many. Whitman's readers have historically
praised his sympathy as being everything from a personal magnetism or
characteristic self-sacrifice to a central component of his politics, poetics,
and sexuality. An 1856 review in the *Christian Spiritualist* approvingly
commented that everywhere in *Leaves of Grass,* the poet's "sympathy is with
man, and not with conventionalisms."[12] Reviewing the 1860 edition, the
New York Times saw the quality as being integral to Whitman's character.
"In his hearty human sympathy, his wonderful intensity, his fullness of
epithet, the author shows that he is a man of strong passion, vigorous in
thought and earnest in purpose."[13] Whitman's sympathy became particularly evident to reviewers of the 1867 editions of *Drum Taps* and *Leaves
of Grass,* thanks in part to O'Connor's hagiographic portrait of the poet's
wartime service. A reviewer for *Broadway* used the term four times in
praising the books, finally concluding that the "greatest" of Whitman's
many attributes was "his wondrous sympathy with men as men."[14] Writing about *Drum Taps* in *Galaxy,* John Burroughs declared that Whitman
contained "almost in excess, a quality in which every current poet is lacking
. . . the faculty of being in entire sympathy" with both nature and "rude,
abysmal man."[15]

That so many reviewers remarked on this feature should not be surprising, for not only was sympathy commonly perceived to be an important social value, but in both his prose and poetry, Whitman had applied the term to himself. Although it presumably went unnoticed, the practice had begun as early as 1846, his first year of editing the *Daily Eagle*. He celebrated the quality in an editorial inaugurating a new font type for the paper: "There is a curious kind of sympathy (haven't you ever thought of it before?) that arises in the mind of a newspaper conductor with the public he serves. He gets to *love* them. Daily communion creates a sort of brotherhood and sisterhood between the two parties."[16] Whitman presents sympathy as a kind of republican camaraderie that an editor and his readers come to enjoy over time. A year later he returned to the theme, this time emphasizing the public's reception of him: "We feel a hearty sympathy with each woman, man, and child, who communes with us, and we with them, every day; for what is giving up one's attention to another's thoughts, even in print, but communion."[17] Expressions of sympathy are usually meant to comfort the receiver, but in Whitman's case they shaded into self-promotion. The editor feels sympathy with an audience that had given its thoughts up to him. If publicity were the means by which the famous nurtured their public selves, sympathy suggested their absorption in other lives.

In sympathy, Whitman found a nexus of appealing commercial and political values: a commercially successful posture associated with a number of well-known writers, a political sentiment employed and developed by such abolitionists as Angelina Grimke and Lydia Maria Child, and an aesthetic virtue that would distinguish his poetic qualities from other nations and their art.[18] As a younger poet, Whitman had found this quality lacking in the literature around him, and he scribbled in the margins of an essay on Milton that "Wordsworth lacks sympathy with men and women— that does not pervade him enough by a long shot."[19] When he turned to writing the 1855 Preface, he made the quality the center of his national aesthetic. Americans were distinguished from other nationalities by "their self-esteem and wonderful sympathy" (*LG* 1855, 6). "The inmost secrets of art"—and hence, the greatest poet—slept between sympathy and pride (*LG* 1855, 12). Having set this new critical standard, Whitman announced in "Song of Myself" that he met the critical challenge. "I am he attesting sympathy," he declares, offering what would become an important epithet for helping readers navigate his work (*LG* 1855, 46). By 1876, Whitman asserted that sympathy was his driving force in writing *Leaves of Grass:* "To this terrible, irrepressible yearning, (surely more or less down underneath in most human souls)—this never-satisfied appetite for sympathy, and this boundless offering of sympathy—this universal democratic comradeship —this old, eternal, yet ever-new interchange of adhesiveness, so fitly emblematic of America—I have given in that book, undisguisedly, declaredly, the openest expression" (*WPP*, 1011). Whitman turned sympathy into a kind of trademark for his verse, a quality that, as Burroughs argued in 1866, distinguished his work from that of other poets.[20]

Despite Lawrence's objections, the book's stated interest in other people's suffering has led contemporary critics to continue the practice of treating Whitman's sympathy as the pinnacle of his achievement. Martin Klammer places it at the center of Whitman's poetic, arguing that, like Frederick Douglass's *Narrative*, the 1855 *Leaves of Grass* importantly links sympathy with the imagination. Klammer wonders whether the "radically sympathetic depiction of blacks" in *Leaves of Grass* compelled Whitman toward "his equally radical and new poetic form," namely the development of his "long-line free verse."[21] The legal theorist Martha Nussbaum places even more weight on the poet's sympathy as she examines how it can instruct contemporary jurists. Although her comprehension of Whitman's career is limited, she quotes passages from "Song of Myself" and "By Blue Ontario's Shore" to support her argument that Whitman's sympathy with the degraded should be the "norm of democratic judgment" in the American legal system.[22] Sympathy emerges as an unquestioned poetic value, a cardinal virtue expressing the poet's sincere and decisive sentiments. Whitman himself had made similar statements about sympathy's moral and political import. As "Song of Myself" explains, "whoever walks a furlong without sympathy walks to his own funeral, dressed in his shroud" (*LG* 1855, 82).

However, sympathy for Whitman was not a simple quality, and despite his confidence in *Leaves of Grass*, he did not always find it to be self-evident or easily possessed. As we saw in chapter 2, sympathy was one of the personal attributes that Whitman felt a community of sane or insane people needed to recognize in order for it to exist. In his notebook entry, he had inverted the most common dynamics of the feeling. Rather than the gift to imagine the experience of someone else, he had seen sympathy as a ratification of the self. The poet's identification with others and his compassion for their experience become a stunning and abiding consequence of his rhetorical ingenuity. The runaway slave, the excluded prostitute, and the apprehensive reader all signify not their individual conditions but the poet's personality. Whitman may be an excellent judge, but he also campaigns for the office, skillfully claiming his seat on the bench through the regular profession of sympathy.

The appeal of shared intimacy comes from its suggestion that, in an atomized society, we might enter into someone else's private experience. Despite the emphasis on privacy, antebellum Americans enjoyed this sentiment largely through cultural productions, through books, lithographs, the theater, and newspapers. In these and other media, sympathy appeared as two distinct inflections of a common emotional theme. The first was a kind of charitable love and respect. When Klammer and Nussbaum praise Whitman's sympathy, they highlight the compassion he feels for others, a compassion that reflects the state of his soul as much as it does the depravity of human conditions.[23] Whitman resembles contemporaries such as Stowe and Longfellow, who sought to redeem themselves and their audiences through their respectful, often tender portraits of the poor, enslaved, and dispossessed.

In making sympathy a defining quality of American poets, in emphasizing his affinity with readers, Whitman was also drawing on a different aspect of antebellum popular culture: that celebrities nurtured feelings of sympathy or correspondence with their audience. The intimacy people felt toward well-known individuals was directly related to the pose of good-natured mutuality that the famous had learned to cultivate with the people who followed them. When Whitman writes, "I own publicly who you are, if nobody else owns . . . . and see and hear you, and what you give and take," he employs a rhetoric of intense emotional identification that was prevalent in the celebrity columns of antebellum newspapers (LG 1855, 88; Whitman's ellipsis).

The most prominent of these papers was Bonner's New York Ledger, which in 1855 became the regular home of such celebrity columnists as Fern, Beecher, and the lecturer Edward Everett.[24] The celebrity columns in the Ledger and other papers found a way to commercialize their authors' sympathy, effectively commodifying the "language and sensations of sympathy among an audience hoping for personal attachment."[25] Fern highlighted this aspect of her celebrity in *Ruth Hall* by having Ruth receive a series of fan letters from readers across the country. Among a number of comic messages proposing marriage, expressing outrage, and asking for money, she includes a moving letter from a pregnant woman who fears that she will die in childbirth. The woman asks Ruth to adopt the child after it is born. She broaches this request by drawing on the sympathy she has found in reading the columnist: "Dear Madam: I address a stranger, and yet *not* a stranger, for I have read your heart in your many writings. In them I see sympathy for the poor, the sorrowing, and the dependent; I see a tender love for helpless childhood."[26] Ruth's celebrity becomes the site at which two versions of sympathy combine; her compassion for the downtrodden first reveals her soul to the reader and then nurtures the belief that the two share an intimate, personal relationship. Schickel's phrase "intimate stranger" is directly applicable here, for in the context of this semiautobiographical novel, Fern presents herself as performing precisely that cultural role.[27] She is cherished by a public that seems to think it knows her.

A keen student of this environment would learn that while expressions of sympathy can personalize famous writers, making celebrities appear to be intimate friends, they could also serve to make them more renowned. If sympathy were the distinguishing characteristic of a celebrity columnist, then a would-be celebrity might appropriate that quality as well. Fame, as Baker notes, had once involved performing before nobility, but in the era of sentimental celebrity, it required individuals to perform symbolically before a diverse and fragmented audience. Fern's pregnant correspondent is indicative of the many followers of people such as Beecher, Lind, and Willis who "longed to achieve a sense of wholeness through emotional identification with their parlor idols."[28] Whitman strove to maintain his own public intimacies through his sympathetic address to readers. "Talk honestly," he coaxes us in "Song of Myself," "for no one else hears you, and I stay only a minute longer" (*LG* 1855, 85). Whether readers are searching for love, compassion, adventure, or wholeness, he is the one to whom they should turn. In "Crossing Brooklyn Ferry," he projected his sympathy across time, assuring successive generations that he too had felt vanity, greed, and lust, that he too had had suspicions about himself. As he peers into the innermost secrets of other souls and desires, Whitman opens up his private experience. Not only do readers receive the poet's compassion, they become his confidants as well. Whitman's confession speaks to an audience eager not just for acceptance but for access to his private self.

THE SEA WHISPERED ME

In the 1860 edition of *Leaves of Grass*, Whitman offset his eagerness to merge with other lives by asserting a self seemingly remote from the public man. The book's first two editions had created the impression of a platform speaker gifted with the faculty of personal address, but the book rarely depicted an authentic private self beyond the programmatic representative bard. While "Song of Myself" assumes an autobiographical posture, its *I* is so large and multitudinous that it resists identification with any individual life. The hint of self-revelation we get in "Crossing Brooklyn Ferry" was unusual for the first two editions, but it did suggest a new direction for *Leaves of Grass:* the construction of a private, intimate voice, an interior in which the lyric would thrive.

Whitman's experiment with an autobiographical self occurred alongside the growing hunger for knowledge about the renowned. As England and the United States produced a cadre of trans-Atlantic celebrities, fans in both countries were possessed by the desire to understand such figures beyond their public personae. Unsatisfied with knowing the work of a Stowe or Lind, they viewed the celebrity less as a cultural producer than as a product. The antebellum celebrity, as Newbury writes, "was defined not by the audience's desire for his cultural productions or by the possibility of an economically profitable exchange between the celebrity and audience but rather by the audience's irrational drive to see, touch, hold, possess, and consume the celebrity body itself."[29] Celebrity status had less to do with one's merit or wealth than with the public's desire for private contact with public individuals. When fans harassed Lind in her hotel room in New York City, when crowds pressed into the courtroom to hear the details of the Forrests' divorce trial, they were helping to create a model of celebrity that emphasized the publicity of intimate knowledge.[30] Fed by the democratization of photography and a growing interest in personality, antebellum celebrity culture was marked by a desire to pierce through its own inauthenticity, to reach beyond the fabrications and mediations that both connected and separated the crowd from the persons it admired.

The celebrity-based lecture series that emerged after the Civil War responded to these desires. As the publisher turned promoter James Red-path explained, "We want more from a man or woman than books can give—the living voice, at least electric with enthusiasm or earnestness."[31] When a writer in the *Galaxy* compared "Star course" lectures with print, he focused on the medium's success in conveying human personality: "Lectures have also this advantage over books, that they give you not only the matter but the man—the soul behind the substance, the worker to-gether with his work. Print can never vie with personality; and one of the ends served by lectures is to put on exhibition people more or less il-lustrious."[32] In 1855, *Leaves of Grass* had claimed precisely these attributes as the foundation of American poetry, but even then, Whitman made these claims by asserting that his poems were different than poems, that his was an art that incorporated other cultural modes. He envisioned ways to put himself "on exhibition," metaphorically suggesting that readers encountered a speaker, a performer, or a rebellious auctioneer. With those metaphors came a corollary insistence that readers must see in those public figures a somatic presence and personality. "I pass so poorly with paper and types," he writes in "A Song for Occupations," "I must pass with the contact of bodies and souls" (*LG* 1855, 87). In short, Whitman developed a poetry that tried to escape the conditions of poetry in striving for a sense of immediacy.

The market for celebrity lectures in the 1870s grew out of the strong interest in public figures before the Civil War. The hoopla Barnum orga-nized around Jenny Lind's arrival in Manhattan—the welcoming parades, ticket-buying auctions, and charity performances—are part of American cultural lore. Indeed, when the English and American press caricatured the Jenny Lind affair, they depicted Barnum in the midst of blaring trum-pets, gaudy banners, and unruly, indiscriminate crowds. However, the showman was equally adept at creating for Lind a personal life with whom her audiences would identify. He hired N. P. Willis to write a biography of the singer that purported to provide special insight into both her talent and character. Stitching together articles he had previously published in the *Home Journal,* Willis mixed a nationalistic defense of Lindmania from its European detractors with an earnest revelation of the singer's "Private Habits and Manners." "[S]howing the celebrity off her pedestal," Willis confidently wrote, "will by no means diminish the interest of her recep-tion in America."[33] In fact, it did the reverse. Only months before her debut, *Harper's* published a profile of Lind that traced her rise from humble origins to international stardom. The profile began with a portrait of the singer as an impoverished, misunderstood child: "There was once a poor and plain little girl dwelling in a little room in Stockholm, the capitol of Sweden. She was a poor little girl indeed, then; she was lonely and neglected and would have been very unhappy, deprived of the kindness and care so necessary to a child if it had not been for a peculiar gift. The little girl had a fine voice, and in her loneliness, in trouble or in sorrow, she consoled herself by singing."[34] Although *Harper's* satirized the humbug over Jenny Lind, it eagerly extended that publicity to a sentimental rendering of her life. Invoking the sympathy of its readers, the article approaches its subject with the tenderness befitting a deserted little girl who has found consolation in song. We follow the birth of this artist through her lonely years studying as an *élève* in Paris (the author has the same fondness for the word that Whitman does) to her triumphant return to Sweden, the homeland she dearly loves. Like Willis's *Memoranda*, the profile personalizes the public figure Lind, providing a compelling narrative backdrop to her international acclaim.

In the mid-1850s, publishers produced a number of highly successful books that profiled well-known personalities or reveled in their private and even scandalous secrets. In March 1855, Fanny Fern's former publisher William Moulton published an exposé of the famous columnist, detailing with particular relish the divorce she had sought from her second husband.[35] Despite its unflattering portrait, the book actually increased Fern's popularity, and the publication of *Ruth Hall* in December of that year met with brisk sales. (The novel left out any reference to the failed marriage.) Perhaps one reason for the novel's success was that the Christmas season of 1855 was a particularly busy time for celebrity memoirs and biographies. Joining *Ruth Hall* as best sellers that season were James Parton's biography of Horace Greeley and the first edition of Barnum's autobiography.[36]

Whitman may have been trying to duplicate this successful timing when in December 1859 he published "A Child's Reminiscence" in Henry Clapp's weekly newspaper, the *New York Saturday Press*. Later titled "Out of the Cradle Endlessly Rocking," the poem was the poet's most intimate and seemingly autobiographical publication to date. Whitman and Clapp drew attention to the poem's appearance in the December 24 issue through a series of advertisements promoting it as the *Press*'s "Christmas present" to its readers. (The poet's handwritten draft of the advertisement has been preserved in the Berg Collection of the New York Public Library.) The poem recreates the poet's encounter with a pair of mockingbirds and the mournful aria one of them sings when his mate flies out over the ocean and does not return. As in many romantic works, Whitman's most prominent concern is the event's impact on the poet, the ways in which it transformed him into the soul that would write *Leaves of Grass*. Like the *Harper's* profile of Lind, the poem creates a biographical intimacy based on the consolation of song.

With its operatic lines and high sense of drama, the poem provides a compelling, almost numinous account of the poet's birth. Whitman invokes the "mystic play of shadows" and the ocean's "secret hissing" as the child seeks a "clew" that will help him understand the bird's disappearance (*LG* 1860, 269, 275, 276). Such images mark the scene as being fundamentally private and unknowable, and they therefore underscore the special, privileged nature of the poem's revelations. The poem translates the deathly clue the poet receives from the mockingbird's aria into a clue the audience receives about the poet's character. From the poem's beginning, Whitman would have his readers know that the experience produced a "thousand responses" in his heart and a "myriad thence-aroused words" (*LG* 1860, 269, 270). Describing himself at times in the third person and at others in the first, he is character and narrator, observer and participant, the child and the lyric *I*. This multiplication of the poet's identity heightens our attention to the transformative aspects of the experience, and rather than produce a fragmentary effect, it emphasizes the ways in which the poet's consciousness originated in the child's life.

As an etiology of the great American bard, the poem seems organized around the Wordsworthian principle that "the child is father of the man," but what Whitman celebrates in the weeping boy is the sensibility that produced *Leaves of Grass*.[37] When the bird sings its mournful dirge, the poet nominates himself as the only audience fit for such a song:

> He called on his mate,
> He poured forth the meanings which I, of all men, know.
>
> Yes, my brother, I know,
> The rest might not—but I have treasured every note.
>   (*LG* 1860, 271–72)

The importance of the experience lies in how it has fathered this singularly sympathetic poet. Others may overlook the song's significance, but the poet ostensibly wants the bird to know that he values every note.

My point here is not to downgrade the poem but to demonstrate how inextricable its intimacy is from the project of promoting *Leaves of Grass*. At the end of the poem, Whitman turns the bird's song into the defining moment of his life, and in the process, he rivals the she-bird as the song's principal addressee:

> Bird! (then said the boy's Soul,)
> Is it indeed toward your mate you sing? or is it mostly to me?
> For I that was a child, my tongue's use sleeping,
> Now that I have heard you,
> Now in a moment I know what I am for—I awake,
> And already a thousand singers—a thousand songs, clearer,
>   louder, more sorrowful than yours,
> A thousand warbling echoes have started to life within me,
> Never to die. (*LG* 1860, 275–76)

The poet places himself at the front of this scene of dramatic loss. As the mockingbird sings and the sea hisses, the entire setting collaborates on making this new poetic self. "O you demon," Whitman calls out to the bird, "singing by yourself—projecting me" (*LG* 1860, 276). He concludes the poem, "That strong and delicious word which, creeping to me my feet, / The sea whispered me" (*LG* 1860, 277). The syntax of the last sentence suggests that the experience has not just spoken to the poet; it has somehow *articulated* him, given him a fundamentally linguistic identity. The poet's sympathy with the natural world results in his bardic capacity to sing for the thousand others who warble inside him.

"Out of the Cradle" embeds its publicity within what is at heart a melodramatic conversion narrative. Among the shadows and moonbeams that have marked his mystical birth, the poet regards the bird as both a brother and a "demon," for its song transforms the sympathetic boy into the artist who suffers from his gifts: "The dusky demon aroused —the fire, the sweet hell within, / The unknown want, the destiny of me" (*LG* 1860, 276). Dickinson invites readers to see her soul at the white heat; Whitman allows them to gaze at "the sweet hell within." The autobiographical mode suggests a kind of revelatory personal confession. Ac-

cording to Helen Price, Whitman claimed that the episode actually occurred.[38] However, when the *Cincinnati Daily Commercial* attacked the
poem, he anonymously came to its defense, suggesting that the mocking-
bird—not the boy—was a persona for the author of *Leaves of Grass*.[39] The
poem's autobiographical frame reminds the public of the poet's values,
predilections, and astonishing musicality. Advertised as a present to the
Saturday Press's readers, the poem invites us to observe the poet before he
is conscious of being observed, to project ourselves into his past as a way
of understanding his present-day contributions.

EXPOSURE AND CONCEALMENT

"Out of the Cradle" appeared in the 1860 edition of *Leaves of Grass* along
with what is commonly regarded as Whitman's most revealing and confessional set of poems: the much-discussed Calamus cluster. Both works
fuse autobiography and publicity, though in contrast to the sustained
intensity of the childhood reminiscence, the forty-five lyrics that made up
the original Calamus actively and at times ironically suggest that their
intimacy is fleeting and unreliable. In Calamus 3, later titled "Whoever
You Are Now Holding Me in Hand," Whitman writes,

> I will certainly elude you,
> Even while you should think you had unquestionably caught
>   me, behold!
> Already you see I have escaped from you. (*LG* 1860, 346)

Though on the surface they caution readers against identifying too closely
with the poet, the lines underscore that desire, turning Whitman into a tantalizing, mysterious figure whose self-revelations seem to contain pre-
ciously tantric significance. The poems' coy indirection creates a zone of
hushed and fragile intimacy, making its revelations seem personal and unguarded. Far from signaling a retreat from public life, the Calamus poems
oscillate between exposure and concealment, between public and private
selves. His experiments with the confessional mode reveal the falseness of
such oppositions, for through Calamus, publicity and intimacy feed off each
other, inspiring a private lyric address that we are privileged to overhear.

　　The central narrative of the Calamus poems has been clear since the
1950s. Having reached a personal crisis that corresponded to the national crisis over slavery, Whitman backs away from his public persona,

preferring instead the seclusion and intimacy of private relationships. At the center of this movement toward the interior is the poet's renunciation of fame for a world of male camaraderie and affection. In the past decades, attention to this world has grown considerably, as readers have focused on the homosexual desire at the heart of Whitman's notion of adhesiveness. Although their emphases have differed, they have generally agreed that the values of this private affectionate world are meant to be an antidote to the Union's imminent collapse. Rather than the states being held together by lawyers, papers, and arms, Whitman proposes a stronger union grounded in the invincible power of male friendship, what Erkkila has characterized as the "unpublished standard of homosexual love."[40] Reynolds explains that the Calamus poems "were at once intensely 'private,' in the sense of retreating from institutions he thought were ineffective or corrupt, and 'public,' in the sense of replacing them with the kind of passionate friendship other reformers of the day were elucidating."[41]

Interest in the public dimensions of Calamus has led to the politicization of the poems. Thus when Erkkila in a more recent essay writes about the poem's fusion of intimacy and publicity in Calamus, she focuses on the ways in which the cluster "seeks to express, enact, and incite new 'types' of 'manly attachment' and 'athletic love' as the source and ground of a fully realized democratic culture."[42] Calamus does not privatize homosexuality, she argues, but instead makes it the foundation of public democracy. Erkkila's understanding of publicity is firmly rooted in the critical forms of publicity that in the 1840s began to include the manipulative kinds of social display common today. As in *Leaves of Grass,* the Calamus cluster is suffused with two distinct meanings of the concept. The intimacy Whitman invokes may have the political purpose that Erkkila and others suggest, but the only way to achieve that purpose is through a promotional campaign, the carefully manipulative act of selling the poet's personality.

In positing the Calamus sentiment as a genuine, albeit utopian, counterpart to the divided public world, critics have essentially followed the terms that Whitman himself set forth. The poet's prophecy that affection "shall solve every one of the problems of freedom" grows out of his self-portrait as a solitary singer pining for lovers and comrades ("For You O Democracy," *LG* 1860, 349). This interpretation mirrors the composition process, for as a cluster, Calamus evolved out of the twelve-poem "Live Oak, with Moss" sequence that Whitman had privately drafted in the late

1850s. Although there have been intense disagreements about its portrait of homosexuality, the early sequence clearly suggests deep personal sorrow after a failed love affair, a sorrow that the poet offers as a personal confession. It is only later that the poet contextualized this introspection with his endorsement of democratic camaraderie.

This originating intimacy bears reexamination in the Calamus cluster —not only because it offers a gratifying model of politics by other means, but because it is indispensable to the poet's publicity. From the cluster's beginning, "In Paths Untrodden," Whitman promotes the poems as a retreat from public life. As a variation of his well-known symbol of grass, he situates the calamus plant in remote and isolated terrain:

> In paths untrodden,
> In the growths by margins of pond-waters,
> Escaped from the life that exhibits itself,
> From all the standards hitherto published—from the pleasures,
>   profits, conformities,
> Which too long I was offering to feed my Soul . . .
> Here, by myself, away from the clank of the world,
> Tallying and talked to here by tongues aromatic,
> No longer abashed—for in this secluded spot I can respond as I
>   would not dare elsewhere,
> Strong upon me the life that does not exhibit itself, yet contains
>   all the rest. (*LG* 1860, 341)

The opening lines create a remarkable sense of place, a sense that the poem exists in a *here* that is secluded from the rest of the world. The poet has "escaped" from public life and personal display. He speaks from a marginal and safe retreat where he will reveal secrets that he has kept from the public at large. The rhetoric of intimacy is so strong that it may obscure the irony of Whitman's publicizing Calamus precisely because it is free of publicity. As Terry Mulcaire explains, "what appears to be a movement towards a radically private, unitary state . . . turns out to be a move from one form of publication to another, equivalent form."[43] The poet's intimate relation with his readers enhances the value of the poems themselves, distinguishing them as being uniquely authentic compared to his platform efforts. Perhaps more important, these opening lines transform Whitman's readers from individuals engaged in a public exercise to highly privileged confidants sharing in an ostensibly private exchange. "[I]n this secluded spot I can respond as I would not dare elsewhere," Whitman writes, as if his revelations were neither as crafted nor public as the rest of *Leaves of Grass.* The intimacy of Calamus is simultaneously constructed with the advertisement of that intimacy.

This doubleness is particularly apparent in Whitman's purported rejection of fame. As might be expected from a cluster of poems dedicated to preserving and delineating interior space, Calamus makes regular reference to the hollowness of popular praise, elevating the genuine affection of comrades over the glories of celebrity. When Whitman surveys an array of accomplishments in Calamus 28—the fame of heroes, generals, and presidents—all seem unfulfilling next to the brotherhood of manly love ("When I Peruse the Conquer'd Fame," *LG* 1860, 370). The prevalence of this theme has led many readers to take Whitman's pronouncements in Calamus literally. Braudy, who is perhaps our most distinguished and learned commentator on fame, has seen the cluster as Whitman's obsessive rejection of a cultural system rooted in recognition and praise.[44] The appearance of that rejection, however, ultimately foregrounds fame as a useful, viable category in which to understand the real man. The lyric becomes all the more powerful because it rejects earthly glory for the satisfactions of intimate address.

Calamus 11, "When I Heard at the Close of the Day," invokes fame as a backdrop for understanding Whitman's interest in love, but he emerges from the poem as a man grown skeptical of his cultural legitimacy:

> When I heard at the close of the day how my name had been
> received with plaudits in the capitol, still it was not a happy
> night for me that followed;
> And else, when I caroused, or when my plans were
> accomplished, still I was not happy . . .

What makes the poet happy is not the fulfillment of his project, nor the fame that he has accrued, but the intimate moment shared with his lover as he lay awake in a seaside room:

> And that night, while all was still, I heard the waters roll slowly
> continually up the shores,
> I heard the hissing rustle of the liquid and sands, as directed to
> me, whispering, to congratulate me,

For the one I love most lay sleeping by me under the same cover
   in the cool night,
In the stillness, in the autumn moonbeams, his face was
   inclined toward me,
And his arm lay lightly around my breast—And that night I was
   happy. (*LG* 1860, 357–58)

As Greenspan has noted, "The familiar Whitman circling action is here all inward, self-contained," with the poem moving from the external world of the capitol to the internal world of the soul.[45] In the process, the poem reintegrates Whitman into the natural world, as he moves from psychological stasis—"still I was not happy"—to psychological calm, the stillness of the night reflecting his new emotional state.

Though the poem clearly encourages readers to think in this vein, the sea's congratulations do not cancel out the capitol's praise. Rather, the image of Whitman's fame permeates the entire work, turning this narrative of emotional fulfillment into a momentary glimpse into the private life of a renowned and celebrated man. The opening line may allude to a positive review Whitman had received from the *Washington Daily National Intelligencer*, which in 1856 praised his work and concluded that he was "the 'representative-man' of the 'roughs.' "[46] If indeed he was referring to the review, he wildly exaggerates the event, turning it into a formal, almost official, celebration of his accomplishment: a newspaper has not merely recommended his book; the capitol has applauded his name. Whether real or fictional, the fame Whitman repudiates serves the purpose of establishing the poet as the recipient of public acclaim. Though they profess disinterest, the lines suggest that Whitman had attained the legitimacy he wished for in other parts of *Leaves of Grass*. Indeed, when Whitman announces that he would rather be remembered as a lover of comrades than as a poet in Calamus 10, he couches his desire in the explicitly public terms of portraiture, fame, and posterity ("Recorders Ages Hence," *LG* 1860, 356). At the thought of death, Keats saw love and fame sinking into nothingness. Although he initially presents them in conflict, Whitman joins these desires in imagining a way to counter death's annihilating effects. As Tenny Nathanson has put it, the poet poignantly recalls "what feels like a specially valued intimacy," but he carefully situates that intimacy within our recognition of his value as an icon and personality.[47]

Whitman's exploration of the psychological toll inflicted by fame is central to his realization of a new lyric voice in the 1860 *Leaves of Grass*. The world becomes a platform for the poet's self-doubt, a check against the broad promotional orations of his earlier poems. In "Bardic Symbols" (later titled "As I Ebb'd with the Ocean of Life"), Whitman's desire to impress himself on others turns into a struggle between his public and private identities. The poem discloses the psychological division of a man who sees himself removed from his own public performance:

> Oppressed with myself that I have dared to open my mouth,
> Aware now, that, amid all the blab whose echoes recoil upon me,
>   I have not once had the least idea who or what I am,
> But that before all my insolent poems the real ME still stands
>   untouched, untold, altogether unreached,
> Withdrawn far, mocking me with mock-congratulatory signs
>   and bows,
> With peals of distant ironical laughter at every word I have
>   written or shall write,
> Striking me with insults till I fall helpless upon the sand.
>   (*LG* 1860, 196–97)

The poem records a moment of painful self-recognition in which he comes to know the emptiness and superficiality of hype. "Song of Myself" marveled at the "blab of the pave" (*LG* 1855, 31). Five years later, Whitman casts a cold despairing eye at the blab of his alter ego.

In its highly stylized and dramatic fashion, "Bardic Symbols" seems to offer a direct and unmediated view of the poet's emotional state. What readers encounter in the 1860 edition is the real poet, the one who suffers beneath the burden of his publicity. In his gesture toward "the real ME," Whitman anticipates the work of later nineteenth-century writers such as Jack London and Mark Twain, who treated their audiences, as Braudy describes it, to "endless Chinese boxes, each one claiming to be the really personal under the last seemingly personal."[48] Whitman presents his revelations as the antithesis of self-promotion. If readers have grown skeptical of public imagery, if they have seen how hype can distort their perception of well-known public figures, then what they can value in the 1860 *Leaves of Grass* is its window into a genuine person. The poem appeared in the April 1860 issue of the *Atlantic*, certainly the most prestigious magazine publication of Whitman's early career. For all of the platform confidence in *Leaves of Grass*, one wonders whether the poem's exploration of self-doubt was responsible for its highly successful placement.

The intimacy that many of the 1860 poems cultivate is part of the identification at the heart of celebrity. In Calamus, Whitman problematizes the private experience of renown by questioning the false nature of public performance. Indeed, the illusory value of fame emerges as one of the touchstones of Whitman's intimacy. In Calamus 40, he observes the shadow of himself chattering and chaffering on the public stage and begins to doubt his identity ("That Shadow My Likeness," *LG* 1860, 376). The experience is common among people who perform their own celebrity. Mark Twain described his public identity as "my double, my partner in duality, the other and wholly independent personage who resides in me."[49] While Twain acknowledged this partner in the privacy of his notebooks, Whitman, stunningly, made it part of his aesthetic practice. The poet's questions heighten his authenticity, depicting a seemingly private self who exists beyond the tiresome public charade. In these carols, he concludes, "I never doubt whether that is really me" (*LG* 1860, 376). That Calamus's portrait is as publicly oriented as anything in the Chants Democratic series does not seem to trouble the poet. He invokes the artifice of privacy to counter the artifice of publicity, but both, in effect, are inverse expressions of the same promotional energy.

The backdrop of discarded fame plays an important role in Whitman's pioneering use of the confessional mode. Byron and Shelley received such wide attention that they were forced to evade their celebrity before an eager public, publishing their books anonymously, for example, while still acknowledging their authorship.[50] In 1860, Whitman's situation was the reverse: with a small bohemian following, he depicted himself as evading the trials of publicity on a well-lit public stage. No matter how intimate they initially appear, Whitman's confessions double back upon themselves, leading us to recall the degree to which they have been performed. As Greenspan has commented, very often in Calamus, "One mask would peel off, only to reveal, often as not, another one beneath it."[51] Although not part of the original "Live Oak" cluster, Calamus 15 is fervently confessional in that the poet addresses the blood, tears, and other bodily fluids that "stain" every song he sings ("Trickle Drops," *LG* 1860, 361). Whitman initially titled the poem "Confession Drops," but the poem confesses nothing but the act of confession itself. For this reason, its claims to intimacy may seem somewhat forced and undeveloped. But the trope of bloodstained words radiates into other parts of the cluster, proclaiming the special nature of their revelations. Expressed in bodily form, Whitman's confession turns the lyric into a relic of the self. The words on the page become meaningful because of their somatic connection to the poet. Calamus encourages the same sentiment that would inspire Whitman's English followers to treasure anything associated with his person. The stuffed canary, the broken fountain pen, the "confession drops" of Calamus, all these things take their meaning from their connection with the poet's body.

Its claims to transparency notwithstanding, Calamus's promotional vigor rests on the complex erotic interplay between exposure and concealment. For every image of a bloodstained word, there is one cautioning readers not to trust what they have read. "But these leaves conning, you con at peril," Whitman warns in Calamus 3. "For these leaves, and me, you will not understand" (*LG* 1860, 346). Kennedy's reaction to the publishing of Whitman's autopsy reproached the poet's executors for not maintaining the mystery that comes with both decorum and concealment.[52] Unlike his executors, Whitman understood that the illusion of his intimacy would only be valued if it seemed rare, unintended, and difficult to possess. When he reads "the biography famous," he praises the cunning soul (both his soul and others') for keeping its secret so well. The allusion to secrets tantalizes readers with the knowledge that there is more to Whitman than initially appears. The "faint clews and indirections" address an audience he hoped would be eager for information about his "real life" and personality, though the poem strongly questions whether a book could capture the particularity of any man's experience.[53]

Faced with such coy expressions of intimacy, critics have understandably looked to Calamus for insights into Whitman's personal life. From Reynolds to Schmidgall to Loving, recent biographers have tried to discover the details of Whitman's sexuality by plumbing the poems' vision of a nation grounded in the camaraderie and erotics of same-sex love.[54] The neglected topic of Whitman's homosexuality makes such efforts laudable, but Calamus does not expose for us what Whitman felt he had to conceal. The cluster's faint clues may be less significant in shielding the poet from a homophobic world than they are in establishing the poems' appeal; they sensationalize the poet's inner life, attracting speculation about his erotic experience. This critical tendency is especially clear in recent efforts to see the handwritten "Live Oak, with Moss" sequence as possessing more authenticity than the published Calamus cluster.[55] When we look at the poems for insights into the poet's life, when we prize them for their revelation of a secret sexuality, we seek to break the barrier of publicity that separates us from him. Such inquiries into Whitman's personality put us in the position of being both critics and fans.

CONSTITUTING THE FAN

Calamus emerges from a culture that was adapting to the new significance of publicity. As midcentury audiences grew distrustful of the public figures they encountered in newspapers and politics, they became interested in stories and profiles that placed these men and women in distinctly private settings. Amid his discussion of concerts, negotiations, and charity contributions, Willis follows Lind to various villas and apartments where we see her kindness to humble admirers and her distaste for fashionable society.[56] The authenticity seemingly afforded by such profiles was consistent, as Ponce de Leon explains it, with a prevailing cultural belief that, among the famous and nonfamous alike, the "real self . . . was a private self, one that men and women protected from view and revealed only under special circumstances."[57] Calamus directly appeals to this belief in its portrait of a poet who appears before the reader exposed, revealed, and authentic.

The "special circumstances" under which Calamus suggests its revelations extend beyond the poet's private, confessional language. In earlier poems, Whitman had depicted his readers as needing to be awakened. To this familiar mode of address, he added the fantasy that his audience had grown inquisitive about him, that it had developed a hunger to know more about his personality. In Calamus 16, he wonders who is reading his book and what they have learned about his past life ("Who Is Now Reading This?" *LG* 1860, 361). In Calamus 12, he asks, "Are you the new person drawn to me?" addressing the reader as a personal admirer (*LG* 1860, 358). In Calamus 3 he tells readers that they are merely "candidates" for his affection before warning them that if they would know him, they must contend with danger, stealth, and his own unreliability (*LG* 1860,

346). The poems present the author as a source of intrigue and inquiry, a figure who eludes our comprehension:

> Do you see no further than this façade—this smooth and
>   tolerant manner of me?
> Do you suppose yourself advancing on real ground toward a real
>   heroic man?
> Have you no thought, O dreamer, that it may be all maya,
>   illusion? O the next step may precipitate you! (Calamus 12,
>   *LG* 1860, 358)

The lines encase Whitman in the mystery of his mediation, creating both the need and desire for intimacy. The poet warns us that we will struggle to get beyond his illusions, but such warnings simply pique our interest in the "real heroic man" who may—or may not—be waiting for us.

Calamus strategically makes the prospect of intimacy appear both implausible and real. In "Song of Myself," Whitman declared that he was either beneath our boots or walking by our side; in 1860, he described the poet's affection as a tantalizing dream. Calamus 3 warns the poet's "novitiates" that their path is so "long and exhausting" that they have little chance of achieving their goal. "Release me now, before troubling yourself any further," Whitman commands. "Put me down, and depart on your way" (*LG* 1860, 345). Such lines promote the rare and exceptional nature of the poet's camaraderie. They sensationalize the poet's intimacy to the extent that any difficulty seems worthwhile next to the poet's promise that alone on a beach or high on a hill, he might someday recognize us with "the comrade's long-dwelling kiss or the new husband's kiss" (*LG* 1860, 345). The metaphor turns reading into a fantasy in which Whitman will select a true and genuine comrade from among his many admirers. Readers not only have the opportunity to remark upon the poet, but just possibly, the poet might remark upon them as well. Alone on an island or sailing on the sea, he will kiss the few who have followed him with particular devotion, stamina, and goodwill.

The intensity with which Whitman promoted this intimacy was so strong and commanding that some readers took it for being real. Frequently described as Whitman's "English admirer," Anne Gilchrist was one such reader, and her story reveals the substantial power of his address. After losing her husband, Alexander, in 1861, Gilchrist completed

and published his unfinished biography of William Blake, while also rais-
ing their four children. In 1869, she discovered Whitman in William
Rossetti's English edition of the poems and experienced a profound revolution of consciousness, a revolution that only deepened after she read an
unexpurgated version of the 1867 *Leaves of Grass*. Gilchrist wrote an elegant and important defense of Whitman's poems in the *Radical*, but her
fascination with the poet was deeply personal. Having counted "Whoever
You Are Now" among her favorite poems, Gilchrist presented herself as
being precisely the reader to whom Whitman should grant the "new
husband's kiss."[58]

In September 1871, Gilchrist wrote the first of a series of passionate
letters to the poet that confessed her deep love and willingness to bear
him a child. Whitman did not respond to the first two letters, so she sent a
third that made clear her belief that she was the true recipient of his
poems: "Do not say I am forward, or that I lack pride because I tell this
love to thee who have never sought or made sign of desiring to seek
me. . . . Besides, it is not true thou has not sought or loved me. For when I
read the divine poems I feel all folded round in thy love: I feel so often as if
thou wast pleading so passionately for the love of the woman that can
understand thee—that I know not how to bear the yearning answering
tenderness that fills my breast."[59] The letter prompted a response from
Whitman, and a steady correspondence ensued in which Whitman acknowledged Gilchrist's special friendship while he also tried to curb her
romantic attachment. Undeterred by the poet's lack of interest, Gilchrist
eventually moved her family from London to Philadelphia with the "deep,
strong faith" that their relationship would blossom and that she and her
children would be "shone upon, vivified, strengthened by" his presence.[60]
Upon meeting Whitman, Gilchrist quickly realized that he would never
match her ardor, and the two settled into what would become a lifelong
friendship.

Thinking about Gilchrist as one of the first Whitmaniacs is an important step in correcting the tendency to see her infatuation merely as a
comic chapter in the life of a gay man. Though she understood her attraction in the Victorian discourse of husband and wife, Gilchrist's combination of spiritual and sexual obsession draws on the same eroticized energy
that binds celebrities and their followers.[61] Exhibiting the kind of devotion
associated with the most zealous of modern-day fans, she had fallen in

love with Whitman's illusion, and she radically altered her life to become close to and noticed by him. Celebrities and their followers have what psychologists describe as a parasocial relationship.[62] Fans may feel that they "know" a star, but they almost always comprehend that that relation exists outside of any social context. Although they may fantasize about such encounters, they rarely expect to be recognized themselves. In insisting on her connection to Whitman, in reading the poems as if they were destined for her, Gilchrist challenged the boundaries that separate public figures from their followers. She claimed the right to turn the illusory intimacy at the heart of *Leaves of Grass* into a substantially personal bond.

In the decades surrounding the Civil War, many assumed the kind of intimacy with the famous that Gilchrist did with Whitman. The sweeping language and heated passion of Gilchrist's letters are consistent with the marriage proposals and confessions of love that celebrities received from their admirers in the nineteenth century (and continue to receive today). Writing to the Norwegian violinist Ole Bull in 1847, one fan expressed a sense of personal completion she received from the musician:

> I have never found one to love with my whole soul . . . and perhaps it is well, for I should die and be consumed with the intensity of that passion, but friendship is as beautiful as love and that I cannot live without, though even here I have never been satisfied. I have never met a nature who could return to me the half of what I could give, and so my life has been one long famine and my heart the cannibal of itself. If I seem to you too enthusiastic in my expressions of friendship for you, remember that my heart has been frozen for a whole lifetime and it must naturally overflow on meeting one so large and so noble as your own. Ah, Ole Bull! If I could tell you the history of my life, so cold, so barren without and so volcanic within![63]

Stars from the stage, the newspapers, and the lecture circuit received similarly passionate letters from their admirers. As Baker describes it, antebellum celebrities offered "the semblance of an extraordinary friendship" that many fans interpreted romantically.[64]

In 1872, Whitman warned Gilchrist that she had fallen in love with an illusion: "Dear friend," he wrote. "You must not construct such an unauthorized & imaginary ideal Figure, & call it W.W. and so devotedly invest your loving nature in it. The actual W.W. is a very plain personage, & entirely unworthy such devotion."[65] Such warnings meant little to a reader who not only had accepted the poet's claims to intimacy but had begun to envision Whitman as the fulfillment of her desires. By the 1870s, Anglo-American culture was still charting the new terrain of stardom and renown, and as Newbury has explained, audiences tended to focus not on the products created by celebrities but on "the act of very literal self-presentation and the audience's pure pleasure in and valuation of the act of consumption."[66] In recent years, we have learned a lot about the ways in which fans appropriate cultural products to fashion their own meaning. Scholars such as Michel de Certeau, Harry Jenkins, and Constance Penley have suggested that fans do not passively receive popular culture—instead, they tactically re-create and, in one sense, *produce* popular culture to suit their particular needs.[67]

Thinking about fans as cultural producers becomes especially complicated when we turn to Whitman. Throughout *Leaves of Grass*, he encourages us to make the poems our own. In "Song of Myself," he commands: "You shall not look through my eyes either, nor take things from me, / You shall listen to all sides and filter them from your self" (*LG* 1855, 26). The poet expects his followers to transform his work, to appropriate *Leaves of Grass* in the same way that students should strive to outdo their masters (*LG* 1855, 81). Whitman's openness to innovation makes him a difficult figure to rework. Not only does he instruct readers to reject him, he is so large and comprehensive that he seems both to produce and contain any act of subversion. When we look at Gilchrist and her Whitmaniac peers, however, their principal act of transgression seems to have been reading *Leaves of Grass* devotedly. Gilchrist was on solid ground when she read Whitman as a fan. She didn't stitch together her image of the poet as much as she took his self-mythologizing literally. Whitman objected to Gilchrist's "unauthorized" portrait of himself, but clearly he had authored the feelings she conveyed back to him.

For decades biographers have puzzled over the fact that of all the works in *Leaves of Grass,* the ones that most moved Gilchrist were the Calamus poems, the love poems he directed toward other men.[68] But in filtering their revelations through the language of secrecy, the poems eroticize the poet's relationship to any reader who regards the book affectionately. Later titled "A Glimpse," Calamus 29 offers a particularly valuable example of how Whitman sensationalized his intimacy by offering a fleeting—and thus precious—look into his private life. The poem invites the audience to view a carefully staged moment of male camaraderie:

> One flitting glimpse, caught through an interstice,
> Of a crowd of workmen and drivers in a bar-room, around the
>   stove, late of a winter night—And I unremarked, seated in a
>   corner;
> Of a youth who loves me, and whom I love, silently approaching,
>   and seating himself near, that he may hold me by the hand;
> A long while, amid the noises of coming and going—of drinking
>   and oath and smutty jest,
> There we two, content, happy in being together, speaking little,
>   perhaps not a word. (*LG* 1860, 371)

The distinctly masculine and working-class setting becomes the backdrop for the poet's quiet communion with the boy. Amid the din of joking and drinking, he makes contact with a single individual, and both experience the calming, emotional fulfillment that he celebrated in Calamus 11 ("When I Heard at the Close of the Day").

Whitman frames the scene carefully, using both space (the gap in the wall or interstice) and time (the hurried observation) to underscore the special, privileged nature of this vision. Both images would seem to indicate the opposite of publicity in suggesting that the public has been excluded from this view. In "The Two Vaults," Whitman looked from the vantage of a basement saloon on the busy scene on Broadway. In Calamus 29, readers peer into a barroom that is only briefly accessible to them. The fact that the poet sits in the corner "unremarked" only further enhances the scene's authenticity, though of course he reverses that condition as soon as he mentions it. Of particular note is the word *flitting*, which Whitman used in Calamus 22 ("To a Stranger") to describe the movement of a stranger passing him on a city street. As the two men flit by each other, Whitman is filled with affection and desire. Calamus 29 retains the sexual dimensions of this encounter but applies it to the quality of observation. The poem eroticizes the observers' hurried view, offering a kind of antebellum peep show in which we look through the interstice into a scene charged with male sexuality. Drawing heavily on Jacques Lacan, Michael Moon has argued that the poem creates a kind of "split subjectivity" between Whitman and the observer. The poet sits in the corner focused on the boy. Mutually desired and desiring, the couple shares an intensive homoerotic affection that anchors the poem.[69]

But what exactly does the observer desire? Amid the sexual jests, the bonhomie, the quiet moment of intimacy, the poem anticipates the observer's thrill at moving beyond the poet's facade. Unlike the boy seated next to the poet, readers gaze upon a scene in which they can only imaginatively participate. Outside the barroom, outside the circle of familiarity, we are limited to the interstice that the poem has opened for us. The poem rests on the fantasy that we will want to exchange our "flitting glimpse" for the steady, direct contact that the poet shares with the boy. We desire to be recognized as the poet's one true friend, to be drawn into this genuinely personal moment of affectionate camaraderie. The scene's eroticism lies in the suggestion that we have not quite rent the public veil; our desire for an authentic Whitman has been only partially satisfied.

It is easy to imagine a reader such as Gilchrist coming upon Calamus 29 and replacing the boy with herself. Publicizing privacy and establishing intimacy, the Calamus poems encouraged precisely the kind of desire that they produced in this English admirer. "Among the the Multitude," originally numbered Calamus 41, profoundly appealed to Gilchrist, for it explicitly promoted the illusion that Whitman was speaking to her:

> 1. Among the men and women, the multitude, I perceive one,
>   picking me out by secret and divine signs,
> Acknowledging none else—not parent, wife, husband, brother,
>   child, any nearer than I am;
> Some are baffled—But that one is not—that one knows me.
>
> 2. Lover and perfect equal!
> I meant that you should discover me so, by my faint
>   indirections,
> And I, when I meet you, mean to discover you by the like in you.
>   (LG 1860, 376)

The poem cultivates the fantasy that one of us will see beyond the interstitial view, that one of us will replace the quiet young man, that one of us will be fit enough to hold the poet's hand. The trope is now a staple of the public relations industry, but in the 1870s, it was new and powerful enough to convince this mother of four that, through secrets and indirections, she had discovered the Walt Whitman that no one else knew. In time, she hoped, he would discover the same in her.[70]

For a man so immersed in his own publicity, Whitman was surprisingly naïve about its most intimate effects. In old age, he considered himself a failure for never connecting with the masses, but he found it easy to dismiss individuals who professed great devotion to his work. Gilchrist's fundamental intelligence and respectability made her difficult to reject, and in the end, he elegized her in " 'Going Somewhere' " as "My science-friend, my noblest woman-friend" (WPP, 627). In sharp contrast was his ready rejection of Susan Garnet Smith, a woman from Hartford who had written the poet an erotic fan letter in 1860. Like Gilchrist, Smith confessed her deepest sexual desires:

> Know Walt Whitman that I am a woman! I am not beautiful, but I love you! I am thirty-two years old. I am one of the workers of the world. A friend carefully lends me Leaves of Grass for a day. Stealing an hour from labor I take it out for a walk. I do not know *what* I carry in my arms pressed close to my side and bosom! I feel a strange new sympathy! a mysterious delicious thrill! . . .
>
> Know Walt Whitman that thou hast a child for me! A noble beautiful perfect manchild. I charge you my love not to give it to another woman. The world demands it! It is not for you and me, *is our child,* but for the world. My womb is clean and pure. It is ready for thy child my love. . . . Our boy my love! Do you not already love him? He must be begotten on a mountain top, in the open air. Not in *lust,* not in mere gratification of sensual passion, but in holy ennobling pure strong deep glorious passionate broad universal love. I charge you to prepare my love.
>
> I love you, I love you, come, come. Write. (WWC, 4:312–13)

Whitman wrote "?insane asylum" on the cover of Smith's envelope, but Traubel defended Smith's fanaticism with unusual fervor. "It sounds like somebody who's taking you at your word," he argued. "You should have been the last man in the world to write 'insane' on that envelope. . . . her letter itself is extraordinary in what it offers, in what it imposes" (WWC, 4:313).

Traubel saw that Whitman's merger of intimacy and publicity demanded Smith's response. If Whitman envisioned a kiss on a hilltop, then Smith would invite him to make love on a mountain summit. If he boasted of his power to jet the stuff of future republics, then she would provide him with a fertile womb (*LG* 1855, 71). Susan Garnet Smith was profoundly influenced by the things Whitman had said about himself, and it was his professions of intimacy that led to her zealously presumptuous correspondence. Traubel's comments reveal a deep understanding of this relationship. "Isn't it crazy?" Whitman asked—to which Traubel replied, "No: it's Leaves of Grass" (*WWC*, 4:313).

CHAPTER FIVE

Campaigns

POLITICS AND THE SUBLIME

AMONG WALT WHITMAN'S PAPERS at the time of his death was an 1849 article from the *Edinburgh Review* titled "The Vanity and the Glory of Literature."[1] The article describes the explosion of print culture in the first half of the nineteenth century and speculates on the possible consequences it would have on British society. The author lamented that facing an astonishing number of choices, people might read in a desultory manner, moving from book to book without design or purpose. Worse yet, they might indulge in the desire to gain "encyclopedic knowledge" and simply sample the learning represented across a variety of fields (150). Certainly the reign of the universal scholar had passed, the author conceded, but taking its place he saw the emergence of the minute philosopher, the specialist who had little interest in connecting his work with general truths (151). More than any of these consequences, the author worried about the plight of good books when surrounded by so many competitors. Struck by the mortality of genius, he wondered which books would survive and which would enter oblivion as this already prodigious mass of texts multiplied over the years.

We would not initially expect the young Walt Whitman to be sympathetic to such concerns, for in the decades before the Civil War, he regularly championed America's production of newspapers, magazines, and popular books. Referring to the nation's twelve thousand print shops, three thousand newspapers, and countless adventure stories, novels, and biographies, he had confidently written Ralph Waldo Emerson in 1856: "All current nourishments to literature serve" (*WPP*, 1329). As evidenced by his many annotations and markings, however, Whitman read the article carefully and returned to it both before and after the 1855 publication of *Leaves of Grass*. The commentary occurs throughout the text, but it is most densely concentrated on those pages that address questions of posterity. When the author proclaimed, "Hardy must those be who shall venture to hope for the *permanent* attention of mankind!" Whitman not only underlined the statement, he drew a hand in the margins that pointed to it as well. When the author mourned the "beautiful poetry" and "thousand bright names" that will be "forgotten in the crowd," Whitman again marked it with a pointing hand (155). Borrowed from the practice of antebellum newspapers and advertisements, these hands—along with the associated commentary—reveal an ambitious young writer eagerly consuming advice about how to achieve immortality.[2]

An especially revealing annotation occurs midway through the article when the author replies to Benjamin Disraeli's assertion that a philosopher "would consent to lose *any* poet to regain a historian." Whitman's response was twofold, and he wrote in the margin, "Then poets must arise to make future D'Israeli's unable to say this" and underneath it in a different pen, "Why the best poets are the *real history*" (158). The idea that poets are the true historians, that a Homer or Virgil could supply the ages with a more genuine and universal history than their scholastic counterparts, is common enough. Whitman's initial reaction merits more attention, though, for it suggests that at first he agreed with Disraeli's evaluation. Rather than attack the statesman for his lack of literary understanding, the poet accepted Disraeli's opinion and quite significantly shifted his attention to the task facing poetry. Poets must learn to rival historians as the most esteemed writers in a community. Poetry must be more accountable as a genre, so that figures such as Disraeli would see its authors differently. Whitman saw in Disraeli's remark both a contest and a challenge: poetry must prove its superiority to other forms of discourse; poets must convince the public of their value and vitality.

The marginalia is indicative of Whitman's political grasp of celebrity and his sense that poets must prove their worth by campaigning for

cultural legitimacy. What matters to Whitman is not a philosophical rank-
ing of genres (nor its corollary suggestion of transcendent, hierarchical
categories), but the capacity for poetry to compete with other genres, for it
to be selected by people such as Disraeli as the most desirable and steadfast form of discourse. Whitman's annotations appear to have been made
in 1854 and 1856 and thus are roughly contemporaneous with his declaration, "The proof of a poet is that his country absorbs him as affectionately
as he has absorbed it" (*LG* 1855, 24). Taken together, the annotation and
pronouncement form two parts of a premise underlying Whitman's career: if countries can prove poets by absorbing them affectionately, then
poets must arise to capture that affection. The burden of recognition
shifts to the poet rather than the audience. As printing in the nineteenth
century became more efficient and productive, poets faced competition
from writers in both their own time and the future. As the republic of
letters transformed itself into a liberal and capitalist democracy, they
could not assume positions of prominence: they had to rely on rhetoric,
salesmanship, and persuasion.[3] Like their political counterparts, they
would have to achieve their office through the quality of their works and
the effectiveness of their campaigns.

Amid the many studies of the poet's politics, there is little discussion
of the need in a democracy to canvass the public in search of supporters
and votes. Whitman's conception of power and his response to various
power-related issues have received more attention than his thinking about
elections themselves. And yet, the importance of competition and pol-
iticking was fundamental to the poet's appreciation of democracy. "Always America will be agitated and turbulent," he wrote Emerson in the
"letter" he appended to the 1856 *Leaves of Grass*. "This day it is taking
shape, not to be less so, but to be more so, stormily, capriciously, on native
principles, with such vast proportions of parts! As for me, I love screaming, wrestling, boiling-hot days" (*WPP*, 1335–36). It was in the turbulence
of American politics, in the screaming and wrestling of its citizens and
parties, that Whitman saw the animating energy of democratic society. As
he both experienced and celebrated it, democracy depended on a carefully
structured competition, a national ritual that began in arrogance and
culminated in "moral grandeur": "What is the philosophy of American
politics? Out of the chaos of vulgar excitements and selfish aims and
automatic spasms, that make the [content?] of one of our national elec-

tions, beginning at first the primaries, continued in the great nominating conventions, and on through the tumultuous canvass running through five or six months, and culminating in the moral grandeur of the singularly quiet national election day—What is there I say beneath all these that may serve to illustrate the great dicta of history and philosophy & the Deific purpose, the finale of all."[4] Though wary of political ambition, Whitman viewed the electoral system with wonderment and pride. Although somewhat confusing in this notebook entry, the questions do not express skepticism about a political process emanating from "vulgar excitements and selfish aims." Rather, they pose the personal challenge of how he might illustrate that system as the fulfillment of human history.

Although Whitman would eventually conclude that democracy required the unifying force of spiritual and physical camaraderie, his enthusiasm for elections and electioneering lasted into old age. Alluding to the brass bands and drum beats that marked a Camden political rally, Traubel was amazed to find that the poet had been following the intricacies of the 1889 New Jersey gubernatorial campaign (*WWC*, 6:97).[5] The significance Whitman saw in elections is especially apparent in *Democratic Vistas* (1871). "What is more dramatic," he wrote, "than the spectacle we have seen repeated, and doubtless long shall see—the popular judgment taking the successful candidates on trial in the offices?" (*WPP*, 954). Castigating the nation during the corruption of Grant's presidency, the essay gravely expresses the poet's disappointment with the course of American democracy. In the midst of this jeremiad, however, Whitman praises the presidential election as the hallmark of democratic society: "I think, after all, the sublimest part of political history, and its culmination, is currently issuing from the American people. I know nothing grander, better exercise, better digestion, more positive proof of the past, the triumphant result of faith in human kind, than a well-contested American national election" (*WPP*, 954). Harold Aspiz has demonstrated that *Democratic Vistas* employs somatic imagery to signify a diseased body politic in which individuals are "canker'd," the moral vertebrae are "enfeebl'd," and the culture is afflicted with a "hectic glow."[6] In the presidential contest, though, Whitman sees "better exercise, better digestion"—in short, an internal system that works. The national election achieves the sublime through a tangible corporate process.

Campaigns were a vital component of Whitman's engagement with celebrity, for they provided an overarching structure to his publicity. Whitman not only celebrated the principle of election, he internalized its rituals and hype, using them as the basis for his lifelong efforts to make *Leaves of Grass* publicly significant. The word *campaign* originally denoted the time that armies spent "in the field" actively pursuing their territorial objectives rather than quartered in a town or fortress. American politicians and political writers appropriated the concept from the military and were followed by others interested in public relations and advertising.[7] Charles Dickens used the term in 1868 when he described his preparations for "a final reading campaign," by which he meant the last of his many reading tours in England, Scotland, and Ireland.[8] In using the term, he was making an analogy between the conquering of a country through military force and the persuading of hundreds of British readers through his charismatic performance. Politics and publicity merge in campaigns, for as publicly directed rituals, they marshal symbols, discourses, and personalities into a coherent pattern or narrative, all with the purpose of influencing the popular will.

In the campaign for *Leaves of Grass*, Whitman inhabited the roles of general, candidate, and publicist. He was the poet who would lead an army, seek election, and shape public opinion through the press. The poet's contemporaries were comfortable associating the virtue of public commitment with the exhibition of identities and commodities. "Song of the Answerer" describes a culture rooted in the struggle for public attention: "Books friendships philosophers priests action pleasure pride beat up and down seeking to give satisfaction" (*LG* 1855, 130). The multiple applications of the word campaign capture that competitiveness, that sense of "beating up and down," as democratic republicanism began to incorporate the culture of a market economy. The merger appears quite vividly in the logic of Whitman's self-promotion. Readers elect the poet into prominence by consuming his poems with the kind of gusto and commitment they could never have mustered for other cultural products. In the boiling-hot days of democratic society, promoting *Leaves of Grass* proved to be a contest, a competition for public favor against the many occupations and institutions that Whitman subordinated to his project: "The talented, the artist, the ingenious, the editor, the statesman, the erudite . . . they are not unappreciated," he writes in the 1855 Preface, "they fall in their place and do their work" (*LG* 1855, 24; Whitman's ellipsis). *Not unappreciated* and *falling in their place* are rather anemic terms of praise. He encloses these real-life rivals into the poet's vision where they signify his worth.

In structuring his campaigns, the biggest problem Whitman faced was hostility and indifference. With his goal of transforming the republic by putting *Leaves of Grass* on the public stage, the poet had to draw attention to both himself and his book. I have already discussed how he used Emerson's endorsement of the 1855 edition and how he fabricated his own endorsements through a series of anonymous self-reviews. This chapter turns to the campaigns he developed around the theme of neglect, the sense that the public and its representatives had reached a critical rupture or crisis. Spurred by his frustration with the lack of White House leadership, Whitman's writings from the 1850s repeatedly campaign against the presidency, forming a tenacious (albeit one-sided) rivalry with the nation's most legitimate public representative. The parameters of this campaign would shift with the emergence of Abraham Lincoln, and in the years that followed the Civil War, Whitman raised his public profile by attaching himself to the martyred president. As we will see, the effectiveness of this strategy did little to allay the poet's feelings of resentment, and in his last decades he began to publicize himself by exaggerating his neglect, creating a kind of jeremiad around his treatment by the American public. For a poet who had begun his career cultivating the image of popularity, this shift in strategy was both radical and ironic. It also proved to be remarkably successful. Whitman's embrace of his critical and popular failings complicates his early association of popularity with legitimacy. The poet's disillusionment suggests his growing skepticism about the democratic potential of fame.

LAUNCHING AT THE PRESIDENCY

After the publication of the 1856 edition of *Leaves of Grass,* Whitman found himself directionless. Frustrated by the disappointing reaction to his poems, he returned to editing newspapers, working at the *Brooklyn Daily Times* from 1857 to 1859. During this period he experienced both a personal and vocational crisis—the chief feature of which was a growing disillusionment with *Leaves of Grass.* The Calamus poems express that disillusionment quite poignantly, but despite the moody withdrawal that hangs over parts of the cluster, Whitman never really relinquished his desire for the national stage. For a while he entertained the prospect of traveling from state to state offering lectures for fifteen cents. Thinking back on the period, he later told Traubel, "I thought I had something to say—I was afraid I would get no chance to say it through books: I was to lecture and get myself delivered that way" (*WWC*, 1:5).[9] Combining a sense of both birth and redemption, Whitman's phrasing is quite revealing, for it suggests that the process of delivering himself to the populace was a kind of radically transformative experience. The nation's political conflicts may have made the poet's message especially urgent, but in many respects he was the core of that message.

The combination of political frustration and personal desire appears in a notebook entry from April 1857 in which Whitman fantasized about positioning himself at the center of popular consciousness:

> That the mightiest rule over America could be thus—as for instance, on occasion, at Washington to be launching from public room, at the opening of the session of Congress—perhaps launching at the Presidency, leading persons, Congressmen, or judges of the Supreme Court—that to dart hither or thither as some great emergency might demand—the greatest Champion America ever would know, yet holding no office or emolument whatever—but first in the esteem of men and women. *Not* to direct eyes or thoughts to any of the usual avenues, as of official appointment, or to get such any way—To put all those aside for good—But always to keep up living interest in public questions,—and *always to hold the ear of the people.*[10]

Whitman places his familiar populism against the elected and appointed officials that make up the federal government. To borrow from Emerson's description of Thoreau, he seems to "feel himself" in opposition to legitimate authority, using Washington to define his own ambitions and power. He would be the "greatest Champion," a celebrated defender of American democracy, a political watchdog whose popularity would allow him to "launch" at the government. The power Whitman visualizes for himself stems from the people's esteem for his work—his ability to command their attention in a national emergency. In this informal, quixotic campaign, the poet's fame would make him a critical representative of the public good. Launching at the president, he would conflate his own heroic venture with the sting of a military attack.

Although it presumed a departure from poetry, Whitman's proposal is consistent with his treatment of the presidency in the antebellum editions of *Leaves of Grass*. He had long viewed the president as the paragon of democratic fame. As a boy, Whitman had thrilled to the sight of Andrew Jackson arriving in Brooklyn after crossing the East River from Manhattan. Years later in a newspaper editorial, he recalled how the president literally drew the people out of isolation and into public life:

> Noble! Yet simple-souled old man! We never saw him but once. That was when we were a little boy, in this very city of Brooklyn. He came to the North, on a tour while he was President. One sweet fragrant morning, when the sun shone brightly, he rode up from the ferry in an open barouche. His weather beaten face is before us at this moment, as though the scene happened but yesterday—with his snow-white hair brushed stiffly up from his forehead, and his piercing eyes quite glancing through his spectacles—as those rapid eyes swept the crowds on each side of the street.
>
> The whole city—the ladies first of all—poured itself forth to welcome the hero and the Sage. Every house, every window, was filled with women, and children, and men—though the most of the latter were in the open streets. The President had a big-brimmed white beaver hat, and his arm must have ached some, from the constant and courteous responses he made to the incessant salutations which greeted him every where—the waving of handkerchiefs from the females, and shouts from the men.[11]

Here are the embryonic beginnings of Whitman's fascination with the crowd. On both a symbolic and institutional level, Jackson had defined the president as the center of popular democracy.

In 1855, Whitman depicted the poet in similar terms, converting the wide-brimmed hat, the celebratory citizens, and the rustic face into icons of himself. The Preface makes the connection explicit by frequently turning the presidency into an image of the poet. Like the president, the poet communes with the masses yet remains unconstrained: "Cleaving and

circling here swells the soul of the poet yet is president of itself always"
(*LG* 1855, 14). Free from self-restriction, the poet "does not stop for any
regulation . . . he is the president of regulation" (*LG* 1855, 9; Whitman's
ellipsis). The Preface borrows the president's civic prestige in promoting
the poet's independence and cultural authority. At times Whitman invokes the office to demonstrate his own democratic philosophy, dismiss-
ing the distinctions that divided the chief executive from common men
and women. "Who has been wise, receives interest," he comments in
"Song of Prudence." "Savage, felon, President, judge, farmer, sailor, me-
chanic, young, old, it is the same, / The interest will come round—all will
come round" (*LG* 1860, 212). Such comparisons invite readers to focus
their attention equally on the president and the bard.

Whatever importance the president possessed as a model in *Leaves of
Grass* paled in comparison to his role as the poet's rival and competitor.
The 1855 Preface explains that the essence of unrhymed poetry—and
hence, democratic art—lies in the president's taking his hat off to the
people (*LG* 1855, 6). But in the years before the Civil War, Whitman
regularly implied that the president had forgotten the central meaning of
that gesture, that as a representative he had failed. In "A Boston Ballad" he
appears as a distant, amoral leader who sanctions the capture of a runaway slave. In "A Song for Occupations" his power has led the citizenry to
doubt its own worth. In "To the States" he reminds the poet of "Scum
floating atop of the waters" (*LG* 1860, 400). In "To a President," he is
accused of dangling mirages in front of the nation (*LG* 1860, 402). In
each of these poems, the president exerts his official power without regard
for the electorate and the public good. The 1860 poem "Thought" imagines a president grown fearful that the people would revolt and exercise
their rightful power:

> Of Public Opinion,
> Of a calm and cool fiat, sooner or later, (How impassive! How
>   certain and final!)
> Of the President with pale face asking secretly to himself, *What
>   will the people say at last?* (*LG* 1860, 286)

Having cut himself from Jacksonian cloth, the poet is outraged by the
antidemocratic drift of the presidency. Expressing his deep respect for all

people on the continent, the poet rivals the president as a more faithful representative of the nation's democratic ideals.

The portrait of the presidency offered by these poems captures Whitman's frustration as the nation veered toward civil war. The fullest expression of his anger comes from "The Eighteenth Presidency!" an 1856 pamphlet that was set in type but never published. Throughout the pamphlet, Whitman denounces the state of the presidency. Charging that party politics had corrupted the electoral process, he argued that the nominations of Millard Fillmore and James Buchanan had come not from poets, miners, and farmers but from "political hearses, and from the coffins inside, and from the shrouds inside of the coffins; from the tumors and abscesses of the land; from the skeletons and skulls in the vaults of the federal almshouses" (*WPP*, 1313). In a nation rife with sectional and partisan conflict, the president had failed the popular will with a politics of denial and avoidance: "The President eats dirt and excrement for his daily meals, likes it, and tries to force it on The States" (*WPP*, 1310). The pamphlet's coarse and grotesquely satirical language may seem unusual for Whitman, but in "Starting from Paumanok" he committed himself to precisely this form of political critique. "I will make a song for the ears of the President, full of weapons with menacing points, / And behind those weapons countless dissatisfied faces" (*LG* 1860, 10). In both texts, Whitman draws on the campaign's military origins in positioning himself against the presidency.

Whitman's sense of anger and betrayal was no doubt sincere, but as with any candidate involved in an electoral race, the differences between political commentary and self-promotion become blurred. Subtitled "Voice of Walt Whitman to each Young Man in the Nation, North, South, East, and West," the pamphlet reveals the same broad-based desire to capture the nation's attention that appeared in his notebooks, prefaces, and poems. "Circulate and reprint this Voice of mine for the workingmen's sake," he writes. "I am not afraid to say that among them I seek to initiate my name, Walt Whitman, and that I shall in the future have much to say to them" (*WPP*, 1323). While the pamphlet does not refer to its author's poetry, its vision of a redeemer president shares much in common with Whitman's description of the poet in *Leaves of Grass*: a healthy-bodied, bearded, working-class reformer intent on saving the nation that supports him. As Kerry Larson has argued, the essay's political program is "hopelessly divided," but in it "we find Whitman autobiographically campaigning for a 'Redeemer President'" whose policy resembles his own.[12]

In his private and public writings, in his prose and poetry alike, Whitman publicized his opposition to the presidency, inviting readers to compare the president's failures with his own civic commitments. As he suggested in 1855, the visionary goal of his campaign was to replace the president as the point of civic convergence: "Their Presidents shall not be their common referee so much as their poets shall. Of all mankind the great poet is the equable man. . . . He bestows on every object or quality its fit proportions neither more nor less. He is the arbiter of the diverse and he is the key. He is the equalizer of his age and land . . . he supplies what wants supplying and checks what wants checking" (*LG* 1855, 8; the second ellipsis is Whitman's). The poet assumes the president's role as the ultimate referent of the people, and in the process he becomes a government to himself, the single individual who "supplies what wants supplying and checks what wants checking." "Poetry is a rival government always in opposition to its cruder replicas," William Carlos Williams wrote in the 1930s.[13] In the years between 1855 and 1860, Whitman maintained a particularly aggressive form of that rivalry—though instead of launching missiles at the president, he was launching himself.

HE LOOKS LIKE A MAN

Whitman moved away from his early campaigns against the presidency after the Civil War. On both a political and promotional level, the poet's rivalry with the White House had been futile, and perhaps some suspicion of this futility guided the decision not to publish "The Eighteenth Presidency!" after it had been set in type. In the decades following the Civil War, Whitman engaged in an equally vigorous campaign to associate himself with Lincoln, a campaign that proved to be critical to his reputation and celebrity. His 1856 vision of a redeemer president rising out of the West had seemed to prophecy Lincoln's arrival on the American political scene; by 1876, he was presenting himself as the president's most sympathetic and authoritative interpreter. The success of that strategy is evident in T. S. Eliot's pithy comparison of the poet with his leading English counterpart: "Tennyson liked monarchs, and Whitman liked presidents." To Eliot, this parallel suggested the poets' fundamental conservatism, by which he meant that each believed that "progress consists in things remaining much as they are."[14] We need not agree with Eliot to recognize that when he (and many of his contemporaries) reflected on Whitman, they did not think of the menacing radical who hurled his weapons at the White House. They thought of Lincoln's elegist.

There is a long tradition in Whitman studies of exploring the relations between the poet and the president.[15] Not only did the two men share a general political orientation but, as many have pointed out, the rhetoric of *Drum Taps* is remarkably compatible with that of Lincoln's most important speeches. Whitman himself invited such comparisons among his disciples, telling Traubel in 1889 that "Lincoln gets almost nearer me than anybody else" (*WWC*, 1:38). Although he did not support the president initially, his admiration shines forth from an 1863 letter in which he described Lincoln as having a face like a "hoosier Michel Angelo, so awful ugly it becomes beautiful." In Congress, Whitman could discern no "masterful" men, but in the president he saw a "fountain of first-class practical telling wisdom." Using the imagery he would later employ in "O Captain, My Captain," he praised Lincoln's "almost supernatural tact in keeping the ship afloat at all, with head steady, not only not going down and now certain not to, but with proud and resolute spirit, and flag flying in sight of the world, menacing and high as ever." In Whitman's estimate, there had never been a ruler who had encountered such a perplexing, dangerous task as Lincoln: "I more and more rely upon his idiomatic western genius, careless of court dress or court decorums."[16]

Whitman's identification with the president is as much a story of cultural performance as it is aesthetic awareness, for he used Lincoln's image to ratify himself and his book. In the poet's memory as well as publicity, the president emerges not as a rival but as a highly reliable running mate. He once commented, "Lincoln is particularly my man, particularly belongs to me; yes, and by the same token, I am Lincoln's man: I guess I particularly belong to him; we are afloat on the same stream—we are rooted in the same ground."[17] The sense of ownership is astonishing—especially in the assertion of an exceptional, almost exclusive, bond between the two men. Whitman profoundly admired Lincoln, and his admiration was fueled by the memory of the Fillmore and Buchanan presidencies. But the poet's sense of ownership does more than express the reverence and awe that many Americans felt toward the martyred president; it links *Leaves of Grass* with his monumental prestige and renown. Whitman's efforts to cultivate the association suggest a markedly different understanding of fame and publicity than his earlier writings displayed. The poet no longer expected the people to elect him to the position of popular representative. Rather, he would descend to the public as a great and enigmatic man, a compatriot of such Christlike immortals as Lincoln and Columbus; his greatness would be recognized and certified by his proximity to these widely celebrated men.

The president first appeared in one of Whitman's promotional campaigns after the poet had been dismissed from his position with the Department of the Interior. According to Whitman's supporters, the poet was fired after the secretary of the department, the clergyman James Harlan, found a copy of the 1860 edition of *Leaves of Grass* in Whitman's desk and concluded that it was immoral. Many workers lost their jobs when Harlan became secretary of the Interior, and within twenty-four hours Whitman had found a new post with the Attorney General's Office. Nevertheless, the episode prompted William Douglas O'Connor to write *The Good Gray Poet*, the lengthy defense of Whitman against the charges of indecency that Harlan had apparently leveled at him. O'Connor's essay positions the poet's sacrificial wartime service, his "sublime ministration," against his unfair treatment at the hands of a prudish, intolerant bureaucrat. He invites readers to see among the rows and rows of wounded soldiers a vision of Whitman walking "in the spirit of Christ, soothing, healing, consoling, restoring, night and day, for years; never failing, never tiring, constant, vigilant, faithful; performing, without fee or reward, his self-imposed duty; giving to the task all his time and means, and doing everything that it is possible for one unaided human being to do."[18]

As if the portrait of a Christlike Whitman did not possess enough rhetorical power, O'Connor drew Lincoln into his argument, deploying the recently assassinated president as a kind of sanctifying cultural authority. The essay's third paragraph culminates in an account of Lincoln's marveling at Whitman's character and manliness: "I treasure to my latest hour, with swelling heart and springing tears, the remembrance that Abraham Lincoln, seeing him [Whitman] for the first time from the window of the east room of the White House as he passed slowly by, and gazing at him long with that deep eye which read men, said, in the quaint, sweet tone, which those who have spoken with him will remember, and with a significant emphasis which the type can hardly convey, 'Well, he looks like a MAN!' Sublime tributes, great words; but none too high for their object, the author of *Leaves of Grass*, Walt Whitman, of Brooklyn."[19] The story not only vindicates the poet from Harlan's charges of indecency, it serves to consecrate his character as well. Whitman the citizen, Whitman the nurse, Whitman the representative man—all these identities are confirmed by the voice of the martyred president. The poet took deep personal satisfaction from the account. After Traubel expressed some skepticism about the story's veracity, the poet produced a letter that seemed to confirm its truth. "I think that letter will convince," he said to the beaming Traubel. "I have sometimes thought you had an idea we were romancing a bit in telling that story about Lincoln: now you can see for yourself that we've kept literally prosaically to the figures—have added nothing to them" (*WWC*, 3:177–80). Whether Whitman knew it or not, the letter's authenticity is quite suspect—though its power to confirm his gifts remained quite strong.[20]

O'Connor's use of the passage presumes a different conception of fame than the populist celebrations Whitman had envisioned in 1855. In poems such as "Song of the Answerer," "To a Pupil," and "The Sleepers," Whitman imagined the poet at the center of the crowd, a man whose magnetic personality resulted in his being spontaneously celebrated by it. In O'Connor's account, the president assumes this nominating role; he is the one who selects the poet out of the men and women walking outside the White House. The people may have been unwilling to recognize the poet's cultural significance, but with O'Connor's help, Whitman had an example of the nation's most prestigious representative doing that important ratifying work. Whitman had shrewdly used this strategy when he publicized Emerson's private letter of congratulations in advertisements, circulars, and the 1856 copy of *Leaves of Grass*, and the results immediately gave the book a public profile. The sanctifying power of Lincoln pushed the approach to a new level. The disciples would later cultivate that sense of election, of one famous American bringing another into the fold. They propagated the legend that Lincoln had kept a copy of *Leaves of Grass* in his Springfield law office and that he had praised it as inaugurating a new school of poetry. As late as 1926, William Sloane Kennedy was repeating the story with satisfaction. When he compiled the names of Whitman's "Wholehearted Accepters," he brazenly placed Lincoln at the top of the list.[21]

While the telling of exaggerated apocryphal stories resulted in some success, it was in the actual cultural arena that Whitman scored the most points as Lincoln's complement and interpreter. By the 1880s, the poet's domestic reputation rested firmly on his association with Lincoln. Despite its being his weakest and least original poem about the president (a fact that Whitman himself recognized), "O Captain, My Captain" forged that link in the popular imagination, moving from the pages of *Drum-Taps and Memories of President Lincoln* to anthologies and text books within two decades. Whitman built on this association in delivering what would come to be known as his Lincoln lecture. According to Reynolds, the poet delivered the lecture over nineteen times in eleven years.[22] Identifying himself with Lincoln's accomplishments, character, and tragedy proved to be essential to the poet's rising celebrity.

The lecture offered a dramatic retelling of Lincoln's assassination, and having gone through many drafts, the narrative gains considerable power from its sharp and vivid details. Whitman brings us directly into Ford's Theater and into the president's entertainment that evening, the British play *Our American Cousin*. For a story his audience knew quite well, the poet creates a surprising amount of suspense. We see the headlines announcing the president's attendance at the theater. We watch as the play unfolds, counterposing the ridiculously portrayed Yankee and his stiff English acquaintances. We see the actors exit the scene, clearing the stage for a moment (*WPP*, 1042). We hear "the muffled sound of a pistol shot" and learn that not "one-hundredth part of the audience" heard it at the time (*WPP*, 1042–43). We see the assassin dressed in black, his raven hair full and glossy above his mad, animalistic eyes (*WPP*, 1043). We see Mrs. Lincoln's "ashy cheeks and lips" as she points to Booth, crying, "*He has kill'd the President*" (*WPP*, 1043).[23]

Whitman was in New York on the night of Lincoln's death, but his details are so finely wrought that his audience would have been justified in concluding that he had participated in the event himself. The poet seems to have encouraged such misunderstandings. He may have been responsible for an advertisement that appeared a few days before his 1886 lecture in Elkton, Maryland. Placed in the *Whig*, the advertisement proclaimed that Whitman had been "upon terms of close intimacy with Mr. Lincoln and occupied a seat by his side when the fatal shot that killed the martyred President was fired."[24] A year later, a flyer promoting Whit-

DON'T FAIL TO ATTEND

THE LECTURE BY

Walt Whitman

ON

Abraham Lincoln

AT

UNITY CHURCH, Benson above Fourth.

Tuesday Evening, April 5, 1887.

The lecture is a prose poem and is now regarded as a classic. Whitman was at the Theatre when Lincoln was assassinated, and graphically describes the most terrible event in American history.

Miss Weda Cook, the favorite contralto, will sing some popular selections. The poem of Whitman's "My Captain, oh, my Captain," will be recited.

It is proposed to make this a Lincoln evening, as we are nearing the anniversary of his death,

An advertisement for Whitman's 1887 Lincoln lecture in Camden. The flyer falsely claims that Whitman was in Ford's Theatre on the night of Lincoln's assassination. Courtesy of the Charles E. Feinberg Collection, the Library of Congress.

man's appearance at Unity Church in Camden relied on similar false-hoods. The program was held only blocks away from the home on Mickle Street and included not only the Lincoln lecture but a vocal performance by the widely respected contralto Weda Cook. A Camden native, Cook was a frequent visitor to Whitman's home; she would later pose for Thomas Eakins's painting *The Concert Singer* (1890–92). It seems unlikely that Whitman wrote the program advertisement himself (the title of "O Captain! My Captain!" is incorrect), but he surely must have influenced its content and style. The advertisement is strongly reminiscent of the self-assured declarations and deceptions he had issued from Brooklyn in the 1850s: "The lecture is a prose poem and is now regarded as a classic," the flyer reads. "Whitman was at the Theatre when Lincoln was assassinated, and graphically describes the most terrible event in American history."[25]

The promotional fictions were ironic because the lecture's most significant theme was how impoverished the arts appear next to the high drama of actual history. Whitman recalls seeing the president at the theater on several occasions and thinking "how funny it was that he, in some respects the leading actor in the stormiest drama known to real history's stage through centuries, should sit there and be so completely interested and absorb'd in those human jack-straws, moving about with their silly little gestures, foreign spirit, and flatulent text" (*WPP*, 1041). As the poet presents it, Lincoln's death was the climax to the greatest crisis since the beginning of time. With the "historic Muse" and the "tragic Muse" at opposite ends of the stage, the assassination would stir the imagination for centuries on end. It would act as a "cement to the whole people," condensing them into a single, lasting Nationality in a way that the Constitution, courts, and armies never had or could (*WPP*, 1046). Whitman had once assumed that role for himself, promising in Calamus to bring the nation together through affection rather than constitutions, lawyers, and arms (*LG* 1860, 349). With the poet as its interpreter, Lincoln's death would now create those bonds—not through love but through sacrifice.

Whitman's performance of the Lincoln lecture put him before the leading writers, artists, and citizens of his time. While it did not appeal to the masses, it became an important cultural ritual in which the members of polite society could pay homage to both the president and the poet. The most famous of Whitman's performances occurred on April 14, 1887, at

Madison Square Theatre in New York. The performance was organized as a benefit for the poet by a group of businessmen and intellectuals committed to improving his fortunes. As William Pannapacker remarks, the evening "was the culminating coup in a long career of self-promotion as a journalist, poet, lecturer, and self-conscious literary celebrity."[26] Whitman felt triumphant at the number of luminaries who appeared in the audience and attended the reception afterward. Not only had Andrew Carnegie contributed 350 dollars toward the evening (although he did not attend), among those in the audience were the writers Mark Twain and James Russell Lowell, the sculptor Augustus St. Gaudens, the art historian Mrs. Schuyler Van Rensselaer, Lincoln's secretary and biographer John Hay, the Cuban revolutionary and poet José Martí, and the president of Johns Hopkins University.[27] All had come to pay their respects to Whitman and his singular dedication to the slain president. Repeating the apocryphal story that the two men had been friends, the *New York Times* distinguished the poet's reverence from the neglect of his countrymen: "Yesterday was the anniversary of the death of this country's greatest President. There was no public evidence of the fact, however. The majority of men in the pressure of personal affairs forgot it entirely. But a poet, an old man bent with years and tottering through the summer of life to the twilight and the dark, came feebly forth from his retirement to lay his wreath upon the grave of his friend. The Poet was Walt Whitman and the President was Abraham Lincoln."[28]

With only five hundred seats and an unusually situated orchestra pit, the Madison Square Theatre was one of the most intimate venues in New York, and gathered together in the late afternoon, the audience members no doubt felt themselves distinguished to be in each other's company. At 4:00 p.m., the curtain went up, revealing a drawing-room scene with a plush chair and table set beside it. A wreath of laurels decorated with red, white, and blue ribbons stood to the left side. Whitman walked onstage with the help of a young Camden friend and a well-worn shepherd's crook that he used as a cane. Wearing a velvet coat and elegant open-collared shirt, sporting long white hair and a full white beard, he could no longer claim the role of the good gray poet, nor the workingman radical of decades before. To one reporter, he resembled nothing short of Jove (*DN,* 2:428). Whitman began the lecture slowly, fumbling for his eyeglasses

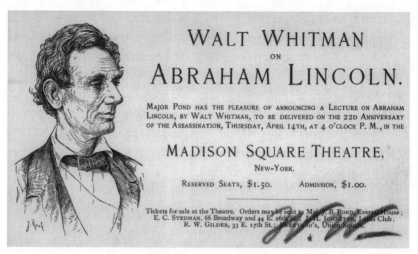

An advertisement for the Lincoln lecture at Madison Square Theatre in 1887. Although the lecture was arranged as a benefit for Whitman, the ticket subsumes the poet to an image of the young man Lincoln. Courtesy of the Henry W. and Albert A. Berg Collection of English and American Literature, the New York Public Library, Astor, Lenox and Tilden Foundations.

and adjusting his high-keyed voice, but his narrative was audible and clear. He spoke, the *New York Times* reported, as "a venerable patriarch in his study talking to the friends who had gathered around."[29]

Weaving himself into the fabric of national memory, Whitman reminisced about Lincoln's preinaugural visit to New York City before taking the audience through the details of the tragedy and his own reflections on the deaths of important leaders in human history. He spoke without gestures, but when a passage elicited an emotional reaction from the audience, he would look in its direction "in a way that was better than any gesture and impressive in the extreme."[30] As was his custom, he ended the lecture with an emotional recitation of "O Captain, My Captain," which brought many in the audience to tears. But in this tribute to both the poet and the president, the organizers did not forget Whitman's most powerful elegy "When Lilacs Last in the Dooryard Bloom'd." As the applause subsided, a little girl appeared on stage and presented a basket of the blossoms with the line, "I've brought you some lilacs that in our door yard bloomed" (*DN,* 2:418).[31] The audience delighted in this fusion of patriotic sentiment and piety. As the *Times* reported, "It was December frost and Maytime blossom at their prettiest contrast as the little pink cheek shown against the snow-white beard, for the old man told his appreciation mutely by kissing her and kissing her again."[32] The lilacs that had served for many as icons of the slain president now became icons of the poet who remembered him. At a crowded reception in the Westminster Hotel, one man looked at Whitman and remarked, "He looks like a god." The reporter from the *Evening Post* agreed, describing the poet as having the appearance of a "man of magnetism" (*DN*, 2:428). Whether the reporter knew it or not, Whitman had been proclaiming the virtues of a magnetic personality for over thirty years.

Although frequently presented as the pinnacle of his career, the Manhattan lecture was just one of many that Whitman delivered on the East Coast, each one displaying his determination to align *Leaves of Grass* with the nation's love of the martyred president. An equally revealing portrait comes from the poet's final performance of the lecture in April 1890 when he ferried across the Delaware River to speak at the Art Club in Philadelphia. Whitman had been unwell all spring, and it took enormous effort to support him as he walked up the stairs to the second floor. (The building's elevator was inoperable that evening.) Exhausted by this exertion, Whitman paused at the top of the staircase, feeling dazed, his head in a whirl. A friend found a chair, and the old poet sat for a few minutes before moving to the lecture room. When Whitman made his entrance, he had difficulty seeing his manuscript, and finding the lilacs distracting, he asked for them to be removed. While the effects of aging were clear to all, the performance, as Traubel tells it, was "grand": "It was an extraordinary gathering—from 3 to 4 hundred. A victory his, after 3 decades of scorn and slander—brought into the very citadel of literary fashion and bequeathed the hour's (and future's) triumph. He was applauded several times—once responding with a wave of the hand. At times he would throw his body back in order the more sharply to define his emphases. After he had finished the address, he read, 'O Captain!' with greatest effect—power and pathos" (*WWC*, 6:365). In many ways this final performance was no different from its predecessors: the presence of lilacs, the recitation of "O Captain," the triumph over exaggerated memories of slander and scorn all had their place in the lecture's history.

However, it was the poet's perseverance in the face of obvious suffering that made the evening so meaningful to Traubel. Only a week before, he had asked the ailing poet whether they should cancel the event, echoing the concerns of several friends who thought him too ill for such a strenuous task. Whitman declined, explaining how personally significant the Lincoln lecture had become to him: "No: I doubt if even you or Doctor Bucke know just the egotism that backs me in such an undertaking as this. It is in part the explanation of my work—*of Leaves of Grass* . . . I feel pledged to it [the lecture]—not to you but to myself. It will probably be its last deliverance. I hope to be identified with the man Lincoln, with his crowded, eventful years—with America as shadowed forth into those abysms of circumstance" (*WWC*, 6:353). The poet's desire "to be identified" with Lincoln conveys both a respect for his character and an understanding of his place in the hearts of the nation. The ultimate homage to Lincoln was to integrate his image into the campaign for *Leaves of Grass*. Whitman recognized that not only had the lecture become an annual performance of his fame, it remained vital to his permanent achievement of that state.

STAR-FEVER

The assimilation of Lincoln into Whitman's public identity is indicative of a broader shift in the culture of American celebrity. In place of the popularly elected heroes of the 1840s and 1850s, the Gilded Age produced a class of luminaries whose wealth and prestige set them apart from the rest of society. Fame was in the process of becoming a category of social identity, one that granted its bearers access to other famous people. Whitman's performance at Madison Square Theatre testifies to this change, for when his disciples described the evening as triumphant, they referred to the number of dignitaries in the audience, passing over the fact that the theater had plenty of empty seats. The artisan representative hoping to be celebrated by the masses evolved into the star who kept company with other cultural luminaries. When the *Evening Post* reported on the event, it devoted most of its coverage to the dress and appearance of the admirers who greeted Whitman at a reception after the show (*DN*, 2:418). And while it did not attract the number of national dignitaries he had seen in New York, Whitman was surprised by how "tony" the crowd was at the Philadelphia Art Club in 1890. The audience was dressed so elegantly, he remarked, with women of all ages wearing evening dress, that he hoped he had added a touch of the outdoors—the sea, the woods, the river—to the refined proceedings (*WWC*, 6:366). Celebrity was emerging as the kind of republican aristocracy that N. P. Willis had envisioned in the 1840s, a class of fashionable individuals engaged with each other at extravagant dinners and benefits. The spectacle they provided may have occupied the newspapers and entertained the masses, but it had little of the democratic fervor that Whitman had witnessed Edwin Forrest create among audiences at the Old Bowery.

From the editor's desk at *Scribner's*, J. G. Holland regularly grumbled about fame's role in precipitating cultural decline. According to the editor, the star system had created mediocrity in the theater, and it was ruining the lecture series. Audiences and organizers alike had become afflicted with a "star-fever" that valued notoriety over education and accomplishment: "Men were summoned to the platform simply because they would draw, and not because the people expected instruction or inspiration from them. A notoriety had only to rise, to be summoned at once to the platform. If he could lift a great many kegs of nails; if he was successful as a showman; if he was a literary buffoon, and sufficiently expert in cheap orthography; in short, if he had been anything, or done anything, to make himself an object of curiosity to the crowd, he was regarded as a star, and called at once into the lecture field for the single purpose of swelling the receipts at the door." Like countless cultural commentators after him, Holland warned against the transformation of culture into a spectacle organized around frivolity. "The lecture room must cease to be a showroom of fresh notorieties, at high prices," he wrote, in longing for a return to the values of the pre–Civil War lyceum.[33]

Holland was additionally troubled by the influence of celebrity on American politics. The election of Ulysses Grant in 1872 occasioned the complaint: "We run our politics on the starring system. A man becomes a star, and we make him president." With the exception of a few archaisms, Holland's concern about the conflation of politics and celebrity seems as penetrating today as it must have in the 1870s: "Not statesmanship, not personal character, not intellectual culture, not eminent knowledge, not anything and not any combination of things that constitute superlative fitness, fixes the American choice for the chief magistracy. The star which, for the moment, can attract the greatest number of eyes, becomes the lord of the heavens and the earth. Votes must be had at any sacrifice; and votes can only be counted on for stars. . . . The starring system in politics is a failure. It is bad for the country, it is bad for politics; it is a discouragement to personal and political worth, it is a nuisance." Afflicted with "star-fever," Americans had begun to see fame as being desirable in itself, elevating the well-known and popular into positions of power and authority. Holland had little patience for the democratic promise that some had viewed in celebrity; the starring system had perverted the workings of democracy, creating an elite with little regard for virtue, talent, or the public good. The problem was that the appetite for stardom had outgrown its supply. The public wanted cultural luminaries to follow and admire, but there were not enough people to fill that role. With great exasperation, Holland remarked on the rise of the public relations industry. Stardom had become such the fashion that actual businesses had arisen "for the manufacture of fictitious reputations."[34]

Fifteen years later, Whitman echoed Holland's complaints about the meretricious foundation of celebrity. "The world goes daffy after phantom great men," he told Traubel in 1889, "—the noisy epaulette sort. . . . if you have the real stuff in you, you've got to wait for it to be recognized: and you are far more likely to die than to live in waiting" (WWC, 3:562). In making this statement, Whitman was drawing a careful distinction between popularity in the marketplace and the kind of genuine recognition he now saw as coming only with time. The distinction became especially meaningful to the poet after the Civil War. As much as he distrusted the fluctuations of contemporary society, however, Whitman certainly did not wait for posterity to confirm his achievement. His scorn for phantom greatness aside, the poet immersed himself in the kind of promotional campaign that offended critics such as Holland. Greenspan has noted that Whitman's textual attention to the reader declined in the postwar editions of *Leaves of Grass*. Not only did he refrain from addressing his reader as a lover or compatriot, the poet edited out many of those passages from earlier poems. He simultaneously began to court the reading public with new enthusiasm and commitment: "If less went into the poems themselves," Greenspan observes, "more went into the external means of their presentation and into the advocacy of their reception."[35]

Even when confined to the areas around Camden in the last few years of his life, Whitman exhibited a breathtaking preoccupation with getting his name before the public. Although disappointed by his books' sales, he expressed great faith that the right publicity could bring the volume into public consciousness. Among collectors of rare books, Whitman's older editions steadily climbed in value, but the poet remained focused on the prospects of a future popular edition. As he told Traubel in 1889, "I feel sure . . . that if a hustler got hold of *Leaves of Grass* the book would make the fur fly in many places it don't touch at all" (*WWC*, 6:130). Who that hustler might be was unclear, though only months before, Whitman was mourning his inability to assume such a role himself. Sounding like a presidential candidate and his key adviser embarking on a national campaign, he and Traubel spoke of their difficulties in reaching Whitman's "constituency"—a core group of readers spread out across the land. "The natural thing to do would be for me to go about myself—go from city to city—New York, Chicago, St. Louis—take quarters—locate for a few days, weeks—see the publishers—sell: whack about, solicit, bargain myself" (*WWC*, 5:439–40). Whitman may have invented the puff when he placed Emerson's compliments on the spine of the 1856 *Leaves of Grass*. In 1889, he seems to have anticipated the modern book tour in imagining himself on the road—not as a lecturer but as a publicist.

Prepared to bargain himself in the cultural marketplace, Whitman reflected the Gilded Age's enthusiasm for the commodification of personality. Interest in personality had grown in the antebellum period, manifesting itself in autograph collections, daguerreotype and photography studios, and lithographed images in the newspapers. Fueled by changes in the technology, the importance of personality grew dramatically in the 1860s. The decade saw the rise of the carte de visite craze as Americans collected and traded pictures of the renowned on two-by-three-inch calling cards. The "public's fascination with certain personalities" was so high that "hundreds of thousands of cartes of a single image might be sold in a few months."[36] Some celebrities were popular enough that they could demand sitting fees or royalties from the sale of their images to people across the nation who collected and pasted their images into family photo albums. While the technology and format would change over the next decades, the fascination with the celebrity's image would remain quite steady. By the 1870s, collectors had turned from the carte de viste to larger "images of celebrated actors and actresses, businessmen, clergymen, and political leaders" that were printed on cardstock and either sold separately or bound together in books.[37] By the 1880s, stores were selling

3-D stereographs (also known as stereoscopes) through which consumers could see three-dimensional images of their favorite stars.

Whitman's vision of the book tour as a kind of whistle-stop campaign indicates his eagerness to cultivate interest in his book and personality. Although he complained about the autograph seekers and photographers, he himself encouraged such attention and tried to meet the market's demand. He and Traubel worked together on a small album of photographs, planning to release the volume as a private edition titled "Portraits of Life from Walt Whitman." Negotiations with photographers are sprinkled throughout the volumes of *Walt Whitman in Camden*, with Whitman ordering sometimes hundreds of extra photographs of himself for distribution in England and the United States (*WWC*, 5:73). The transAtlantic nature of Whitman's publicity was particularly important, for the British press was perhaps more interested in the poet than its American counterpart. Traubel records an amusing evening in December 1889 when Whitman commented on and criticized his various portraits in the London newspapers, speaking about his image with detached and calculating objectivity (*WWC*, 6:171). If the fur was going to fly around *Leaves of Grass*, it would come from its author—a great man eager to influence posterity's decision before his looming death.

THE SANCTION OF NEGLECT

The most prominent and successful theme in Whitman's publicity after the Civil War was that the poet suffered from cultural neglect. The poet who had seen popularity as a ratifying force, who had exaggerated his sales figures and fantasized about his overtaking the president in an orgiastic campaign, now sought to promote his failures and misfortunes. The shift in both temperament and strategy is clearly expressed in a passage from "A Backwards Glance o'er Travel'd Roads." The essay pointed to the future where the poet's audience waited to redeem him:

> I look upon "Leaves of Grass," now finish'd to the end of its opportunities and powers, as my definitive *carte visite* to the coming generations of the New World, if I may assume to say so. That I have not gain'd the acceptance of my own time, but have fallen back on fond dreams of the future—anticipations—("still lives the song, though Regnar dies")—That from a worldly and

business point of view "Leaves of Grass" has been worse than a
failure—that public criticism on the book and myself as author
of it, yet shows mark'd anger and contempt more than anything
else—("I find a solid line of enemies to you everywhere,"—letter
from W. S. K., Boston, May 28, 1884)—And that solely for publishing it I have been the object of two or three pretty serious official buffetings—is all probably no more than I ought to have
expected. I had my choice when I commenc'd. I bid neither for
soft eulogies, big money returns, nor the approbation of existing
schools and conventions. (*WPP, 656–57*)

The passage briefly gathers up many of the grievances Whitman felt in his
last years. He alludes to his dismissal from the Department of the Interior
in 1865 and the suppression of his book in Boston in 1882. He cites a
letter from Kennedy attesting to the many enemies still lingering in the
city. He reminds us that in refusing to bend to convention, money, and the
popular taste he has suffered both poverty and calumny. With their elegant leather covers, autographed title pages, and frontispiece photographs, Whitman's books are his cartes de visites to posterity, his letters to
a future world that would recognize merit more than meretriciousness.

The passage draws on a fascinating cross-section of cultural attitudes
about fame, popularity, and the arts. Emboldened by a rhetoric of failure,
Whitman cites his lack of popularity as evidence of his artistic integrity.
He rejects not only the bravado of the 1855 Preface but also the promise
that celebrity could reliably index his cultural value: his virtue as an artist
now resides in his alienation from the times. In renouncing the crowd
and contemporary judgments, Whitman inhabited the world of founders
such as John Adams and Benjamin Rush, who viewed popularity as the
cheap and fickle cousin of everlasting fame. Though he was clearly divided over the subject, the poet's failure to achieve popularity becomes a
sign of his virtuous commitment to aesthetic and political revolution.
Borrowing from Jean Baudrillard, Pannapacker has suggested that during
this period Whitman employed the "rhetoric of exclusion" associated with
being avant-garde.[38] While the Lincoln lectures attest to a good deal of
ambivalence about such a choice, "A Backwards Glance" exemplifies the
ways in which Whitman began to exaggerate his failure in order to claim a
different kind of legitimacy.

Writing about the eighteenth and nineteenth centuries, Braudy has used the term "sanction of neglect" to describe this political and aesthetic pose. In Braudy's discussion, Whitman joins Emerson, Thoreau, and Dickinson—as well as Washington, Jefferson, and Paine—in understanding fame to be "a turning away from time itself," a democratic spirituality that challenged the values of commerce, technology, and incessant change. From this perspective, a work such as "Crossing Brooklyn Ferry" reflects the stance of many American authors who "wrote directly and often explicitly for the future and so paid their present readers the compliment of standing with them outside the accidents of time and place."[39] The poet would descend to future generations who would discover the timeless sympathy that eluded his contemporaries.

Whitman's embrace of posterity broadly evokes the posture of his romantic predecessors, poets and novelists who professed to value their aesthetic reputations more than popularity. Braudy describes how this rejection of publicity arose in direct reaction to the sense of an ever-widening audience: "A crucial element of Romantic art was the effort to make an impression on a public audience, that is, one that was not personally known to the poet but was, in theory, his psychic kindred. The look of destiny, the sanction of neglect, thus made a public assertion that was overheard by an audience rather than forced upon it. Neglect confirmed originality and genius by demonstrating that true art was unappreciated by the new commercial audience."[40] The romantic embrace of failure would later appear in the United States in a host of private and public declarations, perhaps the most memorable of which was Melville's statement that "it is my earnest desire to write those sort of books which are said to 'fail.' "[41] As distinguished from popularity, fame became "a kind of revenge on society for its neglect of 'true' values." The stance allowed writers and artists to develop their marginality into "a social role itself," occupying what would later be known as the role of the avant-garde.[42] Wrapping himself in the sanction of neglect, Whitman suggests that the ultimate proof of the poet was the public's indifference and mistreatment. The poet had not failed the nation as much as the nation had failed him.

To say that Whitman embraced his lack of popularity in his last decades is not to say that he accepted it. As early as 1856, Whitman had been gesturing toward the future, seeking the affirmation denied him by his contemporaries. After the Civil War, he turned this mode of address into a new promotional strategy, publicizing his neglect in order to attract public notice and controversy. A good example comes from an article he published anonymously in the *Washington Star*. The article described a memorial for Edgar Allan Poe, whose remains were reinterred in a Baltimore cemetery in November 1875. Titled "Walt Whitman at the Poe Funeral— Conspicuous *Absence of the Popular Poets*," the piece frankly announced the persistent theme of neglect: "About the most significant part of the Poe re-burial ceremonies yesterday—which only a crowded and remarkably magnetic audience of the very best class of young people, women preponderating, prevented from growing tedious—was the marked absence from the spot of every popular poet and author, American and foreign. Only Walt Whitman was present" (*PW*, 1:231–32). Amplifying his own situation, Whitman positioned his homage to the poorly treated Poe against the callous disregard of their more fashionable counterparts. While he included it in the *Star*, he eliminated the paragraph when revising the article for publication in the *Critic* and, later, *Specimen Days*. Even without the headline and maudlin opening paragraph, the revision highlighted Whitman's frail and impoverished condition, inviting the public to learn from Poe's disreputable fate and repair its relationship with the nearly paralyzed "old gray" (*PW*, 1:232).[43]

At times after the war, Whitman reverted to the habit of exaggerating his popularity. The various press releases, letters, and interviews that came out of his 1879 trip to the West implied that settlers in the plains and mountain states had warmly received the visiting poet. *Specimen Days* reports that the organizers of the Kansas State Silver Wedding had falsely advertised that he had composed a poem for the occasion and would recite it to the twenty thousand celebrants. "As I seem'd to be made much of," Whitman comments, "and wanted to be good-natured, I hastily pencill'd out the following little speech." Exhibiting uncharacteristic nonchalance, the poet then explained that he had such a good time visiting with a local family that he "let the hours slip away and didn't drive over to the meeting and speak my piece" (*WPP*, 853). Shrouded in exaggeration and myth, the poet's descriptions of the event are so deceptive and ambiguous that one of his most current biographers continues to perpetuate the story that in Topeka he delivered a speech to a crowd of fifteen thousand well-wishers.[44]

While the West became a land of distant promise, the geographical embodiment of posterity, Manhattan developed for Whitman into the center of neglect. The city of his youth began to occupy an increasingly large space in his reservoir of resentment. Despite significant evidence to the contrary, the poet tenaciously clung to the belief that the New York literary establishment continued to attack him. R. W. Gilder, who along with his sister Jeannette regularly published Whitman in several New York magazines, had spoken effusively about the poet at a testimonial dinner in Manhattan. But when he received a copy of the remarks by post, Whitman could only see them as an exception to the customary practice: "this speech is very significant and remarkable—coming as it does from New York, right from the cluster of those there who are most engaged in throwing salt water, acid, on our glistening fame" (*WWC*, 5:415). This insistence that New York was against Whitman caused great frustration among supporters such as Edmund Stedman, who contended that he had suffered no more from fame's delay than others in the teeming, fragmented city (*WWC*, 9:392).[45]

As Stedman, Gilder, and others had suggested, by the late 1880s, Whitman had become a poet of great stature, and evidence of his "glistening fame" was obvious and abundant. The British and American press regularly contacted the poet for profiles and interviews. His work appeared in a wide variety of magazines and journals. He received copious letters asking "silly questions" and requesting autographs. "So I am pursued," the poet admitted. "Sometimes I enjoy it—sometimes it infuriates me—though—" he added with a revealing laugh, "the infuriation is not very violent" (*WWC*, 8:196). In what he must have considered an honor, the *Trenton Times* placed the poet alongside such national and personal heroes as Washington, Lincoln, Grant, Emerson, Greeley, and Beecher (*WWC*, 8:223). But this surge in popularity may ironically have come from Whitman's efforts to champion his lack of fame.

In 1876, the poet ignited a controversy in Europe and the United States over the country's allegedly poor treatment of him. Now known as the *West Jersey Press* affair, the incident exemplifies the ways in which the poet came to publicize himself by scolding others for failing to develop a virtuous interest in him. The incident began on January 26, 1876, when Whitman anonymously published an article in the *West Jersey Press* titled "Walt Whitman's Actual American Position."[46] The occasion of the piece was an article in the *Springfield Republican* that praised Whitman and pointed to his growing American and European reputation. In previous years, Whitman might have included the flattering remarks in a promotional pamphlet for *Leaves of Grass.* He may even have exaggerated such support, turning one editor's enthusiasm into that of a half dozen. In 1876, he chose to wrap himself in the mantle of neglect, presenting himself as a revolutionary poet who had received only scorn from his compatriots.

Whitman's article in the *West Jersey Press* does more than exaggerate his hostile reception; it points to that reception as a confirmation of his unique poetic gifts. After describing the "friendly" portrait offered by the *Republican,* the essay corrects the impression that the nation was steadily absorbing Walt Whitman and *Leaves of Grass:* "The real truth is that with the exception of a very few readers (women equally with men), Whitman's poems in their public reception have fallen still-born in this country. They have been met, and are met today, with the determined denial, disgust and scorn of orthodox American authors, publishers and editors, and, in a pecuniary and worldly sense, have certainly wrecked the life of their author."[47] The paragraph succinctly introduces the article's principal theme, the poet's unmerited suffering. As he would later do in "A Backwards Glance," he compiled a list of personal virtues and injustices: his publishing without regard for conventional opinion and profits, his selfless service during the Civil War and its toll on his health, his dismissal from the Interior Department because he was "the author of the 'Leaves.'" In the 1860 poem "To a Pupil," Whitman had proclaimed the power of personality, encouraging his pupils to impress the crowd with their magnetism and elevatedness (*LG* 1860, 400). The article in the *West Jersey Press* is premised on the very different notion that the individual genius is destined for a life of derision and indifference. As he later explained to Traubel, "Now and then a man steps out from the crowd—says: 'I will be myself'—does, because he is, something immense. The howl that goes up is tremendous'" (*WWC,* 1:433). "Walt Whitman's Actual American Position" was ostensibly meant to remind the public that the howl greeting the poet had been loud and continuous.

What made the article so incendiary was that Whitman placed this hostility in a national context. According to the anonymous discussion, the *Republican* may have been correct in viewing the poet's rising reputation overseas, but the United States remained unmoved by his condition and antagonistic toward his work. The bleakness of the portrait is unmistakable. Readers learned that the poet was "pretty well at the end of his rope": publishing houses wouldn't touch him, stores wouldn't sell him, the magazines had snubbed him, and his New York City book agents had embezzled "every dollar of [his] proceeds!" "Old, poor, and paralyzed," he was immersed in preparing a new edition of his works "to keep the wolf from the door" and to give one final "absolute expression before he dies." The only redeeming force in the article was Whitman's faint hint that while Americans had ignored him, the foreign press had provided "the finest general criticism" of his work.[48]

As soon as the article appeared, Whitman sent a copy to his English friend William Michael Rossetti, asking him to "have it put, if convenient, in the *Academy,* or any other literary gazette, your way, if thought proper" (3).[49] Rossetti eventually placed the article in the *Athenaeum,* and after that, newspapers and magazines on both sides of the Atlantic printed excerpts and commentary. Picking up on Whitman's theme of national difference, the Scottish poet Robert Buchanan published a letter in the *London Daily News* attacking the unprincipled behavior of the American literary establishment. The letter ignited a controversy over Whitman's treatment that raged in the London and New York newspapers for over two months. The principal question under debate was whether Whitman had been unfairly treated by his literary contemporaries, whether he was the victim, as Buchanan charged, of the "literary coteries which emasculate America" (8). Both to alleviate the poet's suffering and shame his American counterparts, Buchanan suggested that Englishmen set up a committee to purchase five hundred, perhaps even a thousand, copies of the centennial edition of *Leaves of Grass* and *Two Rivulets.* By late March, the poet Bayard Taylor had become the chief defender of the American literary establishment. In a series of four articles published in the *New York Tribune,* Taylor took exception to the notion that the country had persecuted Whitman for his verse. Whitman's supporters—both in the United States and abroad—seized the occasion to remind the world of Whitman's service and accomplishments, while also offering detailed accounts of his sufferings and mistreatment.

The *West Jersey Press* affair reveals much about the poet's personality, the commitment of his friends, and trans-Atlantic literary relations in the Victorian era. We can also see it as an elaborate form of publicity. As Robert Scholnick has remarked, Whitman originally published the article to kick off an "advertising campaign for himself and the new edition" of his poems, hoping that by stirring up sympathy for himself, he might dramatically improve his sales (5–6). In addition to sending the article to Rossetti, he sent it to at least three other friends in Denmark, Ireland, and the United States, all with the same request for reprinting. An abbreviated version of the piece appeared in the *New York Tribune,* only weeks before Taylor joined its editorial staff and commenced his attacks (6–7). Whether Whitman anticipated it or not, the controversy created by Buchanan's letter significantly raised his public profile. Stedman, who was always a loyal but realistic supporter, saw in the controversy a well-executed promotional campaign. Not only did the debates accelerate Whitman's acceptance in Europe, they brought attention to the centennial edition in newspapers, magazines, and periodicals throughout the United States. "I would give all my literary position for 1/10th the championship & advertising Whitman is having," Stedman wrote in April 1876. "But he *is* a poet, & his new edition is worth all it costs, to any one" (16). The editor at *Appleton's* agreed with the *Saturday Review* in pronouncing the whole affair "an advertising trick."[50]

Although Whitman clearly did not script it himself, the controversy unfolded as an extended jeremiad in which the poet gained ascendancy through castigating his compatriots. He published his initial article in January 1876 when both his book and publicity could draw on the ardent nationalism that would accompany the centennial celebrations. Having exaggerated his economic condition and his contemporaries' hostility, he invoked the nation's failure to shame it into recognizing his work. To Whitman's many friends and supporters, his position in immortality was secure. The problem lay with the literary establishment and their persecution of a poet who, in true republican fashion, had sacrificed everything to his nation and his art. Like the jeremiad, the affair emerged as both a rhetorical form and a cultural rite, and in each of those modes, it touched on many traditional conflicts: the effeminacy of Whitman's enemies versus his manly self-sacrifice, a backsliding public that had forsaken its democratic heritage in failing to realize its most important literary expression, and the remarkable conflation of publicity with pointed social critique.

The jeremiadic tenor of the *West Jersey* campaign becomes particularly evident when read alongside *Democratic Vistas,* long recognized as Whitman's fullest adaptation of the genre. Critics have made much of the essay's portrait of an American society corrupted by materialism and of Whitman's call to reinvigorate that society with more spiritual forms of democracy. The poet argues that, having forgotten its civic heritage, the nation must reconsecrate itself, must fulfill the promise set forth in its founding documents. Whitman's prophetic stance suggests that the past and the present will culminate in a spiritual and political democracy situated in the future. In working within the jeremiad, though, the poet was not only establishing a prophetic chronology, nor simply engaging in the ritual of "continuing revolution" that Sacvan Bercovitch has seen within the form.[51] He was also engaged in the more immediate project of using the past to define and create his own cultural urgency.

As both a political and promotional text, *Democratic Vistas* may have provided a philosophical backdrop for the 1876 controversy. The parallels between the essay and event are striking. *Democratic Vistas* positions "a few coteries of writers" against the "supple and athletic minds" of future literati (*WPP*, 993), just as Buchanan would later argue that "literary coteries" were emasculating America. The threat of effeminacy, which had long played a role in Whitman's writing and in antebellum culture in general, appears in *Democratic Vistas* as the basis for a general literary critique: "What is the reason our time, our lands, that we see no fresh local courage, sanity, of our own—the Mississippi, stalwart Western men, real mental and physical facts, Southerners, &c., in the body of our literature? especially the poetic part of it. But always, instead, a parcel of dandies and ennuyees, dapper little gentlemen from abroad, who flood us with their thin sentiment of parlors, parasols, piano-songs, tinkling rhymes, the five-hundredth importation—or whimpering and crying about something, chasing one aborted conceit after another, and forever occupied in dyspeptic amours with dyspeptic women" (*WPP*, 975).

In the *West Jersey Press*, Whitman had written that *Leaves of Grass* had fallen stillborn into the country. The public, in effect, was toxic to the infant book. Following "one aborted conceit after another," the dandies of *Democratic Vistas* had flooded the nation with sentimental works, their poems never developing in the rush to be born. The essay and event combine to suggest that while America was failing Whitman, other poets were failing America. As he commented in 1871, "the copious dribble, either of our little or well-known rhymesters, does not fulfill, in any respect, the needs and august occasions of this land" (*WPP*, 979).

Whitman's portrait of cultural decay presents a strident compelling case for his relevance. Just as Emerson had sought an American poet who could sing of carnivals and rogues, just as Whitman had sought a redeemer president from the West, *Democratic Vistas* searches for a literature bold enough to resist the commercial age: "where is the man of letters, where is the book, with any nobler aim than to follow in the old track, repeat what has been said before—and, as its utmost triumph, sell well, and be erudite or elegant?" (*WPP*, 975). *Democratic Vistas* never mentions *Leaves of Grass* nor makes reference to its author's reputation. It nonetheless functions as a self-promotional text, depicting the nation as being afflicted with an illness that only Whitman and his pupils could remedy. When Whitman envisions a "divine literatus" who might make the nation whole, he imagines a figure that strikingly resembles an earlier version of himself: "America demands a poetry that is bold, modern, and all-surrounding and kosmical, as she is herself. . . . It must bend its vision toward the future, more than the past. Like America, it must extricate itself from even the greatest models of the past" (*WPP*, 979). The individual as cosmos, the well-shaped heir, the poet who respectfully acknowledges the past and then looks toward the future, all these themes are prominent in the 1855 edition of *Leaves of Grass*. The poet prophecies a new literary class that will maintain "an eye to practical life, the west, the working-men, the facts of farms and jack-planes and engineers," as if "Walt Whitman, one of the roughs" were going to appear in posterity (*WPP*, 962).

Democratic Vistas represents an important step in a promotional campaign that had to contend with the problem of popular letters, a campaign that would have to develop a vertical sanction for the poet after his quest for horizontal support had failed. Throughout the essay, popularity becomes an easy concession to commercial tastes. "Present literature," Whitman writes, "while magnificently fulfilling certain popular demands, with plenteous knowledge and verbal smartness, is profoundly sophisticated, insane, and its very joy is morbid" (*WPP*, 983). "To-day, in books, in the rivalry of writers, especially novelists," he comments, "success, (so-call'd,) is for him or her who strikes the mean flat average, the sensational appetite for stimulus, incident, persiflage, &c., and depicts, to the common caliber, sensual exterior life" (*WPP*, 974–75). Whitman's divine literatus exists in contrast to these more popular writers, speaking to the "high average of men," encouraging them to leave their vulgarity and justify the principles of democracy (*WPP*, 962). While in 1855 he had suggested that poets could be *proven* by their popularity, by 1871 he was proclaiming the risks of letting the crowd's opinions govern aesthetic, if not political, matters. Whitman's stated impulse for writing *Democratic Vistas* was to express his concerns about "the appaling [*sic*] dangers of universal suffrage," presenting the vote as a rite of superficial democracy (*WPP*, 930). No longer ratified by the people, the divine literatus would be sanctioned by his spiritual vision and cultural neglect.

Democratic Vistas was a carefully polished jeremiad and a finished literary work, but as a set of promotional activities, the *West Jersey Press* affair proved to be more effective. Its impact would continue for several years. The advantage Whitman enjoyed in 1876 was that the controversy took place wholly on the public stage and involved an array of different voices, all debating the value and treatment of *Leaves of Grass*. The controversy brought John Burroughs and O'Connor into print, each of whom published lengthy responses to Taylor's attacks. (O'Connor's essay "Walt Whitman: Is He Persecuted?" is noteworthy because the former friends had not spoken since 1872 after Whitman attacked O'Connor's support for the Fifteenth Amendment giving former male slaves the right to vote.[52]) John Swinton responded to Buchanan's nationalist rhetoric by calling on Americans to support its ailing poet. Writing in the *New York Herald,* he asserted that "Walt Whitman's countrymen should not allow him to suffer from penury in his old age. . . . his closing days should be cheered by those kindly memories, which, I hope, are not to reach him wholly from Great Britain."[53] Eventually, in 1880, Stedman would write an essay in *Scribner's* that not only praised the poet, but directly promoted the centennial edition by telling readers how they could purchase it.[54]

While Stedman's essay downplayed the charges of persecution and maltreatment, the sense that the United States had failed its poet persisted in the culture at large and resulted in the organization of benefits such as the Lincoln lecture in New York. No less a figure than Andrew Carnegie found it an outrage that the country had treated Whitman so poorly, saying, "I felt triumphant democracy disgraced" (*DN*, 2:414). Whitman's skeptics were quite insightful in understanding the success of a publicity campaign premised on the lack of popularity. In 1879, the *San Francisco Chronicle* commented that Whitman was "one of the most renowned unknowns" in America.[55] Several years later, the *New York Tribune* made a similar point, commenting, "The celebrity of this phenomenal poet bears a curious disproportion to the circulation of his writings."[56] Perhaps the most perceptive was Taylor himself, who in 1876 summed up the controversy: "No man in this country has ever been so constantly and skillfully advertised by his disciples as Walt Whitman."[57] The poet had built his reputation on his popular failure, establishing himself as the nation's poet not through democratic election but through his sacrifice and neglect.

Rather than focus on the quality of *Leaves of Grass*, the *West Jersey Press* affair relentlessly questioned the degree to which the nation had either supported or mistreated the poet. Buchanan, Swinton, and Carnegie all agreed that the poet's fame and condition were the public's responsibility. Their arguments return us to the logic of Whitman's 1855 pronouncement: "The proof of a poet is that his country absorbs him as affectionately as he has absorbed it." Whitman's lack of popularity became a sign not of poetic weakness but of a nation that had failed to live up to its ideals. The logic behind the pronouncement was now invoked to measure the culture in which he emerged. The arguments underscore the degree to which Whitman's supporters viewed his celebrity as a reflection of the community at large. What comes out of the 1876 controversy is a confirmation of the collaborative nature of celebrity and a fresh acknowledgement that nations had a role in constructing their poets' fame.

It was during this period that Whitman began to think of himself in collective terms. While publicly inhabiting the role of the isolated vanguard artist, he increasingly viewed his reputation as a communal enterprise. The task of promoting *Leaves of Grass* became "the Cause," a term his friends employed with as much frequency as did the poet. The publicly constituted personality of the early *Leaves of Grass* gave way to a corporate identity, with Whitman folding both himself and his supporters into the pronoun *We*. Hearing that a friend desired a manuscript for his collection, the poet indicated that he would certainly give him one: "I would be anxious—to give it him—give it anybody who had staked on us— stood up for us, especially when putting up the actual cash, as he as done" (*WWC*, 6:124). "We seem to be in demand," the poet commented in 1892 (*WWC*, 9:505). The phrasing aptly described the poet in the last decade of his life. Although drawing on the convention of editors and monarchs,

Whitman's *We* expressed the many people drawn into the vast promotional enterprise that extended from Mickle Street. By the 1880s, publicity for Whitman and *Leaves of Grass* involved a network of critics, reviewers, promoters, and financial backers in the United States, Canada, and Europe. When *New England* commissioned Traubel to write a ten-page essay on the poet, both men were delighted about the bonanza of interest. "How do you explain it, Horace?" Whitman asked. "As you say, it is significant. Is it because they are making such a racket about us in England, France, Germany?" (*WWC*, 6:41).

While Whitman's campaign for recognition persisted under the strategy that he had been overlooked by the people and ostracized by the literary establishment, he privately admitted that his position had radically changed. Evidence of Whitman's fame permeates his late conversations, filling the poet with wonder, excitement, and regret. The fame he had envisioned for himself in posterity now seemed to rush at him with stunning, unnerving power. When the American Press Association asked him to submit anything he wanted for publication, he could only reflect on the ironies of his fate: "O the mutations of years! Only a few years ago—five only—I waited for just such orders—wondered, and was willing, able, still with a modicum of strength: but no message came—the world did not want me. *Now*—hardly half a decade after, comes a multitude: comes cry and cry—after my power to respond is gone; after I am wrecked, stranded, left but to look for the end—or near end! And yet there is a sense of satisfaction even in this—though how much of such satisfaction is legitimate, justified—who knows? Can it be a passing fashion?" (*WWC*, 6:373–74). The fame Whitman had achieved was anything but a passing fashion, and while it did not result in the spontaneous celebrations he had fantasized about in his youth, it surely promised increased exposure and publicity. Although filled with regret about his weakening energy, the poet delighted in the attention he was receiving. "There has been a call everywhere for particulars of the life of the critter, Walt Whitman,"—the poet told Traubel in 1891—"the intimate things, which perhaps only a few know, but which are important in any life" (*WWC*, 8:154). To most of these requests, he was willing to comply. As he entered his final year, he approvingly saw the essays, books, and lectures that had been produced about him and the positive attention they were receiving. He saw his own work finding ready publication and soliciting warm words of praise. Turning to Traubel on one such occasion, he triumphantly proclaimed, "It is a *Leaves of Grass* wave!" (*WWC*, 8:44).[58]

POPULISM AND POETRY

In "Song of the Open Road," Whitman envisions his readers as an army marching across the country, and he urges them to follow through "struggles and wars" toward a goal that could not be "countermanded" (*WPP*, 307). Despite various tactical changes, despite victories and defeats, the poet viewed the public as a territory into which he hoped to expand. Through both bravado and skepticism, the campaign for *Leaves of Grass* persisted—with Whitman nourishing active rebellion and inviting the freshly conquered to join in the general celebrity. The poet's vision of fame was populist in nature, for despite enjoying the attention, he was never content simply to play the role of the literary lion, the man feted at dinners and benefits. Whether dressed in workingman's flannel or patrician velvet and lace, whether his hand was defiantly resting on his hip or amiably lifting a cardboard butterfly, he would tirelessly promote his broader ambitions to be a representative voice.

Whitman's immersion in publicity does not rival or compromise the aspects of his work that readers have praised since the nineteenth century: his egalitarian ethic, his giving voice to the body and sexuality, his elevation of marginalized groups, and his bold experiments with poetic form and language. The campaign for *Leaves of Grass* was a campaign for a web of political and aesthetic values that Whitman identified with his public personality. The poet's promotional activities work in concert with his poetry, tirelessly erasing the borders that traditionally separate symbol, theme, and lyric from icon, publicity, and self-advertisement. Within the desert Jeremiah, the new husband and comrade, the Bowery b'hoy, new messiah, and gun-toting abolitionist there is also the poet celebrating himself, convinced that we will join him in that activity. He is the passer of handbills, the voice in the crowd, the impresario who drapes red, white, and blue banners across the pages of his work.

Whitman's final experience of celebrity was one of the many deep ironies that riddled both his life and career. Far removed from the clamorous energy of the public hall or street, he rode the "*Leaves of Grass* wave" in the company of his housekeeper, his nurse, and the ever-faithful Traubel. He had begun campaigning for the role of national poet in 1855, and that campaign had taken him from Broadway to Pennsylvania Avenue to a mining camp high in the Rocky Mountains. With few exceptions, however, this poet of indirection would come to know his celebrity indirectly, through the textual evidence that steadily collected in his home on Mickle Street. The chromatic ovations and "electric force and muscle" he remembered from the crowds at the Old Bowery gave way to letters, press releases, clippings, and the regular visits of a small group of dedicated admirers (*WPP*, 1189). The feverish bodily experience of celebrity that he had envisioned in "Song of Myself" and "The Sleepers" became the promise of a disembodied immortality as the poet saw his physical self overtaken by textuality.

This final chapter in Whitman's life points to both the fragility and the persistence of his association of democratic populism with fame. In 1855, Whitman had made his identity as a poet contingent on the nation's affection for him, and as if to hurry that promise into reality, he had readily supplied his readers with images of their passionate embrace. Whitman's portraits of an ardent attentive crowd arose from a deep faith that his publicity was a form of civic education, and that through his guidance, the public would come to value his democratic achievements. Always a fictive and rhetorical presence in the early editions of *Leaves of Grass*, the public became an increasingly distant abstraction. Mulling over his career in 1891, the poet emphasized his resistance to a crowd that had been so prominent in the pages of *Leaves of Grass:* "I ought to say now—as I have always said—that I care nothing for the public, yet in a sense care for it a great deal. The public has little to do with my acts, deeds, words. I long ago saw that if I was to do anything at all I must disregard the howling throng—must go my own road, flinging back no bitter retort, but declaring myself unalterably whatever happened" (*WWC*, 8:129). Encouraged by a vanguard group of admirers, he viewed himself as a maverick who had bucked the fashionable trends, a man whose commitment to high aesthetic principles and revolutionary consciousness had led him to withstand the public itself.

Whitman's assessment of his career was largely accurate. He had become more conventional with old age and that conventionality appealed to Victorian audiences in both England and the United States. However, in trying to secure the people's interest, in trying to become their beloved bard, he held remarkably little concern for creating the kind of derivative, market-proven verse that his more popular contemporaries were producing. The early editions of *Leaves of Grass* don't seek to accommodate the public with familiar forms of poetry. In his bid for celebrity, the audience would have to come to Whitman, meeting him on his own revolutionary terms. The poet's fame would both fulfill and confirm the radically democratic poetics he saw himself as initiating.

At the same time, Whitman's claim to independence suggests an understanding of poetic fame that diverges from the democratic potential he had seen in celebrity before the Civil War. In this new conception, he had chosen literature, not the public, as his ultimate muse. The man who had once lamented the "howls restrained by decorum" (*LG* 1855, 32) now described the people as a "howling throng," a term he frequently applied to opponents of his work. The prospect of cultural elections seemed quite remote when Whitman distinguished between his reverence for the people and his devotion to art: "Strange as it may sound for a democrat to say so, I am clear that no free and original and loft-soaring poem, or one ambitious of those achievements, can possibly be fulfill'd by any writer who has largely in his thought *the public*—or the question, What will establish'd literature—What will the current authorities say about it?" (*WPP*, 1271–72). Whitman had initially seen revolutionary potential in the public sphere, but he now identified *the public* with the literary establishment. The public was the site of recognized authorities and the literary coteries he chastised in *Democratic Vistas*. The ambition to create a "free and original and loft-soaring poem" exists apart from the community that at one point was expected to support it. This modification is consistent with the sanction of neglect, for in elevating the artistry of his poems, Whitman liberated them from the burden of republican legitimacy. In the process, he liberated himself from the idea that countries would prove their poets. Whitman had expressed such sentiments early on, claiming in 1860 that future poets would be the ones to justify and define him. But at the end of his life he moved toward the familiar role of the isolated, misunderstood artist, the genius who eschews popular and critical endorsements. Expressing the fragility of Whitman's populist aesthetic, this position would eventually be absorbed into the rhetoric of modernism and the search for readers disciplined enough to master the rigor of modern poems: in the new literary landscape, poets might become famous or even immortal, but few would be popularly celebrated.

The final stage of Whitman's campaign indicates a fundamental shift in the culture of American celebrity. In emphasizing his distance from the crowd, Whitman was drawing on the rhetoric of the self-made man as it resurfaced in the late nineteenth century. In the 1840s and 1850s, he and other intellectuals had championed the values of romantic individualism, but as time wore on, increasing numbers of Americans used this language to understand their success in such fields as commerce, industry, warfare, and entertainment. Self-reliant men and women retained their independence in the midst of a stifling consensus. The self-made individual rose to prominence by beating the competition. Fame became a testament to individual power, not the popular will. People paid attention to the famous, but the engine of that fame lay in celebrities themselves. (It would not be until the 1920s that stars would again emphasize their populist roots.) In place of poets being elected into prominence, there would be novelists chronicling the lives of men and women who rose from obscurity to enjoy luxury, fame, and wealth. As Theodore Dreiser presented it in *Sister Carrie* (1900), celebrity was a kind of Darwinian achievement, an honor bestowed on select individuals who rose beyond meager circumstances to press their will upon the world. The democratic potential of fame lay not in its capacity to express popular sovereignty but in the fact that celebrity was a category open to everybody. Just as a Carnegie could rise from the streets to become one of the world's most powerful industrialists, strong and magnetic individuals could survive various misfortunes in rising to fame and glory. *Sister Carrie* expresses the porousness of class boundaries and the promise of upward mobility. It does not suggest the sense of popular election that Whitman witnessed at the Old Bowery.

By the century's end, the culture of celebrity had created a distinct class of social identity. Famous people associated with other famous people, and while potentially anyone could become famous, the company was rather select. In "The Death of the Lion" (1894), Henry James satirized the stature of authorial celebrity at the turn of the century. An English socialite perceives her distinct social advantage in having a renowned author attend a house party. Flattered by the author's company, both the host and her guests do not read the author's work, though they persistently revel in his talent and prestige. In a final irony that anticipates modernist concerns about texts and personality, they carelessly lose the only copy of his final manuscript as he sinks into death. James's allegory is clear: the magnum opus disappears when the author enters into publicity. For the aristocrats, socialites, and popular writers gathered during this house party, celebrity was a new form of distinguished company. The public observed the behavior of this democratic nobility in newspapers, journals, and magazines. The celebrity turned the multitudes not into individuals but spectators.

Whitman imagined fame as a form of political identity. Elected into prominence, the celebrated personality would inspire his fellow citizens into becoming the fitter, more godlike individuals necessary for democracy. On a historical level, his vision never had a chance, for from the beginning it had to compete with the genuine economic potential that others saw in fame. In the 1840s and 1850s, Barnum had intuitively developed ways to create wealth by exhibiting various real and imagined personalities before American and European audiences. By the century's end, celebrities were produced much more systematically. Whitman's early reflections had occurred alongside the rise of the daguerreotype and photograph in antebellum New York. He died in 1892, two years before the first kinetoscope parlor opened in the United States.[59] By 1908, there were four hundred nickelodeon theaters in New York City alone, and magazines such as the *Nation* were calling film "the first democratic art."[60] Over the next decades, as the number of theaters rose and studios wondered how to make their films more profitable, they discovered that audiences were particularly loyal to the actors and actresses who appeared on-screen. Studios developed a star system to cultivate their own celebrities as a kind of corporate aesthetic trademark. To the vast numbers of spectators eager for this fledgling entertainment, celebrity became a dream that might elevate a few individuals rather than redeem a nation.

NOTES

PREFACE

1. A useful study of Whitman's rising reputation is Charles B. Willard, *Whitman's American Fame: The Growth of his Reputation in America after 1892* (Providence: Brown University Press, 1950).
2. Neal Gabler, "Toward a New Definition of Celebrity," The Norman Lear Center, Annenberg School of Communication, University of Southern California, 2001, http://www.learcenter.org/pdf/Gabler.pdf.

INTRODUCTION: FRONTISPIECE

1. *"Leaves of Grass" with "Sands at Seventy" and "A Backward Glance o'er Travel'd Roads"* (Philadelphia: Ferguson Bros., 1889). According to the Department of Rare Books and Special Collections at the University of South Carolina Library, "The 1889 'birthday edition' of *Leaves of Grass* is actually the fourteenth printing of the seventh edition. It is the culmination of Whitman's long-time desire to publish a pocket-size edition of his work." See http://www.sc.edu/library/spcoll/amlit/whitman/ww4.html and http://memory.loc.gov/ammem/today/may31.html.
2. Ed Folsom and Ted Genoways, "The Butterfly Portrait," *Virginia Quarterly Review* 81 (Spring 2005): 118.
3. "Walt Whitman's New Book," *New York Critic*, January 13, 1883, 3, Ed Folsom and Kenneth M. Price, eds., *The Walt Whitman Archive*, http://www.whitmanarchive.org.
4. "Whitman Photographs," special issue, *Walt Whitman Quarterly Review* 4 (Fall–Winter 1986–87): 54.
5. Thomas Donaldson, *Walt Whitman: The Man* (New York: Harper, 1896), 64.

Keller claims to have received Whitman's last autograph, written in blue pencil on a copy of the butterfly photograph. See Elizabeth Leavitt Keller, *Walt Whitman in Mickle Street* (1921; repr., New York: Haskell House, 1971), 172.

6. William Roscoe Thayer, "Personal Recollections of Walt Whitman," in *Whitman in His Own Time*, ed. Joel Myerson (Detroit: Omnigraphics, 1991), 304, 303. Originally published in *Scribner's*, June 1919.

7. "Whitman's New Book," 3.

8. Thayer, "Personal Recollections," 303.

9. According to William Sloane Kennedy, the price rose from five to ten dollars. See *The Fight of a Book for the World* (West Yarmouth, MA: Stonecroft, 1926), 250.

10. Gary Schmidgall, *Walt Whitman: A Gay Life* (New York: Plume, 1997), 283–89.

11. Esther Shepherd, *Walt Whitman's Pose* (New York: Harcourt, Brace, 1936), 250.

12. For an early and bleak expression of this view, see Fisher Ames, "American Literature," in *The Works of Fisher Ames, with a Selection from His Speeches and Correspondence*, ed. Seth Ames (Boston: Little, Brown, 1854), 2:441–42. On the distinction between those arts that might lead to virtue and those that encouraged luxury and vice, see Neil Harris, *The Artist in American Society: The Formative Years, 1790–1860* (New York: George Braziller, 1966).

13. Joel Barlow, preface to *The Columbiad* (1809), Project Gutenberg, http://www.gutenberg.net/etext05/8clmb1oh.htm.

14. As cited in "Whitman Photographs," 54.

15. Michael Davidson, " 'When the World Strips Down and Rouges Up': Redressing Whitman," in *Breaking Bounds: Whitman and American Cultural Studies*, ed. Betsy Erkkila and Jay Grossman (New York: Oxford University Press, 1996), 223.

16. The original photograph featured Whitman with two children, a boy and a girl; in making the photograph an illustration of "Song of Myself," he cropped it so that only the boy was included. See "Whitman Photographs," 52.

17. For a full account of the first edition of *Specimen Days and Collect*, see Ed Folsom, *Whitman Making Books, Books Making Whitman: A Catalog and Commentary* (Iowa City: Obermann Center for Advanced Studies, 2005), 54–56.

18. For example, consider Vivian Pollak's stance toward Whitman's representation of sexuality: "As much recent criticism has demonstrated, Whitman's writings do not fully effect the visionary affiliations he proposes as his ideological goal. His gender and sex democracy remains unachieved; public discourse and private need are not identical; he is less generous and more aggressive than he purports to be." See *The Erotic Whitman* (Berkeley: University of California Press, 2000), xv.

19. R. M. Bucke to Horace Traubel, December 15, 1893, Horace and Anne Montgomery Traubel Collection, Library of Congress. My thanks to Michael Robertson for bringing this letter to my attention.

20. David S. Reynolds, *Walt Whitman's America: A Cultural Biography* (New York: Alfred A. Knopf, 1995). Notable discussions include Kenneth M. Price, *To*

Walt Whitman, America (Chapel Hill: University of North Carolina Press, 2004), 111–12; William Logan, "Prisoner, Fancy-Man, Rowdy, Lawyer, Physician, Priest: Whitman's Brags," *Virginia Quarterly Review* 81 (Spring 2005): 19–33; Heather Morton, "Democracy, Self-Reviews, and the 1855 *Leaves of Grass*," *Virginia Quarterly Review* 81 (Spring 2005): 229–43; Sean Francis, " 'Outbidding at the Start the Old Cautious Hucksters': Promotional Discourse and Whitman's 'Free' Verse," *Nineteenth-Century Literature* 57 (December 2002): 381–406; Terry Mulcaire, "Publishing Intimacy in *Leaves of Grass*," *ELH* 60 (Summer 1993): 471–503.

21. Michael Moon, ed., *Leaves of Grass and Other Writings* (New York: Norton, 2002).

22. On the butterfly's disappearance and recovery, see Gail Fineberg, "LC's Missing Whitman Notes Found in N.Y.," *Library of Congress Gazette*, February 24, 1995, http://memory.loc.gov/ammem/wwhtml/gazette1.html. I borrow the phrase "the occupant and expression of a virtual America" from S. Page Baty's *American Monroe: The Making of a Body Politic* (Berkeley: University of California Press, 1995), 32.

23. "Whitman Photographs," 54.

24. Thayer, "Personal Recollections," 304.

25. Neil Harris, *Humbug: The Art of P. T. Barnum* (Boston: Little, Brown, 1973), 77.

26. Joshua Gamson, *Claims to Fame: Celebrity in Contemporary America* (Berkeley: University of California Press, 1994), 156.

27. Leo Braudy, *The Frenzy of Renown: Fame and Its History* (New York: Oxford University Press, 1986; repr., New York: Vintage, 1997). Citations are to the Vintage edition.

28. Ibid.; Richard Schickel, *Intimate Strangers: The Culture of Celebrity* (Garden City, NY: Doubleday, 1985); P. David Marshall, *Celebrity and Power: Fame and Contemporary Culture* (Minneapolis: University of Minnesota Press, 1997).

29. Jay Grossman, *Reconstituting the American Renaissance: Emerson, Whitman, and the Politics of Representation* (Durham: Duke University Press, 2003). See also Jerome Loving, *Emerson, Whitman, and the American Muse* (Chapel Hill: University of North Carolina Press, 1982); Kenneth M. Price, *Whitman and Tradition: The Poet in His Century* (New Haven: Yale University Press, 1990), 35–52.

30. Braudy, *Frenzy of Renown*, 427.

CHAPTER 1: CELEBRITY

1. Justin Kaplan, *Walt Whitman: A Life* (New York: Simon and Schuster, 1980), 14.

2. For more information on the Whitman calendar, see Joann P. Krieg, "Grace Ellery Channing and the Whitman Calendar," *Walt Whitman Quarterly Review* 12 (Spring 1995): 252–56.

3. On the carnivalized atmosphere of antebellum print culture, see Isabelle Lehuu, *Carnival on the Page: Popular Print Media in Antebellum America* (Chapel Hill: University of North Carolina Press, 2000), 3–10, 156–57.

4. On the development of markets, see Harry L. Watson, *Liberty and Power: The*

Politics of Jacksonian America (New York: Farrar, Straus, and Giroux, 1990), 34–35; Charles Sellers, *The Market Revolution: Jacksonian America, 1815–1846* (New York: Oxford University Press, 1991), 364–95.

5. Benedict Anderson, *Imagined Communities: Reflections on the Origin and Spread of Nationalism* (New York: Verso, 1991), 7.

6. On the forming of class-based identities, see Sean Wilentz, *Chants Democratic: New York City and the Rise of the American Working Classes, 1789–1850* (New York: Oxford University Press, 1984).

7. On the Astor Place riot, see Richard Moody, *The Astor Place Riot* (Bloomington: Indiana University Press, 1958); Dennis Berthold, "Class Acts: The Astor Place Riots and Melville's 'The Two Temples,'" *American Literature* 71 (September 1999): 429–61.

8. All references to *The Compact Edition of the Oxford English Dictionary* (1971), s.v. "celebrity." For additional history of the word *celebrity*, see P. David Marshall, *Celebrity and Power: Fame and Contemporary Culture* (Minneapolis: University of Minnesota Press, 1997), 4–7.

9. Samuel Johnson, *Rambler* 165, in *The Yale Edition of the Works of Samuel Johnson*, ed. W. J. Bate and Albrecht B. Strauss (New Haven: Yale University Press, 1969), 3: 12.

10. Leo Braudy, *The Frenzy of Renown: Fame and Its History* (New York: Oxford University Press, 1986; repr., New York: Vintage, 1997), 371. Citations are to the Vintage edition.

11. Peter Briggs, "Laurence Sterne and Literary Celebrity in 1760," *Age of Johnson* 4 (1991), 263.

12. Ibid., 259.

13. See Braudy, *Frenzy of Renown*, 380–81.

14. Samuel Egerton Brydges, quoted in Ghislaine McDayter, "Conjuring Byron: Byromania, Literary Commodification, and the Birth of Celebrity," in *Byromania: Portraits of the Artist in Nineteenth- and Twentieth-Century Culture*, ed. Frances Wilson (New York: St. Martin's, 1999), 46–47. The ellipsis in the quote is in the original.

15. Mary Shelley, *Frankenstein; or, The Modern Prometheus*, ed. Johanna Smith (Boston: Bedford–St. Martin's, 2000), 21.

16. Frances Trollope, *Domestic Manners of the Americans* (New York: Vintage, 1949). On the use of celebrity, see Thomas N. Baker, *Sentiment and Celebrity: Nathaniel Parker Willis and the Trials of Literary Fame* (New York: Oxford University Press, 1998), 8.

17. "Sketches of Distinguished Females," *Vermont Gazette*, August 28, 1827, 1, Early American Newspapers Database, NewsBank and the American Antiquarian Society.

18. Caroline May, *The American Female Poets: With Biographical and Critical Notices* (Philadelphia: Lindsay and Blakiston, 1853), 15, The American Verse Project, University of Michigan Humanities Text Initiative, http://www.hti.umich.edu/a/amverse/.

19. Ralph Waldo Emerson, *Essays and Lectures*, ed. Joel Porte (New York: Library of America, 1983), 871. Future references to Emerson's essays will be made in the text; they refer to the above edition.

20. Mary Kupiec Cayton, "The Making of an American Prophet: Emerson, His Audiences, and the Rise of the Culture Industry in Nineteenth-Century America," *American Historical Review* 92 (June 1987): 602–3.

21. Baker, *Sentiment and Celebrity.*

22. Charles Dickens to John Forster, February 24, 1842, in *The Letters of Charles Dickens*, ed. Madeline House et al. (Oxford: Clarendon, 1974), 3: 87.

23. See Neil Harris, *Humbug: The Art of P. T. Barnum* (Boston: Little, Brown, 1973), 145, 121.

24. Joan D. Hedrick, *Harriet Beecher Stowe: A Life* (New York: Oxford, 1994), 238; Forrest Wilson, *Crusader in Crinoline: The Life of Harriet Beecher Stowe* (Philadelphia: Lippincott, 1941), 379.

25. *The Federalist Papers*, ed. Bernard Bailyn, *The Debate on the Constitution: Federalist and Antifederalist Speeches, Articles, and Letters during the Struggle over Ratification*, part 2 (New York: Library of America, 1993), 363–64; Alexander Hamilton to James A. Bayard, January 16, 1801, in *The Papers of Alexander Hamilton*, vol. 25, ed. Harold Syrett (New York: Columbia University Press, 1977), 323.

26. James Wilson, quoted in Gary Wills, *Cincinnatus: George Washington and the Enlightenment* (New York: Doubleday, 1984), 129.

27. Douglass Adair, "Fame and the Founding Fathers," in *Fame and the Founding Fathers*, ed. Trevor Colbourn (New York: Institute of Early American History and Culture), 8, 11.

28. John Adams and Benjamin Rush, *The Spur of Fame: Dialogues of John Adams and Benjamin Rush, 1805–1813*, ed. John A. Schutz and Douglass Adair (Indianapolis: Liberty Fund, 2001), 32.

29. Adair, "Fame and the Founding Fathers," 11, 8.

30. *The Adams-Jefferson Letters: The Complete Correspondence between Thomas Jefferson and Abigail and John Adams*, ed. Lester Cappon (Chapel Hill: University of North Carolina Press, 1988), 356.

31. John S. Noffsinger, *Correspondence Schools, Lyceums, Chautaquas* (New York: MacMillan, 1926), 102.

32. Carl Bode, *The American Lyceum: Town Meeting of the American Mind* (New York: Oxford University Press, 1956), 187.

33. Noffsinger, *Correspondence Schools*, 102; *American Lyceum, with the Proceedings of the Convention Held in New York, May 4, 1831, to Organize the National Department of the Institution* (Boston: Hiram Tupper, 1831), 6.

34. The Roll and Minutes of the West Philadelphia Lyceum (from September 28, 1843–April 4, 1844), in Elwood Redman Stokes, "Geological Notes and Verses, 1840–1899," Historical Society of Pennsylvania, Philadelphia.

35. Donald M. Scott, "The Profession That Vanished: Public Lecturing in Mid-Nineteenth-Century America," in *Professions and Professional Ideologies in*

America, ed. Gerald L. Geison (Chapel Hill: University of North Carolina Press, 1983), 19.

36. Bode, *American Lyceum,* 48.

37. Nathaniel Hawthorne, *The Blithedale Romance,* ed. Seymour Gross and Rosalie Murphy (Norton: New York, 1978), 237 (Nathaniel Hawthorne to Sophia Peabody, September 3, 1841); 238 (Nathaniel Hawthorne to Sophia Peabody, September 22, 1841); 5.

38. Ibid., 180.

39. There is some confusion in the terms, as the two are sometimes used synonymously. In the ensuing discussion, I'll refer to the lyceum as the locally organized event and the lecture as the regional or national attractions that later emerged.

40. George William Curtis, "Editor's Easy Chair," *Harper's* 24 (1862): 266–67, Making of America Digital Library, Cornell University Library, http://cdl .library.cornell.edu/moa/.

41. Peter Cherches, "Star Course: Popular Lectures and the Marketing of Celebrity in Nineteenth-Century America" (PhD diss., New York University, 1997), 52–53.

42. Curtis, "Editor's Easy Chair," 266–67.

43. Donald M. Scott, "The Popular Lecture and the Creation of a Public in Mid-Nineteenth-Century America," *Journal of American History* 66 (March 1980): 799–800.

44. Ibid., 807.

45. Cherches, "Star Course," 59.

46. Scott, "Popular Lecture," 793.

47. Curtis, "Editor's Easy Chair," 267.

48. "Lectures and Lecturing," *Putnam's* 9 (March 1857): 317, Making of America Digital Library, Cornell University Library, http://cdl.library.cornell.edu/ moa/.

49. Curtis, "Editor's Easy Chair," 267.

50. Cayton, "Making of an American Prophet," 617–18.

51. Hawthorne, *Blithedale,* 181.

52. Richard H. Brodhead, *Cultures of Letters: Scenes of Reading and Writing in Nineteenth-Century America* (Chicago: University of Chicago Press, 1993), 51–52.

53. Michael Winship provides the sales figures for Hawthorne and many other writers of the decade; see "Publishing *The Scarlet Letter* in the Nineteenth-Century United States," in *The Scarlet Letter,* ed. Rita K. Golin (Boston: Houghton-Mifflin, 2002), 69. For the publishing statistics of Stowe, Warner, Cummins, and Fern see Mary Kelley, *Private Woman, Public Stage: Literary Domesticity in Nineteenth-Century America* (New York: Oxford University Press, 1984), 26, 18, 24.

54. Brodhead, *Cultures of Letters,* 55.

55. Richard H. Brodhead, *The School of Hawthorne* (New York: Oxford University Press, 1990), 71.

56. The source of these book and newspaper statistics is Ezra Greenspan, *Walt Whitman and the American Reader* (New York: Cambridge University Press, 1990), 23.

57. Ibid., 21.

58. Kelley, *Private Woman*, 6.

59. Scott, "Popular Lecture," 798.

60. The Forrest divorce trial lasted from December 1851 to January 1852, though the scandals preceding it stretched as far back as 1848. See Baker, *Sentiment and Celebrity*, 115−57.

61. See Michael Newbury, "Eaten Alive: Slavery and Celebrity in Antebellum America," *ELH* 61:1 (1994): 174, 169, 176.

62. Hawthorne, *Blithedale*, 185.

63. Braudy, *Frenzy of Renown*, 450, 398, 493.

64. Alan Trachtenberg, *Reading American Photographs: Images as History, Mathew Brady to Walker Evans* (New York: Hill and Wang, 1989), 48.

65. Ibid., 60−61; *Harper's Weekly*, as cited in ibid., 42.

66. Tamara Plakins Thornton, *Handwriting in America: A Cultural History* (New Haven: Yale University Press, 1996), 88.

67. See Walter Benjamin, "The Work of Art in the Age of Mechanical Reproduction," in *Illuminations: Essays and Reflections*, ed. Hannah Arendt, trans. Harry Zohn (New York: Schocken, 1968), 223−24.

68. Braudy, *Frenzy of Renown*, 479.

69. Walt Whitman, Autograph MS Annotations, "The Poetical Works of Geoffrey Chaucer," *North British Review* (American edition), February 1849, 158−77, Trent Collection, Duke University Rare Book, Manuscript, and Special Collections Library.

70. Quoted in Kelley, *Private Woman*, 27.

71. Cayton, "Making of an American Prophet," 616.

72. Richard Sennett, *The Fall of Public Man* (New York: Knopf, 1977), 153.

73. *Pittsfield Sun*, December 29, 1859, 2, Early American Newspapers Database; "The Alboni," *New York Public Library*, The Picture Collection Online, http://digital.nypl.org.

74. Robert T. Oliver, *History of Public Speaking in America* (Boston: Allyn and Bacon, 1965), 376.

75. *Brooklyn Daily Eagle*, October 11, 1855, 2, the Brooklyn Public Library, http://eagle.brooklynpubliclibrary.org/.

76. Quoted in Terence Whalen, "P. T. Barnum and the Birth of Capitalist Irony," in *The Life of P. T. Barnum, Written by Himself* (Urbana: University of Illinois Press, 2000), ix.

77. F-260 variant; Emily Dickinson, *The Poems of Emily Dickinson*, vols, 1−3, ed. R. W. Franklin (Cambridge: Belknap, 1998), 279. Unless otherwise noted, future references to Dickinson's poems will be made by number in the text and will refer to the above edition.

78. *Brooklyn Daily Eagle*, October 11, 1855, 2.

79. "Lectures and Lecturing," 318.

80. Scott, "Popular Lecture," 806.

81. David S. Reynolds, *Walt Whitman's America: A Cultural Biography* (New York: Alfred A. Knopf, 1995), 182–83.

82. "The Hutchinson Family," December 4, 1843, *Daily Plebeian*, in Walt Whitman, *The Journalism*, vol. 1, *1834–1846*, ed. Herbert Bergman et al. (New York: Peter Lang, 1998), 176.

83. Reynolds, *Walt Whitman's America*, 155.

84. A particularly good reading of Barnum's exhibits is James W. Cook Jr.'s "Of Men, Missing Links, and Nondescripts: The Strange Career of P. T. Barnum's 'What is It?' Exhibit," in *Freakery: Cultural Spectacles of the Extraordinary Body*, ed. Rosemary Garland Thompson (New York: New York University Press, 1996), 139–57.

85. Jackson Lears, *Fables of Abundance: A Cultural History of Advertising in America* (New York: Basic Books, 1994), 62.

86. Edgar Allan Poe, "Lionizing," in *Collected Works of Edgar Allan Poe: Tales and Sketches, 1831–1842*, ed. Thomas Ollive Mabbott (Cambridge: Harvard University Press, 1978), 178. I am indebted to Braudy's discussion of this story in *Frenzy of Renown*, 465–66.

87. *Southern Quarterly Review*, n.s., 11 (January 1855): 272, Making of America Digital Library, Cornell University Library, http://cdl.library.cornell.edu/moa/. Readers may also be interested in F-481, in which Dickinson contrasts a personal sense of fame with the meaningless acclamations of the crowd.

88. John Keats, "On Fame (I)," in *The Complete Poems*, ed. John Barnard (London: Penguin, 1973), 342. For bibliographic information, see 647–48.

89. David S. Reynolds describes this attraction as the "paradox of immoral didacticism" in *Beneath the American Renaissance: The Subversive Imagination in the Age of Emerson and Melville* (Cambridge: Harvard University Press, 1989), 53–56.

90. Whitman, "Ourselves and the 'Eagle,'" June 1, 1846, in *The Journalism*, 391.

91. Both anecdotes come from David Grimsted, *Melodrama Unveiled: American Theater and Culture, 1800–1850* (Chicago: University of Chicago Press, 1968), 61.

92. Willis, quoted in Baker, *Sentiment and Celebrity*, 11, 99, 89, 101.

93. Bailyn, *The Federalist Papers*, part 1, 411; Willis, quoted in Baker, *Sentiment and Celebrity*, 101.

94. Willis, quoted in Lawrence W. Levine, *Highbrow/Lowbrow: The Emergence of Cultural Hierarchy in America* (Cambridge: Harvard University Press, 1988), 97.

95. Quoted in Baker, *Sentiment and Celebrity*, 101.

96. William Henry Hulbert, "Barnum's and Greeleys Biographies," *Christian Examiner and Religious Miscellany* 58 (March 1855): 246.

97. Scott, "Popular Lecture," 793, 808–9.

98. Bluford Adams, *E Pluribus Barnum: The Great Showman and the Making of American Popular Culture* (Minneapolis: University of Minnesota Press, 1997), 129–39.

99. Edgar Allan Poe, "The Man That Was Used Up: A Tale of the Late Bugaboo and Kickapoo Campaign," in Mabbott, *The Collected Works*, 380, 389.

100. The story specifically comments on the kinds of fame that were produced by the Indian captivity narrative. See David Haven Blake, " 'The Man That Was Used Up': Edgar Allan Poe and the Ends of Captivity," *Nineteenth-Century Literature* 57 (December 2002): 323–49.

101. Jonathan Elmer, *Reading at the Social Limit: Affect, Mass Culture, and Edgar Allan Poe* (Stanford: Stanford University Press, 1995), 50.

CHAPTER 2: PERSONALITY

1. Jerome Loving, *Walt Whitman: The Song of Himself* (Berkeley: University of California Press, 1999), 233.

2. Justin Kaplan, *Walt Whitman: A Life* (New York: Simon and Schuster, 1980), 242.

3. Allen Lesser, *Enchanting Rebel: The Secret of Adah Isaacs Menken* (Port Washington, NY: Kennikat, 1973), 64.

4. On Whitman, bohemia, and Pfaff's, see Christine Stansel, "Whitman at Pfaff's," *Walt Whitman Quarterly Review* 10 (Winter 1993): 107–26. Compare Whitman's description of Broadway with Aleksandr Lakier's: "In the evening Broadway presents a different scene, illuminated by gaslight from street lamps and from rows of magnificent stores, confectioners' shops, amusement and entertainment places. It is then that you think the American can, indeed, enjoy himself. The broad sidewalk is again congested with people, in the midst of whom the richly attired ladies appear in bursts of gay colors; couples swing off the main street either to the theater or to a sumptuously lighted confectioner's; at various places of entertainment flags are fluttering and music is playing; everywhere there are immense playbills and dreadful signs with portrayals of beasts and fantastic wonders. Go into any theater (there are about ten on Broadway) and all are full of people and everyone is enjoying himself in his own way. Parades by militia and especially the fire brigades with their equipment, music, flags, and fireworks are also frequent in the evening." Aleksandr Borisovich Lakier, *A Russian Looks at America: The Journey of Aleksandr Borisovich Lakier in 1857*, trans. Arnold Schrier and Joyce Story (Chicago: University of Chicago Press, 1979), 67.

5. P. David Marshall, *Celebrity and Power: Fame and Contemporary Culture* (Minneapolis: University of Minnesota Press, 1997), 65.

6. Warren Susman, *Culture as History: The Transformation of American Society in the Twentieth Century* (New York: Pantheon, 1984), xxi.

7. Ghislaine McDayter, "Conjuring Byron: Byromania, Literary Commodification, and the Birth of Celebrity," in *Byromania: Portraits of the Artist in Nineteenth- and Twentieth-Century Culture*, ed. Frances Wilson (New York: St. Martin's, 1999), 46.

8. Scott, quoted in ibid.

9. Thomas N. Baker, *Sentiment and Celebrity: Nathaniel Parker Willis and the Trials of Literary Fame* (New York: Oxford University Press, 1998), 5.

10. Trent Collection, Duke University Rare Book, Manuscript, and Special Collec-

tions Library; also in the Trent Collection is Whitman's annotation of the essay "Characteristics of Shelley" from *American Whig Review* (May 1847): 534–36.

11. Susman, *Culture as History*, 273–74, 277.

12. Charles E. Feinberg Collection, Library of Congress, reel 24.

13. Ibid., reel 25.

14. Stephen Railton, " 'As If I Were With You'—The Performance of Whitman's Poetry," in *The Cambridge Companion to Walt Whitman*, ed. Ezra Greenspan (New York: Cambridge University Press, 1995), 14, 16.

15. Walt Whitman, "[A Leisurely Day]," New York Aurora, April 6, 1842, in Walt Whitman, *The Journalism*, vol. 1, *1834–1846*, ed. Herbert Bergman et al. (New York: Peter Lang, 1998), 100.

16. Franck writes, "We cannot bear not playing any role in the other being's consciousness." See Georg Franck, "The Economy of Attention," *Telepolis*, December 12, 1999, http://www.heise.de/tp/r4/artikel/5/5567/1.html.

17. Hans Bergman, *God in the Street: New York Writing from the Penny Press to Melville* (Philadelphia: Temple University Press, 1995), 24.

18. Richard H. Brodhead, *Cultures of Letters: Scenes of Reading and Writing in Nineteenth-Century America* (Chicago: University of Chicago Press, 1993), 57.

19. See Derek Hudson, *Martin Tupper: His Rise and Fall* (London: Constable, 1949), 111–35.

20. John Hollander, *American Poetry: The Nineteenth Century*, vol. 1 (New York: Library of America, 1993), 1005. Halleck's poems appeared in at least eleven anthologies between the years 1840 and 1850. See John W. M. Hallock, *The American Byron: Homosexuality and the Fall of Fitz-Greene Halleck* (Madison: University of Wisconsin Press, 2000), 123.

21. On Whittier's career, see Barbara Packer, "American Verse Traditions, 1800–1855," in *The Cambridge History of American Literature*, vol. 4, *Nineteenth-Century Poetry, 1800–1910*, ed. Sacvan Bercovitch (New York: Cambridge University Press, 2004), 138–42; on Whittier's relation to Whitman, see David S. Reynolds, *Walt Whitman's America: A Cultural Biography* (New York: Alfred A. Knopf, 1995), 318–19.

22. Perry Miller, "John Greenleaf Whittier: The Conscience in Poetry," in *Critical Essays on John Greenleaf Whittier*, ed. Jayne K. Kribbs (Boston: G. K. Hall, 1980), 208.

23. Packer, "American Verse Traditions," 77, 80.

24. Charles H. Brown, *William Cullen Bryant* (New York: Charles Scribner's, 1971), 197, 320, 325, 500–2.

25. William Pannapacker, *Revised Lives: Walt Whitman and Nineteenth-Century Authorship* (New York: Routledge, 2003), 54.

26. Richard Broom Beatty, *James Russell Lowell* (New York: Archon 1969), 91, 102, 130.

27. "*Evangeline—A Poem of Arcadie*," *Brooklyn Daily Eagle*, November 20, 1847, 1, the Brooklyn Public Library, http://eagle.brooklynpubliclibrary.org/.

28. Kirsten Silva Gruesz, "Feeling for the Fireside: Longfellow, Lynch, and the To-pography of Poetic Power," in *Sentimental Men: Masculinity and the Politics of Affect in American Culture*, ed. Mary Chapman and Glenn Hendler (Berkeley: University of California Press, 1999), 50.

29. I offer only a sampling of the sales statistics Longfellow was tracking. All statistics come from Charles C. Calhoun, *Longfellow: A Rediscovered Life* (Boston: Beacon, 2004), 198–99.

30. "A Splendid Picture for the Parlors of Brooklyn!" *Brooklyn Daily Eagle*, January 19, 1847, 2; "Noble Specimen of American Art: Mr. E. Anthony's Engraving of the U.S. Senate Chamber," *Brooklyn Daily Eagle*, October 22, 1847, 1. Both articles are online at the Brooklyn Public Library. http://eagle .brooklynpubliclibrary.org/.

31. "Come Up from the Fields Father" appeared in Richard Chenevix Trench's *A Household Book of English Poetry* (London: Macmillan, 1868). See Ed Folsom. " 'Affording the Rising Generation an Adequate Notion': Whitman in Nineteenth-Century Textbooks, Handbooks, and Anthologies," in *Studies in the American Renaissance*, ed. Joel Myerson (Charlottesville: University Press of Virginia, 1991), 350–51.

32. Henry Wadsworth Longfellow, *The Poetical Works of Longfellow* (Boston: Houghton-Mifflin, 1975), 14–15.

33. "Four Letters on Interesting Subjects" (Philadelphia, 1776), in Charles S. Hyneman and Donald S. Lutz, eds., *American Political Writing during the Founding Era, 1760–1805* (Indianapolis: Liberty, 1983), 1:386. On Paine's authorship of this anonymous pamphlet, see A. Owen Aldridge, *Thomas Paine's American Ideology* (Newark: University of Delaware Press, 1984), 219–39.

34. Thomas Paine, *Rights of Man*, ed. Eric Foner (New York: Penguin, 1984), 219. Future references to *Rights of Man* will be made in the text; they refer to the above edition.

35. Charles E. Feinberg Collection, reel 21.

36. Lawrence W. Levine, *Highbrow/Lowbrow: The Emergence of Cultural Hierarchy in America* (Cambridge: Harvard University Press, 1988), 240.

37. The phrase "strategy of personal abstraction" comes from Michael Warner, "The Mass Public and the Mass Subject," in *The Phantom Public Sphere*, ed. Bruce Robbins (Minneapolis: University of Minnesota Press, 1993), 239. See also Warner's *The Letters of the Republic: Publication and the Public Sphere in Eighteenth-Century America* (Cambridge: Harvard University Press, 1990) for a more extensive discussion of this subject.

38. Walt Whitman, *New York Dissected: A Sheaf of Recently Discovered Newspaper Articles by the Author of "Leaves of Grass,"* ed. Emory Holloway and Ralph Adimari (New York: Rufus Rockwell Wilson, 1936), 171.

39. Peter Briggs, "Laurence Sterne and Literary Celebrity in 1760," *Age of Johnson* 4 (1991): 255.

40. Tenny Nathanson, *Whitman's Presence: Body, Voice, and Writing in "Leaves of Grass"* (New York: New York University Press, 1992), 114–15.

41. Susman, *Culture as History*, 280.

42. William Douglas O'Connor, *The Good Gray Poet: A Vindication* (1866), in Ed Folsom and Kenneth M. Price, eds., *The Walt Whitman Archive*, http://www .whitmanarchive.org.

43. Charles E. Feinberg Collection, reel 25.

44. Ibid.; Whitman's ellipses. Whitman envisions the kind of "collective effervescence" that Emile Durkheim associated with religion and that Chris Rojek has connected to celebrity. See Rojek, *Celebrity* (London: Reaktion, 2001), 56–58.

45. Edmund S. Morgan, *Inventing the People: The Rise of Popular Sovereignty in England and America* (New York: W. W. Norton, 1988), 286.

46. Brian Seitz, *The Trace of Representation* (New York: State University of New York Press, 1995), 5.

47. Daniel Dayan and Elihu Katz, "Electronic Ceremonies: Television Performs a Royal Wedding," in *On Signs*, ed. Marshall Blonsky (Baltimore: Johns Hopkins University Press, 1985), 23–28.

48. James H. Justus, "The Fireside Poets: Hearthside Values and the Language of Care," in *Nineteenth-Century American Poetry*, ed. A. Robert Lee (London: Vision / Totowa, NJ: Barnes and Noble, 1985), 150–55; Longfellow, "The Poet's Calendar," *Poetical Works*, 349; James Russell Lowell, *The Poetical Works of James Russell Lowell* (Boston: Houghton Mifflin, 1978), 321.

49. Gruesz, "Feeling for the Fireside," 50–52. Gruesz refers to Longfellow's poem "Dedication," in *Poetical Works*, 99. It is important to note that the poet also depicts himself as a companion during the reader's seaside walk.

50. Whitman's use of the word *fire* is similarly hostile to domestic comfort. It generally falls into three categories: homes that are in flame, the burning passion of sexual desire, and the discharge of guns and armaments.

51. Susman, *Culture as History*, 277.

CHAPTER 3: PUBLICITY

1. [Henry James], "Mr. Walt Whitman," *Nation*, November 16, 1865), 625–26, Ed Folsom and Kenneth M. Price, eds., *The Walt Whitman Archive*, http:// www.whitmanarchive.org/.

2. Jonathan Franzen's public discomfort about an invitation to appear on *The Oprah Winfrey Show* is just one example of contemporary novelists resisting promotion and publicity. A history of this relationship appears in Joe Moran, *Star Authors: Literary Celebrity in America* (London: Pluto Press, 2000); and Loren Glass, *Authors, Inc.: Literary Celebrity in the Modern United States, 1880–1980* (New York University Press, 2004).

3. "Advertising on the Sly," *New York Daily Times*, April 3, 1854, 4, ProQuest Historical Newspapers database.

4. See, for example, John Updike, "Walt Whitman: Ego and Art," *New York Review of Books*, February 9, 1978: 33; Ivan Marki, *The Trial of the Poet: An Interpretation of the First Editions of "Leaves of Grass"* (New York: Columbia University Press, 1976), 91, 95–96; James E. Miller, *The American Quest for a*

Supreme Fiction: Whitman's Legacy in the Personal Epic (Chicago: University of Chicago Press, 1979), 31–49.

5. Betsy Erkkila, *Whitman: The Political Poet* (New York: Oxford University Press, 1989), 95.

6. Lawrence W. Levine, *Highbrow/Lowbrow: The Emergence of Cultural Hierarchy in America* (Cambridge: Harvard University Press, 1988); Carl Bode, *The Anatomy of American Popular Culture, 1840–1861* (Berkeley: University of California Press, 1959). See also Edward Pessen, *Jacksonian America: Society, Personality, Politics,* rev. ed. (Urbana: University of Illinois Press, 1985).

7. G. Allen Foster, *Advertising: Ancient Market Place to Television* (New York: Criterion, 1967), 66–71.

8. On the emergence of commercial signage in New York City, see David M. Henkin, *City Reading: Written Words and Public Spaces in Antebellum New York* (New York: Columbia University Press, 1998), 39–100.

9. "Extra! Printing for the Million," *Chicago Daily Democratic Press,* , May 14, 1855, American Memory, Printed Ephemera Collection, Library of Congress, http://memory.loc.gov/.

10. *Brooklyn Daily Eagle,* July 12, 1855, 2, the Brooklyn Public Library, http://eagle.brooklynpubliclibrary.org/.

11. Globe Advertising Agency (Boston, Spring 1859), American Memory, Printed Ephemera Collection, Library of Congress, http://memory.loc.gov/.

12. Walt Whitman, *New York Dissected: A Sheaf of Recently Discovered Newspaper Articles by the Author of "Leaves of Grass,"* ed. Emory Holloway and Ralph Adimari (New York: Rufus Rockwell Wilson, 1936), 131.

13. Ezra Greenspan, *Walt Whitman and the American Reader* (New York: Cambridge University Press, 1990), 240.

14. Quoted in Pamela Walker Laird, *Advertising Progress: American Business and the Rise of Consumer Marketing* (Baltimore: Johns Hopkins University Press, 1998), 44.

15. Phineas Taylor Barnum, *The Life of P. T. Barnum, Written by Himself* (Urbana: University of Illinois Press, 2000), 153.

16. P. T. Barnum, *Struggles and Triumph; or, The Life of P.T. Barnum,* ed. George S. Bryan (New York: Knopf, 1927), 196.

17. Barnum tells the story in *Struggles and Triumphs,* 196–97. Neil Harris provides a useful discussion of this incident in *Humbug: The Art of P. T. Barnum* (Boston: Little, Brown, 1973), 22, 53–54.

18. *Brooklyn Daily Eagle,* July 12, 1855, 2, the Brooklyn Public Library, http://eagle.brooklynpubliclibrary.org/.

19. Jennifer Wicke, *Advertising Fictions: Literature, Advertisement, and Social Reading* (New York: Columbia University Press, 1988), 58.

20. As quoted in ibid., 76.

21. Jurgen Habermas, *The Structural Transformation of the Public Sphere: An Inquiry into a Category of Bourgeois Society,* trans. Thomas Burger and Frederick Lawrence (Cambridge: MIT Press, 1991), 184.

22. Richard Salmon, *Henry James and the Culture of Publicity* (London: Cambridge University Press, 1997), 7.

23. Barnum, *Life of P. T. Barnum*, 233.

24. *Brooklyn Daily Eagle*, July 15, 1846, 3, the Brooklyn Public Library, http://eagle .brooklynpubliclibrary.org/.

25. Both advertisements come from the *New York Daily Times*, September 22, 1851, 3, ProQuest Historical Newspapers database.

26. Terence Whalen, "P. T. Barnum and the Birth of Capitalist Irony," in *Life of P. T. Barnum*, xiii.

27. Barnum, *Life of P. T. Barnum*, 153.

28. James, "Mr. Walt Whitman."

29. On the history of *Franklin Evans* (and Whitman's various efforts to distance himself from it), see the editorial comments in Walt Whitman, *EPF*, 124; citations to the novel are to this scholarly edition and occur in the text itself; citations to the *New World* edition are to Walter Whitman, *Franklin Evans; or, The Inebriate: A Tale of the Times*, *New World* Extra Series, November 23, 1842, The Henry W. and Albert A. Berg Collection of English and American Literature, New York Public Library.

30. See Whitman's March 24, 1842 editorial, "Bamboozle and Benjamin," printed in Whitman, *The Journalism*, vol. 1, *1834–1846*, ed. Herbert Bergman et al. (New York: Peter Lang, 1998), 69; on Whitman's stormy relationship with Park Benjamin, see Greenspan, *Whitman and the American Reader*, 44–47.

31. Walt Whitman, *I Sit and Look Out: Editorials from the "Brooklyn Daily Times,"* ed. Emory Holloway and Vernolian Schwarz (New York: Columbia University Press, 1932), 34–35.

32. Alexis de Tocqueville, *Democracy in America*, ed. Richard D. Heffner (1984; repr., New York: Mentor, 1949), 149.

33. P. David Marshall, *Celebrity and Power: Fame and Contemporary Culture* (Minneapolis: University of Minnesota Press, 1997), 58.

34. [Walt Whitman], "Walt Whitman and His Poems," *United States Review* 5 (September 1855): 205–12, Folsom and Price, *The Walt Whitman Archive*.

35. [Walt Whitman], "An English and American Poet" [review of Alfred Tennyson, *Maud, and other poems* and *Leaves of Grass*], *American Phrenological Journal* 22 (October 1855): 90–91, Folsom and Price, *The Walt Whitman Archive*.

36. Ibid.

37. Whitman, "Walt Whitman and His Poems."

38. David S. Reynolds, *Walt Whitman's America: A Cultural Biography* (New York: Alfred A. Knopf, 1995), 344.

39. *Graham's*, Trent Collection, Duke University Rare Book, Manuscript, and Special Collections Library. The quote is from p. 99.

40. Greenspan, *Whitman and the American Reader*, 154.

41. William Wordsworth, *Selected Poetry*, ed. Mark Van Doren (New York: Random House, 1950), 677–78.

42. *Brooklyn Daily Eagle*, December 15, 1860, 1, the Brooklyn Public Library, http://eagle.brooklynpubliclibrary.org/. "ONE OF MRS. SHERMAN'S EXCELSIOR SKIRTS IS WORTH AT LEAST TWELVE OF ANY OTHER KIND. Woven skirts 11

springs. as as low 50cts[*sic*]; 20 springs 87 cts; 30 springs $1.25. Our steel is prepared by a new chemical process, making it tougher and more elastic than any other in use. . . . As to the quality of our Skirts we refer to the ladies of Brooklyn. We have reduced our prices, but the quality of our goods shall be as they ever have been the best."

43. "Root's Daguerreotype" (Philadelphia, 1855), American Memory, Printed Ephemera Collection, Library of Congress, http://memory.loc.gov/.

44. R. H. Macy, "We Sell Good Goods," *Harper's Weekly,* February 12, 1859, 111, http://advertising.harpweek.com/.

45. "Salom's Great Bazaar" (Boston, 1860), American Memory, Printed Ephemera Collection, Library of Congress, http://memory.loc.gov /.

46. "An Appeal to Manhood," Grover and Baker Sewing Machines, *Harper's Weekly,* December 18, 1858, 815, http://advertising.harpweek.com; "An Old Song," Costar's Vermin Exterminators, *Harper's Weekly,* May 12, 1860, 302, http://advertising.harpweek.com.

47. Quoted in Michael Newbury, "Eaten Alive: Slavery and Celebrity in Antebellum America," *ELH* 61:1 (1994): 159. Fields's poem originally appeared in *American Publishers Circle,* September 29, 1855, 74.

48. *Brooklyn Daily Eagle,* November 26, 1855, 2, the Brooklyn Public Library, http://eagle.brooklynpubliclibrary.org/.

49. "Salom's Great Bazaar."

50. On the emergence of this line and the connections between free verse and slavery, see Martin Klammer, *Whitman, Slavery, and the Emergence of "Leaves of Grass"* (University Park: Pennsylvania State University Press, 1995), 118; Kenneth M. Price, *To Walt Whitman, America* (Chapel Hill: University of North Carolina Press, 2004), 12–13.

51. Sean Francis, " 'Outbidding at the Start the Old Cautious Hucksters': Promotional Discourse and Whitman's 'Free' Verse," *Nineteenth-Century Literature* 57 (December 2002): 393; Whitman, "An English and American Poet."

52. Lawrence Buell, "Transcendentalist Catalogue Rhetoric: Vision versus Form," *American Literature* 40 (November 1968): 328.

53. Aleksandr Borisovich Lakier, *A Russian Looks at America: The Journey of Aleksandr Borisovich Lakier in 1857,* trans. Arnold Schrier and Joyce Story (Chicago: University of Chicago Press, 1979), 67.

54. *Brooklyn Daily Eagle,* December 15, 1859, 3, the Brooklyn Public Library, http://eagle.brooklynpubliclibrary.org/.

55. [George Gliddon], "Egypt's Revelations" (1851), The Emergence of Advertising in America: 1850–1920, Hartman Center for Sales, Advertising & Marketing History, Duke University Rare Book, Manuscript, and Special Collections Library, http://scriptorium.lib.duke.edu/eaa/index.html.

56. *Brooklyn Daily Eagle,* November 19, 1846, 2, the Brooklyn Public Library, http://eagle.brooklynpubliclibrary.org/.

57. "Grand Historic Mirror of the American War!" The Emergence of Advertising in America: 1850–1920, Hartman Center for Sales, Advertising & Marketing

History, Duke University Rare Book, Manuscript, and Special Collections Library, http://scriptorium.lib.duke.edu/eaa/index.html.

58. *New York Times*, March 18, 1852.

59. *Brooklyn Daily Eagle*, November 18, 1852, 2, the Brooklyn Public Library, http://eagle.brooklynpubliclibrary.org/. The tone in this advertisement from the Brooklyn Institute is remarkably full of bombast when compared to announcements in previous and subsequent years. I have not been able to account for the discrepancy.

60. *Excelsior: Journals of the Hutchinson Family Singers, 1842–1846*, ed. Dale Cockrell (Stuyvesant: Pendragon Press, 1989), 85. As Cockrell points out in his extensive annotations, the effort to mislead is clear, though by the most strict construction, the sentence was accurate: the songs' *arrangements* had been performed by *other* singers in New York City.

61. C. Carroll Hollis, *Language and Style in "Leaves of Grass"* (Baton Rouge: Louisiana State University Press, 1983), 94–95.

62. *The Federalist Papers*, ed. Bernard Bailyn, *The Debate on the Constitution: Federalist and Antifederalist Speeches, Articles, and Letters during the Struggle over Ratification*, part 1 (New York: Library of America, 1993), 409.

63. Laird, *Advertising Progress*, 21.

64. On the financial aspects of patent medicine advertising, see Edd Applegate, *Personalities and Products: A Historical Perspective of Advertising in America* (Westport, CT: Greenwood, 1998), 77.

65. *Pittsfield Sun*, 25 January 1855, 3, Early American Newspapers Database. Whitman's own promotional pamphlets worked in strikingly similar terms, presenting the poet as an authentic, original voice that would redress the nation's failings, a voice that had produced a significant cultural response.

66. *Brooklyn Daily Eagle*, September 30, 1847, 1, the Brooklyn Public Library, http://eagle.brooklynpubliclibrary.org/.

67. "Other remedies operate as palliations; this strikes at the very root of the disease, with resistless potency and energy, completely purifying the blood, thoroughly cleanses the system, acts in perfect harmony with the laws of life, and leaves the skin in a healthy state, the bowels open and free, and the patient hale, hearty and happy." *The People's Illustrated Almanac* (Clapp & Townsend, 1848), Special Collections, Library Company of Philadelphia.

68. *An Indian Tradition. No Fiction. The Traditionary History of a Narrow and Providential Escape of Some White Men . . .* (Brant's Indian Medicines, 1848), Library Company of Philadelphia.

69. Wicke, *Advertising Fictions*, 58.

70. John Berger, *Ways of Seeing* (New York: Penguin, 1977), 146.

71. Erkkila, *Whitman: The Political Poet*, 101; see also Michael Moon's analysis of section 11 in *Disseminating Whitman: Revision and Corporeality in "Leaves of Grass"* (Cambridge: Harvard University Press, 1991), 37–47.

72. Lauren Berlant, "National Brands/National Life," in *The Phantom Public Sphere*, ed. Bruce Robbins (Minneapolis: University Minnesota Press, 1993), 186.

73. Quentin Anderson, *The Imperial Self: An Essay in American Literary and Cultural History* (New York: Knopf, 1971), ix.

74. Bluford Adams, *E Pluribus Barnum: The Great Showman and the Making of American Popular Culture* (Minneapolis: University of Minnesota Press, 1997), 36.

75. Jacques Derrida, "Call It a Day for Democracy," in *The Other Heading: Reflections on Today's Europe*, trans. Pascale-Anne Brault and Michael B. Naas (Bloomington: University of Indiana Press, 1992), 87.

CHAPTER 4: INTIMACIES

1. On Bucke's vision of Whitman, see Michael Robertson, *Worshiping Walt: The Religion of Walt Whitman* (Princeton: Princeton University Press, forthcoming).

2. William Sloane Kennedy, *The Fight of a Book for the World* (West Yarmouth, MA: Stonecroft, 1926), 85–86.

3. I refer to "Song of Myself," section 3, and "As I Sit Writing Here."

4. The Archives of the Eagle Street College, Bolton, England, can be accessed through http://www.a2a.org.uk/.

5. Beatriz Colomina, *Privacy and Publicity: Modern Architecture as Mass Media* (Cambridge: MIT Press, 1994), 7–8.

6. Jackson Lears, *Fables of Abundance: A Cultural History of Advertising in America,* (Basic Books: New York, 1994), 137–40.

7. Thomas N. Baker, *Sentiment and Celebrity: Nathaniel Parker Willis and the Trials of Literary Fame* (New York: Oxford University Press, 1998), 181, 44.

8. Charles L. Ponce de Leon, *Self-Exposure: Human-Interest Journalism and the Emergence of Celebrity in America, 1890–1940* (Chapel Hill: University of North Carolina Press, 2002). My discussion draws from pp. 29–34; the quotes are found on p. 29.

9. Richard Schickel, *Intimate Strangers: The Culture of Celebrity* (Garden City, NY: Doubleday, 1985), 4, 14–16.

10. Ann Douglas stands at the forefront of these scholars, but her argument that the sentimentality of women's fiction anticipates the bathos of contemporary commercial culture has received much revision. See Ann Douglas, *The Feminization of American Culture* (New York: Avon, 1977), 307–9. For dissenting views, see Jane Tompkins, *Sensational Designs: The Cultural Work of American Fiction, 1790–1860* (New York: Oxford University Press, 1985); Jean Fagan Yellin, *Women and Sisters: The Anti-Slavery Feminists* (New Haven: Yale University Press, 1989); Lauren Berlant, "The Female Woman: Fanny Fern and the Form of Sentiment," in *The Culture of Sentiment: Race, Gender, and Sentimentality in Nineteenth Century America,* ed. Shirley Samuels (New York: Oxford University Press, 1992), 265–81.

11. D. H. Lawrence, *Selected Literary Criticism,* ed. Anthony Beal (New York: Viking Compass, 1966), 403–5.

12. *Christian Spiritualist* (1856). Full bibliographical data is missing; it is reprinted in Whitman, *"Leaves of Grass" Imprints* (Boston: Thayer and Eldridge, 1860),

32–36, and available online at Ed Folsom and Kenneth M. Price, eds., *The Walt Whitman Archive,* http://www.whitmanarchive.org/.

13. "New Publications: The New Poets," *New York Times,* May 19, 1860, supplement, 1, Folsom and Price, *The Walt Whitman Archive.*

14. Robert Buchanan, "Walt Whitman" [review of *Leaves of Grass* (1867) and *Drum-Taps*], *Broadway* 1 (November 1867): 188–95, Folsom and Price, *The Walt Whitman Archive.*

15. John Burroughs, "Walt Whitman and His Drum-Taps," *Galaxy,* December 1, 1866), 606–15, Folsom and Price, *The Walt Whitman Archive.*

16. "Ourselves and the 'Eagle,'" *Brooklyn Eagle,* June 1, 1846, in Walt Whitman, *The Journalism,* vol. 1, *1834–1846,* ed. Herbert Bergman et al. (New York: Peter Lang, 1998), 391.

17. "A Merry Christmas," *Brooklyn Daily Eagle,* December 24, 1847, 2, the Brooklyn Public Library, http://eagle.brooklynpubliclibrary.org/.

18. See Yellin, *Women and Sisters;* Samuels, *The Culture of Sentiment.*

19. Autograph Manuscript Notes on a Magazine Excerpt entitled "Christopher under Canvas," 1849, Trent Collection, Duke University Rare Book, Manuscript, and Special Collections Library.

20. Burroughs, "Walt Whitman and His Drum-Taps."

21. Martin Klammer, *Whitman, Slavery, and the Emergence of "Leaves of Grass"* (University Park: Pennsylvania State University Press, 1995), 118, 136.

22. Martha C. Nussbaum, *Poetic Justice: The Literary Imagination and Public Life* (Boston: Beacon, 1995), 118–20.

23. Klammer, *Whitman, Slavery;* Nussbaum, *Poetic Justice.*

24. Fern wrote serialized fiction for the *Ledger* through June 1855. In January 1856, she began writing her weekly column for the newspaper; this appeared until her death in 1872. See Carolyn L. Kitch, "'The Courage to Call Things by Their Right Names': Fanny Fern, Feminine Sympathy, and Feminist Issues in Nineteenth-Century American Journalism," *American Journalism* 13:3 (1996): 293–94.

25. Deborah Applegate, "Authorship in the 1850s: Sympathy, Celebrity, and the Ideological Formation of the Middle Class" (paper presented at the American Studies Association, Washington, D.C., October 31, 1997). My thanks to Professor Applegate for sharing her paper with me.

26. Fanny Fern, *Ruth Hall* (New York: Penguin, 1997), 213.

27. Schickel, *Intimate Strangers.*

28. Baker, *Sentiment and Celebrity,* 12.

29. Michael Newbury, "Eaten Alive: Slavery and Celebrity in Antebellum America," *ELH* 61:1 (1994): 161.

30. On Jenny Lind's fans, see N. Parker Willis, *Memoranda of the Life of Jenny Lind* (Philadelphia: Robert E. Peterson, 1851), 231–33.

31. Redpath, quoted in Peter Cherches, "Star Course: Popular Lectures and the Marketing of Celebrity in Nineteenth-Century America" (PhD diss., New York University, 1997), 235.

32. Philip Quilbert, "Drift-Wood," *Galaxy* 9 (March 1870): 419, Making of America Digital Library, Cornell University Library, http://cdl.library.cornell.edu/moa/.

33. Willis, *Memoranda*, 169–70.

34. Frederika Bremer, "Jenny Lind," *Harper's* 1 (June–November 1850): 657, Making of America Digital Library, Cornell University Library, http://cdl.library.cornell.edu/moa/.

35. William Moulton's exposé of Fanny Fern, *The Life and Beauties of Fanny Fern*, had appeared earlier that year in March 1855; see Kitch, " 'The Courage,' " 292–93; review of *The Life and Beauties of Fanny Fern*, *United States Democratic Review* (March 1855): 235–36, Making of America Digital Library, Cornell University Library, http://cdl.library.cornell.edu/moa/.

36. Baker, *Sentiment and Celebrity*, 181.

37. William Wordsworth, " 'My Heart Leaps Up When I Behold,' " in *Selected Poetry*, ed. Mark Van Doren (New York: Random House, 1950), 462.

38. Helen Price, quoted in Richard Maurice Bucke, *Walt Whitman*, in *Whitman in His Own Time*, ed. Joel Myerson (Detroit: Omnigraphics, 1991), 27–28.

39. [Walt Whitman], "All about a Mocking-Bird," *New York Saturday Press*, January 7, 1860, 3, Folsom and Price, *The Walt Whitman Archive*.

40. Erkkila, *The Political Poet*, 179. Erkkila alludes to Calamus 5 in making this argument.

41. David S. Reynolds, *Walt Whitman's America: A Cultural Biography* (New York: Alfred A. Knopf, 1995), 401.

42. Betsy Erkkila, "Public Love: Whitman and Political Theory," *Whitman East and West: New Contexts for Reading Walt Whitman*, ed. Ed Folsom (Iowa City: University of Iowa Press, 2002), 126.

43. Terry Mulcaire, "Publishing Intimacy in *Leaves of Grass*," *ELH* 60 (Summer 1993): 488.

44. Leo Braudy, *Frenzy of Renown: Fame and Its History* (New York: Oxford University Press, 1986; repr., New York: Vintage, 1997), 474. Citations are to the Vintage edition.

45. Ezra Greenspan, *Walt Whitman and the American Reader* (New York: Cambridge University Press, 1990), 200.

46. "Notes on New Books," *Washington Daily National Intelligencer*, February 18, 1856, 2, Folsom and Price, *The Walt Whitman Archive*.

47. Tenny Nathanson, *Whitman's Presence: Body, Voice, and Writing in "Leaves of Grass"* (New York: New York University Press, 1992), 416.

48. Braudy, *Frenzy of Renown*, 517.

49. Mark Twain, *Mark Twain's Notebook*, ed. Albert Bigelow Paine (New York: Harper and Bros., 1935), 348–49.

50. Braudy, *Frenzy of Renown*, 432.

51. Greenspan, *Whitman and the American Reader*, 199.

52. Kennedy, *The Fight of a Book for the World*.

53. I quote here the original 1867 version of "When I Read the Book." Whitman

added the line "faint clews and indirections" in 1871. A very similar line appears in Calamus and is discussed below. See *LGV*, 2:561; the poem expresses a growing skepticism about the biographies of public figures, which in the mid-nineteenth century tended to emphasize the representative values that middle-class audiences found appealing. How could anyone describe a life as the genre was then conceived? See Ponce de Leon, *Self-Exposure*, 33–34.

54. Reynolds, *Walt Whitman's America;* Gary Schmidgall, *Walt Whitman: A Gay Life* (New York: Plume, 1997); Jerome Loving, *Walt Whitman: The Song of Himself* (Berkeley: University of California Press, 1999).

55. See Kenneth Price, "Sex, Politics, and 'Live Oak, with Moss,'" in *The Classroom Electric: Whitman, Dickinson, and American Culture,* http://www3 .iath.virginia .edu/fdw/volume3.price/. Price's site offers an account of the debates over the textual history of "Live Oak, with Moss" and its corollary portrait of homosexuality. The site also reproduces two major texts in the debate: Alan Helms, "Whitman's 'Live Oak with Moss,'" in *The Continuing Presence of Walt Whitman,* ed. Robert K. Martin (Iowa City: University of Iowa Press, 1992), 185–205 and Hershel Parker, "The Real 'Live Oak, with Moss': Straight Talk about Whitman's 'Gay Manifesto,'" *Nineteenth-Century Literature* 51 (September 1996): 145–60.

56. Willis, *Memoranda*, 227–38.

57. Ponce de Leon, *Self-Exposure*, 30.

58. See Marion Walker Alcaro, *Walt Whitman's Mrs. G: A Biography of Anne Gilchrist* (Rutherford, NJ: Farleigh-Dickinson University Press, 1991), 160–61. For a discussion of Gilchrist as a reader, see Max Cavitch, "Audience Terminable and Interminable: Anne Gilchrist, Walt Whitman, and the Achievement of Disinhibited Reading," *Victorian Poetry* 43:2 (2005): 249–61.

59. Ibid., 142–44.

60. Ibid., 153. It is important to note that the move to Philadelphia was also beneficial to Gilchrist's daughter Hannah, who pursued medical studies at the University of Pennsylvania.

61. See Robertson, *Worshiping Walt*, for a full discussion of Gilchrist's understanding of sexuality through matrimonial roles.

62. On parasocial relationships, see David Giles, *Illusions of Immortality: A Psychology of Fame and Celebrity* (London: Macmillan, 2000), 126–42; Laura Leets, Gavin de Becker, and Howard Giles, "Fans: Exploring Expressed Motivations for Contacting Celebrities," *Journal of Language and Social Psychology* 14 (March 1995): 102–23.

63. Baker, *Sentiment and Celebrity*, 10.

64. Ibid., 91.

65. Alcaro, *Walt Whitman's Mrs. G.*, 145.

66. Newbury, "Eaten Alive," 168.

67. See Michel de Certeau, *The Practice of Everyday Life* (Berkeley: University of California Press, 1984). In *Textual Poachers: Television Fans and Participatory Culture* (New York: Routledge, 1992), Henry Jenkins demonstrates that television viewers engage in a form of textual poaching in which they empower

themselves as they assimilate various stars and programs into their lives. In *NASA/TREK: Popular Science and Sex in America* (London: Verso, 1997), Constance Penley writes about the emergence of slash identities—fans whose appropriation of mainstream culture is so radically and aggressively provocative that they effectively produce their own set of works. (Penley's chief example is the popularity of *Star Trek* among a specific subculture of women who have used Captain Kirk and Dr. Spock as the basis for an extensive body of homosexual pornography.) The literature on fandom is extensive and is well represented in Lisa A. Lewis, ed., *The Adoring Audience: Fan Culture and Popular Media* (New York: Routledge, 1992).

68. See, for example, Gay Wilson Allen, *The Solitary Singer: A Critical Biography of Walt Whitman* (New York: New York University Press, 1955), 438; Loving, *Song of Himself,* 328; Robertson, *Worshiping Walt.*

69. Michael Moon, *Disseminating Whitman: Revision and Corporeality in "Leaves of Grass"* (Cambridge: Harvard University Press, 1991), 161–62.

70. See Alcaro, *Walt Whitman's Mrs. G.,* 160, on Gilchrist's warm reaction to the poem.

CHAPTER 5: CAMPAIGNS

1. The article itself comes from the *Edinburgh Review* 89 (April 1849): 149–68. Signed "Walter Whitman," the poet's copy of the article is part of the Trent Collection, Duke University Rare Book, Manuscript, and Special Collections Library. Page references are given in the text.

2. Known also as the printer's fist and index, the pointing hand originated in print shops in the fourteenth century and in the pointers used by readers of the Torah. Whitman's acquaintance with the symbol, however, clearly came from his experience in antebellum print shops. Many word processing programs now refer to the symbol as "Barnum."

3. On the prevalence of competition in antebellum print culture, see Isabelle Lehuu, *Carnival on the Page: Popular Print Media in Antebellum America* (Chapel Hill: University of North Carolina Press, 2000), 71–74.

4. Charles E. Feinberg Collection, Library of Congress, reel 24.

5. Despite his knowledge of the gubernatorial candidates, Whitman expressed no inclination to vote for either of them.

6. Harold Aspiz, "The Body Politic in *Democratic Vistas,*" in *Walt Whitman: The Centennial Essays,* ed. Ed Folsom (Iowa City: University of Iowa Press, 1994), 105–19. See especially 107–8.

7. A survey of more than fifty-eight journals in the Making of America database suggests that although the phrase *political campaign* had been used as early as August 1833 (*New-England* 5:2), it began to appear more frequently in the 1840s, particularly in the *Democratic Review.* Making of America Digital Library, Cornell University Library. http://cdl.library.cornell.edu/moa/.

8. Charles Dickens, *The Letters of Charles Dickens, Edited by His Sister-in-Law and His Eldest Daughter,* vol. 2 (New York: Scribner's, 1879), 448.

9. On Whitman's attraction to lecturing, see C. Carroll Hollis, *Language and Style*

in "Leaves of Grass" (Baton Rouge: Louisiana State University Press, 1983), 13, and, more generally, 1–27.

10. "Friday April 24, '57, True Vista Before," The Trent Collection, Duke University Rare Book, Manuscript, and Special Collections Library.

11. Walt Whitman, *The Gathering of the Forces,* ed. Cleveland Rogers and John Black (New York: Putnam, 1920), 2:179.

12. Kerry C. Larson, *Whitman's Drama of Consensus* (Chicago: University of Chicago Press, 1988), xix, xvii.

13. William Carlos Williams, *The Selected Essays of William Carlos Williams* (New York: New Directions, 1969), 180.

14. T. S. Eliot, "Observations on Walt Whitman" (1926), in *A Century of Whitman Criticism,* ed. Edward Haviland Miller (Bloomington: Indiana University Press, 1968), 163.

15. A sampling of criticism on Whitman and Lincoln includes William E. Barton, *Abraham Lincoln and Walt Whitman* (Indianapolis: Bobbs-Merrill, 1928); Mutlu Blasing, "Whitman's Lilacs and the Grammars of Time," *PMLA* 97 (January 1982); Allan Grossman, "The Poetics of Union in Whitman and Lincoln: An Inquiry toward the Relationship of Art and Policy," in *The American Renaissance Reconsidered,* ed. Walter Benn Michaels and Donald E. Pease (Baltimore: Johns Hopkins University Press, 1985); 183–203; Vivian R. Pollak, "Whitman Unperturbed," in Folsom, *Walt Whitman: The Centennial Essays,* 30–47; Helen Vendler, "Poetry and the Mediation of Value: Whitman on Lincoln," *Michigan Quarterly Review* 39 (Winter 2000): 1–18; William Pannapacker, *Revised Lives: Walt Whitman and Nineteenth-Century Authorship* (New York: Routledge, 2003), 19–47.

16. Walt Whitman to Nathaniel Bloom and John F. S. Gray, March 19–20, 1863, in *Selected Letters of Walt Whitman,* ed. Edwin Haviland Miller (Iowa City: University of Iowa Press, 1990), 53.

17. Cited in Barton, *Lincoln and Whitman,* 170.

18. William Douglas O'Connor, *The Good Gray Poet: A Vindication* (1866), Ed Folsom and Kenneth M. Price, eds., *The Walt Whitman Archive,* http://www.whitmanarchive.org.

19. Ibid.

20. See Barton, *Lincoln and Whitman,* 97, on the letter's probable inauthenticity.

21. Kennedy includes all of Henry Bascom Rankin's account of Lincoln and *Leaves of Grass* in *The Fight of a Book for the World* (West Yarmouth, MA: Stonecroft, 1926), 103–5. He lists Whitman's "Friends and Foes" on 287.

22. David S. Reynolds, *Walt Whitman's America: A Cultural Biography* (New York: Alfred A. Knopf, 1995), 531.

23. For a textual history of the lecture, see the introduction to the lecture in Walt Whitman, *Prose Works 1892,* ed. Floyd Stovall (New York: New York University Press, 1964), 2:496–97.

24. Jerome Loving, *Walt Whitman: The Song of Himself* (Berkeley: University of California Press, 1999), 440–41.

25. "Abraham Lincoln Advertisement, April 15, 1887," Charles E. Feinberg Collection, Library of Congress.

26. Pannapacker, *Revised Lives*, 101.

27. "A Tribute from a Poet," *New York Times*, April 15, 1887, 8, ProQuest Historical Newspapers database. The most authoritative scholarly accounts of the event are Pannapacker, *Revised Lives*, 54–62; Justin Kaplan, *Walt Whitman: A Life* (New York: Simon and Schuster, 1980), 29–30.

28. "A Tribute from a Poet," 8.

29. Ibid.

30. Ibid.

31. Of the many bouquets the poet received that afternoon and evening, the *Evening Post* reported, it was the girl's that the old man prized the most (*DN*, 2:418).

32. "A Tribute from a Poet," 8.

33. J. G. Holland, "Star Lecturing," *Scribner's* 8 (May 1874): 110, Making of America Digital Library, Cornell University Library, http://cdl.library.cornell.edu/moa/.

34. Ibid., 110, 111.

35. Ezra Greenspan, *Walt Whitman and the American Reader* (New York: Cambridge University Press, 1990), 221.

36. "Fame after Photography" [exhibition catalogue], Museum of Modern Art, New York (1999), 2. The exhibit was organized by Marvin Heiferman and Carole Kismaric.

37. Ibid., 4.

38. Pannapacker, *Revised Lives*, 51.

39. Leo Braudy, *Frenzy of Renown: Fame and Its History* (New York: Oxford University Press, 1986; repr., New York: Vintage, 1997), 468. Citations are to the Vintage edition.

40. Ibid., 427.

41. Herman Melville, *Correspondence: The Writings of Herman Melville* (Evanston: Northwestern University Press, 1993), 14:139.

42. Braudy, *Frenzy of Renown*, 432.

43. Loving provides a good overview of the article, its different versions, and the circumstances from which it arose in *Song of Himself*, 359.

44. Reynolds perpetuates the story in *Walt Whitman's America*, 532. The most authoritative account of the trip west is Walter H. Eitner, *Walt Whitman's Western Jaunt* (Lawrence: University Press of Kansas, 1986).

45. See also *WWC*, 8:521.

46. The article and commentary appear in Clifton J. Furness, ed., *Walt Whitman's Workshop* (Cambridge, MA: Russell and Russell, 1928), 245–48.

47. Ibid., 245.

48. Ibid., 246.

49. I have based my account of the incident on Robert Scholnick's historical analysis. See his "The Selling of the 'Author's Edition': Whitman, O'Connor, and

the *West Jersey Press* Affair," *Walt Whitman Review* 23 (March 1977). Page references to this work are given in the text.

50. "Editor's Table," *Appleton's*, April 1, 1876, 437, Making of America Digital Library, University of Michigan Library, http://www.hti.umich.edu/m/moagrp/.

51. Sacvan Bercovitch, *The American Jeremiad* (Madison: University of Wisconsin Press, 1978), 141.

52. Loving, *Song of Himself*, 346.

53. Quoted in Scholnick, "The Selling," 12.

54. Edmund Clarence Stedman, "Walt Whitman," *Scribner's* 21 (November 1880): 47–65, Making of America Digital Library, Cornell University Library, http://cdl.library.cornell.edu/moa/. Stedman gives instructions on how to order the centennial edition on 52.

55. *San Francisco Chronicle*, May 19, 1878, as quoted in Greenspan, *Whitman and the American Reader*, 218.

56. "New Publications," *New York Tribune*, November 19, 1880, 6.

57. [Bayard Taylor], "Intellectual Convexity," *New York Tribune*, April 22, 1876, 6.

58. The occasion was the publication of a Walt Whitman number of *Lippincott's*. The issue contained a Whitman portrait, Whitman poems, essays, and a reflection written by Traubel.

59. On the first kinetoscope parlors, see Gordon Hendrick, "The History of the Kinetoscope," in *The American Film Industry*, rev. ed, ed. Tino Balio (Madison: University of Wisconsin Press, 1985), 48–52.

60. Lary May, *Screening Out the Past: The Birth of Mass Culture and the Motion Picture Industry* (New York: Oxford University Press, 1980), 35–36.

INDEX